Footp

Croatia

Foster

Listings

4 About the author
4 About the book
282 Index
288 Credits

Introducing the region

8 Map: Croatia
9 Introduction
10 At a glance
14 Best of Croatia
18 Month by month

About the region

24 History
36 Art & architecture
42 Croatia today
46 Nature & environment
48 Festivals & events
54 Sleeping
60 Eating & drinking
64 Menu reader
66 Shopping
68 Activities & tours
74 Advantage Croatia

Zagreb & inland Croatia

79 Introduction
80 Zagreb & around
82 Map: Zagreb
90 North of Zagreb
96 East of Zagreb
100 Great days out: Plitvice Lakes
102 Listings:
102 Sleeping
104 Eating & drinking
108 Entertainment
108 Shopping
109 Activities & tours

Istria

113 Introduction
114 Pula & around
118 Istria's west coast
124 Inland Istria
128 Listings:
128 Sleeping
131 Eating & drinking
133 Entertainment
134 Shopping
135 Activities & tours

Kvarner

139 Introduction
140 Rijeka & around
144 Island of Krk
146 Island of Cres
148 Island of Lošinj
150 Island of Rab
152 Listings:
152 Sleeping
152 Eating & drinking
157 Entertainment
157 Activities & tours

North Dalmatia

161 Introduction
162 Zadar
166 Island of Pag
168 Paklencia National Park
170 Kornati National Park
172 Listings:
172 Sleeping
173 Eating & drinking
176 Entertainment
176 Shopping
177 Activities & tours

Central Dalmatia

181 Introduction
182 Split & around
184 *Map: Split*
192 Northwest of Split
196 Southeast of Split
200 Island of Brač
202 Island of Hvar
204 *Map: Hvar Town*
208 Island of Vis
210 Listings:
210 Sleeping
214 Eating & drinking
219 Entertainment
222 Shopping
222 Activities & tours

256 Listings:
256 Sleeping
259 Eating & drinking
263 Entertainment
265 Shopping
265 Activities & tours

Practicalities

268 Getting there
272 Getting around
276 Directory
278 Language

South Dalmatia

227 Introduction
229 Dubrovnik & around
231 *Map: Dubrovnik*
240 Great days out:
    Elafiti islands
242 Pelješac Peninsula
246 Island of Korčula
252 Island of Mljet
254 Island of Lastovo

Contents

About the author

Jane Foster grew up in the Yorkshire Dales, then studied Architecture at Oxford Polytechnic. After a stint in Rome, she lived six years in Split, Croatia, before moving to Athens, Greece. She has travelled extensively through the countries of former Yugoslavia, and returns regularly to Croatia both for work and pleasure. She has written about Croatia, Slovenia, Montenegro and Greece for guidebook publishers including Footprint, Insight, DK Eyewitness and Fodor's. She also writes occasional travel articles for British newspapers including the *Telegraph*, *Guardian*, *Observer* and *Independent*. She speaks English, Italian, Croatian and Greek.

Acknowledgements

Thanks to Marina for hosting me in Zagreb, and to her mum for having me and feeding me in Split. Thanks to Duje for arranging for me to stay in Makarska and coming hiking on Biokovo, and to Klaudija for having me to stay in Split. Thanks to Nilla for inviting me to stay on Vis, and to Branka for her local expertise regarding Dubrovnik and to Ivica for cooking a delicious lunch. Thanks to Viktorija and Mladen for taking me hiking in the hills outside Zagreb, and to Tijana and her father and brother for giving me a two-day tour of the island of Brač. Thanks to Anne-Kathrin and Gordan for giving me an excellent tour of the Kvarner region and feeding me well on the way. *Hvala* to everyone at Tri Volte in Split for keeping our glasses filled up, and most of all to Dejan for introducing me to life in Dalmatia.

Thanks to Natali and Filip for helping me endure an extremely weird and eventful overnight train journey from Thessaloniki to Belgrade. Thanks to Azra and Haustor for lifting my spirits on lonely winter evenings in front of the computer. *Efharisto* to Efi and Antonio, Lena and Polly for feeding Mačak (the cat) while I was away. And finally, many thanks to everyone at Footprint, especially Felicity, for bearing with me through the edit.

About the book

The guide is divided into four sections: **Introducing the region**; **About the region**; **Around the region** and **Practicalities**.

Introducing the region comprises: **At a glance**, which explains how the region fits together by giving the reader a snapshot of what to look out for and what makes this region distinct from other parts of the country; **Best of Croatia** lists the top 20 highlights; and **Month by month** is a guide to the pros and cons of visiting at certain times of year.

    About the region comprises: **History**; **Art & architecture**; **Croatia today**; **Nature & environment**; **Festivals & events**; **Sleeping**, an overview of accommodation options; **Eating & drinking**, an overview of Croatia's cuisine, as well as advice on eating out; **Entertainment**, an overview of the region's cultural credentials, explaining what entertainment is on offer; **Shopping**, the region's specialities and recommendations for the best buys; and **Activities & tours**.

    Around the region is then broken down into six areas, each with its own chapter. Here you'll find all the main sights and at the end of each chapter a listings section with all the best sleeping, eating & drinking, entertainment, shopping and activities & tours options.

Map symbols

LEGENDE/LEGEND

🅸	l'Information Information	🚉	Gare Train station
⊙	Endroit d'intérêt Place of interest	🚌	Gare routière Bus station
🏛	Musée/galerie Museum/gallery	Ⓜ	Station de métro Metro station
🎭	Théâtre Theatre	—🚋—	Ligne de tram Tram route
📮	Poste Post office	🏪	Marché Market
†	Eglise/cathédrale Church/cathedral	✚	Hôpital Hospital
〰	Mur de ville City wall	⊞	Pharmacie Pharmacy
🅿	Parking	🎓	Lycée College

Sleeping price codes

Croatian hotel prices are usually posted in euro, even though the official currency is the kuna and guests are expected to pay in kuna

€€€€ over €200 per night for a double room in high season.
€€€ €125-200
€€ €75-125
€ under €75

Eating & drinking price codes

€€€€ more than €40 per person for a 2-course meal with a drink, including service and cover charge
€€€ €30-40
€€ €20-30
€ under €20

Picture credits

Contents

8   *Map: Croatia*
9   Introduction
10   At a glance
14   Best of Croatia
18   Month by month

Dubrovnik old harbour.

Introducing the region

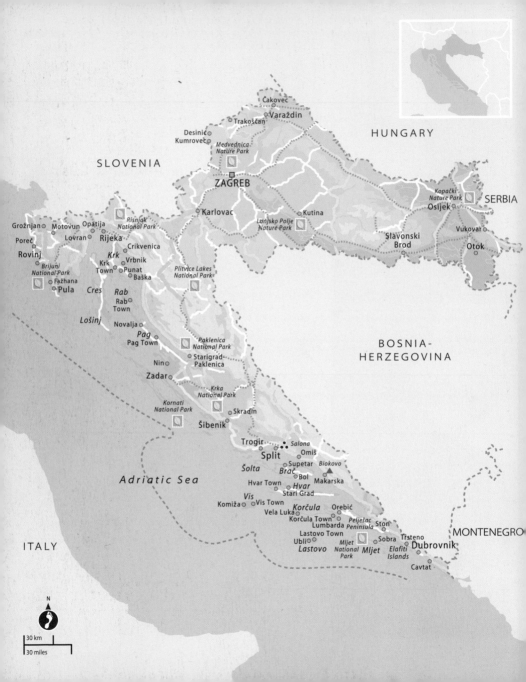

Introduction

"The Mediterranean as it once was", says the national tourist board slogan. And indeed, in Croatia you can still find the wild unexploited nature and genuine hospitality that for most of Europe is a generation past. Picture this: the colours and scent of pine trees, sea air and sun cream mingling to create that late-afternoon *fjaka* – a state of passive contentedness, nearing apathy, unique to Dalmatia. The water is crystal clear and turquoise blue. No pay-as-you go sun beds, no blaring music. Yachts sail across the horizon as the sun begins to sink into the sea. Back in the village, stone houses with green window shutters huddle round a harbour filled with wooden fishing boats. You could be in Hvar Town, Komiža, Makarska or Orebić, but it's certainly Croatia.

Moving north and inland towards Zagreb, elegant Vienna Succession-style buildings are the legacy of years spent under Austro-Hungary. Out of town, sturdy hilltop castles survey wide valleys and undulating vineyards, recalling the centuries lived in fear of Ottoman reprisal. Today's Croatia is proud of its past, eager to preserve its cultural and natural heritage, and moving rapidly towards EU integration.

Zagreb cityscape.

At a glance
A whistle-stop tour of Croatia

Zagreb & inland Croatia

Many visitors bypass the capital, but if you're looking for more than a sea-and-sunshine holiday, and want to understand the country's complexity, spend some time here. Zagreb is culturally and geographically closer to Vienna and Budapest than to the Venetian-influenced coastal regions. While medieval hilltop Gornji Grad is home to the cathedral and parliament, Donji Grad, below it, has several museums, including the Arts and Crafts Museum, the Mimara Museum and the Modern Art Gallery. Pleasant day trips from the capital include hiking on Sljeme in Medvednica Nature Park, exploring the rural villages and medieval castles of Zagorje, and visiting the small baroque city of Varaždin. South of Zagreb, on the way down towards Dalamatia, Plitvice Lakes National Park is the country's most visited inland attraction.

Slavonia, the easternmost region of Croatia, has little of great interest to holidaymakers. However, to get a complete picture of Croatia and its recent tragic history, the largely devastated town of Vukovar, sitting on the west bank of the River Danube, illustrates better than anywhere else the suffering caused by the war of independence. Neighbouring Osijek, with its 18th-century baroque Tvrđa complex, is a more cheerful place to spend the night. Osijek also makes an ideal starting point for visiting the wetlands of Kopački Rit Nature Park, a haven for migrating birds.

From Zagreb, you can take an overnight train directly down to Split to visit Central Dalmatia.

The lowdown

Money matters

Croatia is not a cheap option, with hotel and restaurant prices similar to Greece. Prices rise significantly through July and August with an influx of Italian and German tourists. Private rooms are the best source of low-cost, clean, comfortable accommodation – expect to pay anything between 300Kn and 500Kn for a double, depending on the place, time of year and furnishing. At the really top-class luxury hotels in Dubrovnik and Hvar Town, you can expect to pay over 2000Kn for a double room in high season. Prices in Dubrovnik have escalated out of all proportion, so that even a cup of coffee now costs double what it would cost anywhere else in Croatia. Happily, public transport (buses, trains and ferries) throughout the country is still very cheap by EU standards.

Opening hours & holidays

Many museums are closed on Mondays and public holidays.

Tourist passes

There are very few discount passes – Zagreb has a 'Zagreb Card', but the savings are minimal. However, if you are lucky enough to be a full-time student, an International Student Identity Card (ISIC) will entitle you to reductions at youth hostels, museums and on certain international train and airfares.

Tourist information

All the major cities and even most small towns along the coast and on the islands have a *turistički ured* (tourist office), see the relevant chapters for the contact details of these offices. They provide information about local hotels, sports facilities and public transport, and most can help you find self-catering accommodation. The larger tourist offices provide maps and sightseeing information.

Istria

With its proximity to Central Europe, the Istrian peninsula is Croatia's most developed region for tourism, though happily it retains its unspoilt charm. The largest city is the industrial port of Pula, with its impressive Roman amphitheatre, which makes a good base for visiting the islands of Brijuni National Park. The top resorts are the west coast seaside towns of Poreč and Rovinj. While the former dates back to Roman times, and is home to Euphrasius Basilica, decorated with stunning Byzantine mosaics, the latter is built around a pretty harbour and is visibly Venetian. Both offer a wide choice of hotels and rooms to rent to suit all budgets, excellent seafood restaurants, plus bathing areas and water-sports facilities.

Moving inland, the romantic hill towns of Motovun and Grožnjan rise above undulating vineyards and forests. Come here to savour the best of Istrian cuisine, which has a distinctly Italian influence, with plenty of pasta and seasonal delicacies such as truffles, mushrooms and wild asparagus.

Kvarner

The workaday industrial port of Rijeka is the main city in the Kvarner region. Close by, the restful seaside resorts of Opatija and Lovran are made up of elegant Vienna Secession-style hotels and villas. The nearby island of Krk is joined to the mainland by a bridge, and is home to one of Croatia's biggest and most popular beaches, Veli Plaža in Baška.

Introducing the region

From Rijeka port there are direct boat lines to the islands of Cres, Lošinj and Rab. Wild and rugged Cres is known for its excellent lamb and rare Eurasian griffon vultures, Lošinj is home to the pretty and well-equipped resort of Mali Lošinj, while Rab is well worth checking out for its medieval capital, Rab Town, and its highly publicized nudist beaches.

Moving inland from Rijeka, Risnjak National Park encompasses the rugged mountains and dense pine forests of Gorksi Kotar, offering respite from the heat and hussle of the coast in summer, as well as the opportunity to ski in winter.

From Rijeka, there are regular overnight ferries down the coast to Split and Dubrovnik in Dalmatia.

North Dalmatia

North Dalmatia's chief city, Zadar, centres on a charming old town built on a small fortified peninsula, packed with medieval buildings and several noteworthy Romanesque churches.

From Zadar, regular excursion boats take visitors on day trips around the dozens of rocky, arid, uninhabited islets that make up Kornati National Park. Those in search of a back-to-nature experience might rent a 'Robinson Crusoe-style' cottage here (see page 58), with no electricity or running water, but plenty of solitude. North Dalmatia's biggest and most visited island is Pag, a bizarre moonscape of rocky fields supporting the sheep that produce its highly regarded *paški sir*,

Pag Island.

a salty cheese similar to Italian pecorino. Also on Pag, which is joined to the mainland by a bridge, you'll find the commercial resort of Novalja, known for its 24-hour summer beach clubs.

North of Zadar, part of the Velebit mountain range falls within Paklenica National Park, a haven for hikers and free climbers. Here, the River Zrmanja is also a popular location for whitewater rafting.

Central Dalmatia

In Central Dalmatia, the monumental Roman city of Split is one of Croatia's most fascinating destinations. While the pedestrian-only old town lies within the ancient walls of Diocletian's Palace, looking directly out to sea, the modern high-rise suburbs extend along the coast and into the mountainous hinterland. With incoming ferries from Ancona in Italy, and regular daily ferries and catamarans to the nearby islands of Brač, Hvar and Vis, Split is a key transit point.

On Brač, the top resort is Bol, home to the stunning Zaltni Rat beach. On Hvar, you'll find Croatia's trendiest and most lovely island destination, the Venetian-era Hvar Town. Further out to sea, distant Vis produces organic wines and is much loved by sailing types for its authentic seafood eateries.

Back on the mainland coast, possible day trips south of Split include the seaside towns of Omiš and Makarska. Omiš lies at the mouth of the River Cetina, where you'll find organized whitewater rafting, while the cheerful resort of Makarska is at the foot of Mount Biokovo, whose rocky slopes offer a fierce challenge to seasoned hikers. North of Split, tiny medieval Trogir is home to an impressive cathedral. Further north still, industrial Šibenik is home to yet another noteworthy cathedral, and also makes a good base for visiting the waterfalls of Krka National Park.

The small town of Ston, near Dubrovnik.

South Dalmatia

South Dalmatia is home to Croatia's most expensive destination, the glorious medieval walled city of Dubrovnik. Dubrovnik's attractions, including the city walls, the Rector's Palace, the Franciscan Monastery and Maritime Museum, can easily absorb two or three days of sightseeing. Outside the old town, most of the modern hotels are located on Lapad Peninsula close to Gruž port, which sees regular ferries running back and forth to the tiny Elafiti islands and Mljet. The car-free Elafiti islands can be visited as day trips, while Mljet, home to Mljet National Park with its two saltwater lakes surrounded by dense pine forests, warrants an overnight stay.

Back on the mainland coast, the cheerful seaside resort of Cavtat and Trsteno Arboretum can also both be visited as day trips from Dubrovnik. Further north, Pelješac Peninsula is home to Ston, renowned for its excellent fresh shellfish, while Orebić is the main town in the Pelješac vineyards area. Across the narrow sea channel from Orebić, the island of Korčula is a must-see for its lovely capital, medieval Korčula Town, built on a tiny fortified peninsula.

Further out to sea, the underdeveloped island of Lastovo is a world unto itself. Despite officially belonging to South Dalmatia, both Korčula and Lastovo are served by ferry and catamaran from Split in Central Dalmatia, rather than Dubrovnik.

Best of Croatia

Top 20 things to see & do

❶ Gornji Grad

Zagreb's medieval Gornji Grad, home to the cathedral and St Mark's church with its coloured tiled roof, is a warren of romantic, winding, cobbled streets. It also affords the best views over the modern capital, from Strossmayerova Promenade at the foot of Lotrščak Tower. Page 81.

❷ Plitvice National Park

The 16 emerald-green lakes, connected by a succession of dramatic waterfalls, make Plitvice Croatia's top inland attraction. The surrounding slopes are covered with dense forests of beech and fir, and the entire park is criss-crossed by a series of marked paths and wooden bridges. Page 100.

❸ Euphrasius Basilica

In Poreč, this magnificent sixth-century basilica is decorated with glistening golden mosaics above, behind and around the main apse, making it one of the most important Byzantine monuments in the region, and justly affording it the status of a UNESCO World Heritage Site. Page 123.

❹ Truffle hunting in Istria

Between October and December, the forests and meadows of the Mirna Valley see an influx of people and dogs hunting for truffles. This pungent subterranean fungus is found in damp soils on or near the roots of oak trees and is among the most expensive foodstuffs in the world. Page 126.

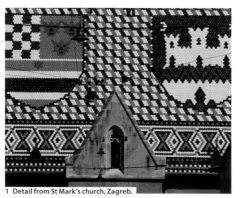

1 Detail from St Mark's church, Zagreb.

❺ Motovun Film Festival
Each year in late July, this five-day international festival attracts some 40,000 cinema buffs from all over Europe, thanks to the standard of the 70 or so avant-garde films that are shown, and its delightful location, in the fortified medieval hilltown of Motovun. Page 133.

❻ Šetalište Franza Josefa
Connecting Volosko to Lovran and running through the seaside towns of Opatija, Ičići and Ika, this 12-km coastal footpath dates back to 1885, coinciding with the opening of Opatija's first hotels. It makes a lovely walk, with plenty of places to stop for a swim or a snack along the way. Page 143.

❼ Rab Town
On the island of Rab, medieval Rab Town is built on a narrow peninsula rising high above the sea. With four elegant bell towers creating a dramatic skyline, it's home to several impressive 12th-century Romanesque churches and a warren of Gothic and Renaissance town houses. Page 151.

❽ Sea Organ
In Zadar, on the tip of the small peninsula that is home to the old town, the Sea Organ is made up of 35 pipes forming whistles that produce sounds according to the movement of the sea. It was installed in 2005, bringing 21st-century culture to a town that is predominantly medieval. Page 164.

❾ Kornati National Park
Daily excursion boats leave from Zadar and Šibenik, taking tourists to explore the 89 islands, islets and reefs that make up Kornati. The Kornati see an influx of chartered yachts through the summer months. Page 170.

❿ Diocletian's Palace
In Split, this magnificent third-century palace was built for Roman Emperor Diocletian as a retirement home. It is entered through four gates and centres on the colonnaded Peristil. Within the walls is a warren of paved alleys packed with Venetian-Gothic buildings. Today it is a UNESCO World Heritage Site. Page 183.

13 Hvar Town.

⑪ Krka National Park

Near Šibenik, Krka encompasses seven magnificent waterfalls, which thunder through a steep-sided, wooded canyon. The most spectacular is Skradinski Buk, made up of 17 cascades plunging over 40 m into a wide emerald-green basin, forming a natural jacuzzi in which it is possible to swim. Page 195.

⑫ Bol

On the island of Brač, Bol is home to the idyllic Zlatni Rat beach. Composed of fine shingle, it juts out into the sea, perpendicular to the coast, and moves and changes shape depending on local winds and currents. It's backed by the rocky heights of Vidova Gora, the highest peak on all the Croatian islands. Page 201.

⑬ Hvar Town

Croatia's most fashionable island resort, Hvar Town on Hvar is made up of old stone houses, built into the hillsides surrounding a small bay. The magnificent main square gives directly onto the harbour and is backed by a 16th-century cathedral. The entire scene is presided over by a hilltop castle. Page 203.

⑭ Blue Cave

Daily excursion boats depart from the fishing harbour in Komiža on the island of Vis, taking visitors to the tiny island of Biševo. Boats then enter the Blue Cave, which is lit a magnificent shade of blue by the sun's rays, which pass through the water and reflect off the seabed. Page 209.

⑮ Dubrovnik City Walls

Any first-time visitor to Dubrovnik should begin their stay by walking a complete 2-km circuit of the medieval city walls. Affording ever-changing vistas over the terracotta roofs of old town and the sea, they are reinforced by a series of towers and bastions. The entire complex is a UNESCO World Heritage Site. Page 229.

⓰ War Photo Limited

In Dubrovnik's old town, which was under siege for seven months during the war for independence, this beautifully designed gallery is dedicated to photo-journalism from war zones around the world. Emotionally gruelling but well worth visiting, it offers a refreshingly impartial look at the human tragedy suffered on all sides during war. Page 236.

⓱ Kayaking round the Elafiti islands

Various Dubrovnik-based agencies arrange one-day sea kayaking tours around the tiny, car-free Elafiti islands of Koločep, Lopud and Šipan. A great way to tone up your torso, it's also possible to opt for pedal-and-paddle, which combines kayaking and mountain biking once ashore. Page 240.

⓲ Wine tasting on Pelješac

Pelješac Peninsula is known for its vineyards, which produce the excellent reds, Dingač and Postup.

Several cellars are open to the public, where you can taste their wines along with platters of appetizers, and then buy bottles to bring home. Page 242.

⓳ Korčula Town

On the island of Korčula, Korčula Town is a compact pedestrian-only settlement of medieval stone houses with terracotta-tiled roofs, built on a small, fortified peninsula, jutting out to sea. The streets are ingeniously set out in a herringbone pattern, protecting the centre from harsh winds. Page 247.

⓴ Mljet National Park

On the island of Mljet, this national park encompasses two interconnected salt-water lakes, set amid indigenous forest of Aleppo pines and holm oaks. You can walk the 9-km perimeter of the lakes, and take a boat ride to a restaurant in a former monastery, which is on an islet in the middle of the larger lake. Page 253.

19 Korčula Town.

Month by month

A year in Croatia

Feast of St Blaise.

January & February

New Year's Day is seen in with a midnight firework display in most towns. The year often begins with snow in the mountains; in areas over 1500 m, winter temperatures average -6°C. But, while skiing may be possible in Gorski Kotar, on the coast (where winters are mild and rainy, with January temperatures averaging 9°C) you may be lucky enough to catch the so-called halycon of clear blue sky and sunshine, albeit with a bracing nip in the air. Meanwhile the capital remains decidedly cold, with winter temperatures averaging 0°C in inland Croatia throughout January. The chilly weather brings hearty, filling dishes to the table, such as *sarma* (sauerkraut cabbage leaves stuffed with meat and rice) and *fažol sa kobasicom* (beans and sausages).

Regarding tourism, low season runs from November through to April, so in winter many hotels and restaurants close down completely, especially on the islands. However, if you do visit Croatia during this period, you can be almost certain there will be few foreigners around, and that locals will be curious to know what you're doing.

In Dubrovnik, 3 February sees the celebration on Sveti Vlaho (Feast of St Blaise), see page 48.

March & April

As spring sets in, while the sun may shine, it can also rain continuously for several days. If you visit during this period, bring a waterproof, a couple of decent pullovers, T-shirts and a choice of footwear.

Easter celebrations see several local peculiarities, the most interesting being the Carrying of the Holy Cross in Jelsa on the island of Hvar. Staged on the night before Good Friday, locals from six neighbouring villages (Jelsa, Pitve, Vrisnik, Svirče, Vrbanj and Vrboska) take part in an all-night procession. At 2200, a group leaves from each parish church, led by a much-honoured (and hopefully very strong) young man carrying a wooden cross. The parties pass through each of the other villages in turn, to return to their respective churches for sunrise on Good Friday morning.

Easter egg in the courtyard of St Mark's Church, Zagreb.

Also at this time of year, open-air markets abound with spring produce and fresh flowers – this is the perfect moment to catch local seasonal delicacies, such as wild asparagus and cherries (which are best in late April).

May & June

May and June can be regarded as the shoulder season for tourism. Summer is in the air but still hasn't quite arrived, and businesses are repainting and opening for the season ahead. In fact, this can be one of the most rewarding times to visit. In June the sea is warm enough to swim in (hardier types will also manage in May) and the beaches are still reasonably peaceful. Hotels and restaurants are open but not overly busy, so you'll tend to get a more personalized service. As temperatures are not unbearably hot, this is also an ideal time for active land sports such as hiking and mountain biking.

In Split, 7 May sees the celebration on Sudamje (Feast of St Domnius), which is a local public holiday, see page 49.

Introducing the region

July & August

Peak season runs through the hottest and busiest months, July and August. The Adriatic coast, blessed with a Mediterranean climate, is hot, dry and brilliantly sunny, with July temperatures averaging between 24°C in the north and 26°C in the south. The sunniest place is said to be Hvar Town, which has 2718 hours of sunshine a year (by comparison, Nice in the south of France has 2706 hours of sunshine). In contrast, in the Dinaric mountains, in areas over 1500 m, summer temperatures average 18°C, while in inland Croatia, with its continental climate, July temperatures average 24°C in Zagreb.

As this is also the period when most Europeans take their summer holidays, accommodation prices rise steeply, and availability may be scarce, so you should book a place to stay well in advance. Likewise, restaurants and bars are so busy you may have to queue for a table, and the beaches can also get horribly crowded. On the upside, all tourism-related businesses are up and running, so you can expect excellent water-sports facilities (scuba-diving, sea kayaking, wind surfing and so on), organized hiking, mountain biking and whitewater rafting tours to be available on a daily basis.

Nightlife is also at its most animated, with big dance clubs and outdoor cocktail bars along the coast. The one-week Garden Festival takes place at Petrčane, near Zadar, attracting international DJs and party people from all over Europe. On a more cultural note, the Summer Festivals in Dubrovnik and Split see the staging of open-air theatre, concerts and opera, each evening from mid-July through to mid-August. The Motovun Film Festival is also staged in late July.

On the food front, stalls at open-air markets are stacked high with tomatoes, peppers, peaches, apricots and watermelons, and seaside eateries do a roaring trade in octopus salad, a light and tasty summer favourite.

September & October

The year's second shoulder season, from September through to October, sees air temperatures drop but the sea remain warm enough for a swim (hardier types will also manage in October). Beaches are now reasonably peaceful, and hotels and restaurants are open but not frantically busy, so you can once again expect a more personalized service after the summer rush. The nights begin to draw in but stay balmy so you can still dine outside. This is also a period for active land sports such as hiking and mountain biking.

In early September, the grape harvest is in full swing and wine producers are hard at work. In Istria, truffle festivals are held in inland hill villages throughout October. With the onset of autumn, leaves take on golden russet hues, making wooded destinations such as Krka and Plitvice national parks, and even the parks and gardens in the capital, Zagreb, exceptionally pretty.

November & December

In Dalmatia and Istria, the tourists have all but departed and the olive harvest takes place. 1 November is All Saints' Day, which is known as Day of the Dead in Croatia – people visit the family grave and fresh flowers are on sale in extraordinary quantities. Shortly after, 11 November sees the celebration of St Martin's Day in Zagorje near Zagreb – the year's new wine is blessed by a priest, and raucous drinking and merrymaking ensue. Then, on 6 December, in Komiža on the island of Vis, St Nicholas Day is celebrated with the ceremonious burning of a fishing boat, outside the church on the hill above the sea.

As Christmas draws near, shops and streets are decorated with fairy lights, and Zagreb is particularly atmospheric for festive shopping. Croatians eat bakalar (salted cod) on Christmas Eve, before attending midnight mass, which is probably the most popular church service of the entire year.

Contents

24 History
36 Art & architecture
42 Croatia today
46 Nature & environment
48 Festivals & events
54 Sleeping
60 Eating & drinking
64 Menu reader
66 Shopping
68 Activities & tours
74 Advantage Croatia

Zut Marina, Kornati.

About the region

History

Temple of Augustus, Pula.

The Illyrians & Greek & Roman colonization

The earliest known inhabitants of the region are the Illyrians, who settled along the Adriatic coast and its hinterland during the Bronze Age. They were divided into various tribes – Liburnians, Histri and Delmati – and built simple hilltop settlements fortified with stone walls.

The Greeks started colonizing the coast in the fourth century BC. The first settlement, Issa, was founded by inhabitants of the Greek colony of Syracuse (Sicily) on the island of Vis, and included a theatre with a capacity for 3000 spectators. Issa later became independent, and founded several more colonies such as Tragurion (Trogir) and Lumbarda (on the island of Korčula). Local Illyrians traded jewellery, metalwork, glassware, salt, wine and oil with the Greeks, and thus Greek colonization induced the development of craftsmanship, the building of towns and more sophisticated farming.

In the mid-third century BC, the southern tribes united to form an Illyrian state, living in part from piracy. Feeling threatened by Illyrian expansion, the Greeks called the Romans for help. When Roman messengers arrived to ask the Illyrians leader, Queen Teuta, to curtail piracy, they were promptly put to death, causing the beginning of a series of wars between the Romans and the Illyrians. In 167 BC, the Illyrian state was defeated and its territory turned into the Roman province of Illyricum.

The first Roman settlers were traders and soldiers. Legions built military camps, roads, bridges and aqueducts, which stimulated the arrival of civilians attracted by the possibility of expanding trade and colonization. This lead to the development of the coastal towns of Pola (Pula), Jader (Zadar), Salona (Solin) and Epidaurum (Cavtat). Croatia's best-preserved Roman monuments are the Arena (amphitheatre) in Pula, and Diocletian's Palace in Split.

When the Roman Empire was divided into the Eastern and Western Empires in AD 395 – a division that was to have far-reaching consequences for the later history of the Balkans – Dalmatia fell within the West. With the fall of the Western Empire in AD 476, the region became part of the Ostrogoth state, then in AD 555 it was made a Byzantine province. During the second half of the sixth century, it was invaded by tribes of Slavs and Avars, who travelled south through Dalmatia, where they demolished Salona.

According to the Byzantine Emperor and historian Constantine Porphyrogenitus, the Croats were invited to present-day Croatia by Emperor Heraclius (AD 575-641) to expel the Avars. This they did, also defeating other Slavic tribes, and they soon became the dominant force in the former Roman province of Dalmatia.

The development of a Croatian state

Very few written documents exist regarding the Croats' early years in the region, although around the year AD 800 we have evidence of one Duke Višeslav, whose court was based in Nin, near Zadar, in North Dalmatia.

Croatian territory covered the hinterland of the coastal towns of Zadar, Trogir and Split, but did not include these towns. It stretched south as far as the River Cetina (near Omiš), and east into Bosnia, and later extended north to include Istria. When the Croatian rulers were at their height, Pannonia was also part of Croatia.

Trpimir, Duke of Croatia (AD 845-864), is deemed as the founder of the dynasty that ruled the country until the end of the 11th century. He considered the entire territory his own property and surrounded himself with a council of hand-picked *župani* (counts), each responsible for a *županije* (county), to help him rule. Trpimir's successor, Domagoj (AD 864-876), built up Croatia's naval strength and came into conflict with Venice over control of the Adriatic. After Domagoj, Zdeslav (AD 878-879) came to power but he was assassinated and was succeeded by Branimir (AD 879-882) who was loyal to the Pope and obtained the first international recognition of Croatia from Pope John VIII.

At that time the 'Apostles of the Slavs', the brothers Methodius and Cyril, were requested by the Byzantine emperor to invent an alphabet for the Slavic languages, thereby spreading the Byzantine influence among these people. The papacy, worried about the strengthening of Byzantium, wanted to keep Croatia under Rome's watch.

The following century is linked with Tomislav's reign (AD 910-928). He started his rule as a *dux* (duke) but changed his title to that of *rex* (king) around AD 925. For his victories over the Bulgarians, the Byzantine emperor awarded him control over the Dalmatian towns and the title of 'proconsul' so he could rule them in the name of the Byzantine Empire. Tomislav defeated the Hungarians and united Coastal and Pannonian Croatia.

In 1054 the 'Great Schism' (the break between Eastern and Western Christian churches) took place, and the border between the Eastern and Western Roman Empires, drawn up in AD 395, became the border between the Roman Catholic and Orthodox churches. The east Adriatic, bisected by this border, was of direct interest to both the Pope in Rome and the patriarch in Constantinople. The papacy was

King Tomislav.

eager to keep Croatia under the Catholic wing. During the rule of Petar Krešimir IV (1058-1074), two church councils met in Split, proclaiming sanctions against clergy who gave sermons in the Croatian language, had beards, were married or in any other way resembled the Eastern Church. Krešimir was recognized as the King of Dalmatia and Croatia by the Pope, and thus the Byzantine theme of Dalmatia was truly united with Croatia. Krešimir was not just a Byzantine official like Tomislav and Tomislav's successors, he was the absolute leader of the entire region.

However, soon after Krešimir's death a conflict blew up, provoked by the Normans, Venetians, Byzantines, Hungarians and the Pope in Rome, who all hoped to gain control over Croatia and Dalmatia. The result was that Zvonimir, the former *ban* (governor) at the time of Krešimir, succeeded to the throne in 1075 and took the title King of Croatia and Dalmatia. Zvonimir was chosen thanks to the support of Pope Gregory VII, and in return he placed the country under papal sovereignty.

After Zvonimir, Stjepan Trpimirović ruled for a short time, but he was too weak to put an end to difficult internal problems. This chaos was used by the Hungarians to take control of Croatia and Dalmatia and finally fulfil their long desire to open up their land-locked territories with access to the sea. Rome favoured the Hungarians, and so in 1091 Hungarian King Ladislas succeeded in taking Pannonia (which from then on became known as Slavonia) too. In 1102, Ladislas' successor, Koloman, oversaw the signing of the Pacta Conventa, in which the heads of the 12 most powerful Croatian families recognized him as their leader, and accompanied him to Biograd-na-Moru (near Zadar) where he was crowned King of Croatia and Dalmatia.

Croatian history from 1102 until 1991 finds the country divided into three administrative areas that had little contact with each other – Croatia, Slavonia and Dalmatia – under various foreign powers.

In the 14th century, the Ottoman Turks began expanding towards Croatia. The Holy Roman Emperor and King of Hungary, Sigismund I (1387-1437) organized a crusade against the Turks, but was defeated at the Battle of Nicopolis in 1396. It was an evil omen that signified the forthcoming wars between Croatia and the Ottoman Empire that would last for centuries.

After the fall of neighbouring Bosnia in 1463, the Croatian borderlands lay open to Turkish attack. The first defeat took place in Lika in 1493, when the Turks achieved victory over the Croatian army. Constant Turkish attacks on Croatian lands brought great disruption. Peoples from Serbia and Bosnia fled the Turks, seeking refuge in Croatia, and these migrations affected food production, resulting in poverty and famine. Croatia's western neighbours, namely Venice and the Hapsburgs, recognized the danger for their own countries and started worrying about how to defend Croatia in order to defend themselves. By the end of the 15th century, conflicts between the ruling Hungaro-Croatian aristocracy culminated in the aristocracy opposing the king and the lower nobility, and the burghers opposing the clergy. In 1526, a catastrophic defeat of the Hungarian army by the Turks at the Battle of Mohacs brought about the problem of electing a new king, as Louis II had somewhat ignominiously drowned in a river as he tried to escape the battle.

On 1 January 1527, the Croatian nobles elected Ferdinand Hapsburg as their king. He thus became the leader of Croatia, Dalmatia and Slavonia, and the entire territory was absorbed into the Holy Roman Empire of the German people. At the time the Hapsburgs were the kings of Czech, Hungary, Spain, the Netherlands, Naples and even Mexico.

To defend the region against the Turks, the Hapsburgs established the *Krajina* (military border) in the 16th century. In 1578, work began to build Karlovac as a major defence nucleus – Turkish skulls were thrown into the foundations of Karlovac as a sign of the mood of the times. Other defence posts were later built to the south and east. To guard these positions, a special borderline army was formed, made up largely of Vlahi, Orthodox Serb cattle farmers who had fled the Turks from the east. By this time the Hapsburgs were overriding the authority of the *ban* (Croatian governor) and the *sabor* (Croatian parliament), and the *Krajina* was put under German officers who took their orders directly from Vienna.

The rule of the first Hapsburgs was devoted to defending the region against the Turks. When the Turks took Klis in 1537, they effectively had control over the entire Dalmatian hinterland all the way south to the River Neretva, leaving Dalmatia divided between Venice and the Ottoman Empire. In October of the same year, the Turks defeated Ferdinand's armies in Slavonia, and thus opened their way to the Croatian lands in the west.

The Turks achieved their greatest victories at the time of Sultan Suleiman the Magnificent (ruled 1520-1566). On his campaign against Vienna, his army was detained by the Croatian *ban*, Count Nikola Zrinski, and his army at Szeged (southern Hungary). Even though Szeged was eventually conquered in 1566, Zrinski's heroic defenders aroused doubts about Turkish invincibility. In 1593, the Turks suffered defeat near Sisak, marking the beginning of a 13-year war against Croatia and Hungary. This war ended with a peace treaty in 1606, proving the decline of Turkish power. During the first half of the 17th century, the Croatian nobles considered that the *Krajina* (military border) had fulfilled its task, and demanded that it should come back under the authority of the Croatian *ban*.

The *Krajina* had physically divided Croatian territory in two, which made national integration difficult. The Emperor's Court in Vienna had two reasons not to disband the military border. on the one hand, it was an infinite source of cheap, well-trained, loyal soldiers and, on the other hand, Vienna feared that national integration would strengthen the Croatian aristocracy. The Hapsburgs decided to keep the border soldiers to serve their own interests.

During the 200-year fight to hold back the Turks, Croatia lost not only three-quarters of its territory, but also the same proportion of its population. People either died in battle, or were captured by the Turks and taken away to be used as slaves. The survivors moved to the north and the west of the country, and even beyond its borders. The aristocracy also migrated northwards, thus displacing the centre of the Croatian state from Coastal Croatia to Upper Croatia.

Two Croatian aristocratic families in particular distinguished themselves in the wars against the Turks: the Frankopans and Zrinskis. These two families were related by blood and held similar political beliefs. In the 17th century, Petar Zrniski, together with a group of Hungarian aristocrats, lead a mission to free Croatia of Hapsburg domination. But the conspiracy was discovered and Vienna sentenced Petar Zrinski and his brother-in-law Franjo Frankopan to the guillotine. They were executed on 30 April 1671, and their extensive estates became property of the Hapsburgs.

By 1718, Croatia had reclaimed all of Slavonia and much of Lika from the Turks. The Hapsburgs did not want to strengthen Croatia, so on the pretext of having been won in war, these lands were placed under military authority, effectively becoming part of the *Krajina*. The Hapsburgs also started to give away large estates in liberated Slavonia to foreign (German and Hungarian) families, to the obvious detriment of the Croatian nobility. Therefore, the Croatian parliament became disaffected, and fewer and fewer noblemen participated in its meetings, attending the Hungarian parliaments instead, where they solved Hungaro-Croatian matters together with the Hungarian nobles.

Ironically, with the expulsion of the Turks, Croatia's position became even more uncomfortable, as the Hapsburgs tightened their grip on the country. By this time a sizeable Serbian population (of the Orthodox faith) were living in Croatia, and when Russia began to show interest in the situation, the so-called Eastern Question evolved: when the Turks finally left the Balkans, who would rule, Catholic Austria or Orthodox Russia? Later this would be one of the factors that contributed to the escalation towards the First World War.

Another powerful empire also held Croatian lands: Venice. By the mid-16th century, the Turks had conquered all of Dalmatia apart from the islands and the coastal cities of Zadar, Šibenik, Trogir and Split, which were under Venetian control. By the late-17th century, Venice had extended its territory along the entire coast and into the hinterland. The Venetians applied the name Dalmatia to all these parts and, like the Hapsburgs, declined to return territories liberated from the Turks to the Croatian aristocracy.

In 1718, the peace treaty of Požarevac awarded Venice the hinterland territory eastwards up to the Dinara Mountains and south to Kotor (in present-day Montenegro). The Independent Republic of Dubrovnik now found itself surrounded by Venetian territory. However, the citizens of Dubrovnik were very skilful diplomats and, not wanting the Venetians as neighbours, they gave the area to the north around Klek (present-day Neum) and the area south around Sutorina (close to Herceg Novi in Montenegro) to the Turks, thus forming a buffer zone between the republic and the Venetian Empire.

This was later to cause great difficulties in defining the geographical limits of Croatia. The borders of today's Croatia were drawn up according to the peace treaty in Požarevac. As Bosnia and Herzegovina remained under the Ottoman Turks until 1878, part of the territory of medieval Croatia is now western Bosnia, and the area around Neum has been awarded to Bosnia as access to the sea, thus cutting across the Croatian coast. Croatian nationalists have always resented this; during the war of the 1990s Tudjman described Croatia as a croissant-shaped country that needed a filling.

The arrival of Napoleon & the eventual fall of the Hapsburgs

With the demise of the Venetian Empire in 1797, Dalmatia was handed to the Hapsburgs. In 1806, Napoleon took Dalmatia, bringing to the region a series of progressive reforms, but also imposing hefty taxes and recruiting local men to participate in his army and navy. In 1809, Napoleon united Dalmatia with parts of Slovenia and Croatia, calling the new region the Provinces Illyriennes (Illyrian Provinces). During the Napoleonic Wars, the English navy defeated the French fleet near Vis, and subsequently took the island from 1811 to 1815, using it as an important strategic base on the Adriatic. After Napoleon's downfall in 1815, Dalmatia came back under the Hapsburgs.

In 1827, a new law was passed making the Hungarian language obligatory in all Croatian secondary schools. As a reaction against increasing Germanization and Hungarianization of the region under Austro-Hungary, Ljudevit Gaj (1806-1872) founded the Illyrian Movement. Gaj believed that unification of the South Slavs was essential, and aimed at doing this through a reawakening of the national consciousness, primarily through language and literature. Gaj's movement was renamed the National Party in 1843, the name Illyrian having been prohibited.

The National Party rapidly gained popularity on county assemblies and as a counter-Hungarian wing in the parliament. The ideas the Illyrians cherished were expressed in the so-called 'Demands of the People', which included the union of Dalmatia, Slavonia and the *Krajina* (military border), the institution of Croatian as the official language, and the foundation of a Croatian people's army.

The National Party also voted for Josip Jelačić as *ban* (governor), and he was instated on 4 June 1848. Croatia was now in a difficult position because the revolutionary movement in Hungary refused any possible agreement with the Croats. The Hungarian revolutionary leader, Lajos Kossuth, famously said: "Where is Croatia? I do not see it on the map." In September 1848, Jelačić thus lead his army into

battle with the Hungarian revolutionaries, in the defence of both Croatia and the Hapsburgs. He wasn't protecting the empire, but rather he hoped that by so doing he would be able to procure certain favours from the Austrians.

The situation became more complicated than had been expected, and in December 1848 Emperor Ferdinand abdicated in favour of his teenage son Franz-Josef I. With the revolution in Hungary finally over (with the help of the Russian Tsar) Jelačić's dream of a 'Slavic Austria' also ended. In August 1849, the Hapsburgs returned to their old ways, with Emperor Franz-Josef I eliminating the new constitution he had formulated and imposing a centralist-absolutist regime accompanied by Germanization that eliminated all political freedom.

One of the National Party's demands that was eventually implemented was the integration of the *Krajina* (military border) into Croatia in 1881, which extended Croatian territory by one-third. This brought a considerable Serb population into the sphere of Croatian politics, a situation that was immediately abused by the new pro-Hungarian *ban*, Khuen Hedervary (1883-1903), who played off the ongoing competition between Croats and Serbs to weaken the Slav position by inciting conflicts between them. At this time there were 103 Serb representatives in the Croatian parliament, of whom 101 were pro-Hungarian.

On 16 May 1895, during a state visit by Francis Joseph, the Hungarian flag was burnt in Zagreb, reflecting a mood of discontent. Soon after that, the Croatian Peasants' Party, led by Stjepan Radić, entered the Croatian political scene. It represented a sizable force, as about 80% of the population were peasants. All the progressive parties united into one party in 1902, and the so-called Croatian Question, dealing with the destiny of Austro-Hungarian Slavs and the monarchy, moved more and more to the centre of politics.

Meanwhile, in Serbia, King Alexander, of the pro-German Obrenović Dynasty, was assassinated in 1903, and substituted by Petar, of the Karadjordjević Dynasty, which was more orientated towards Russia, France and Britain. The change of dynasty brought about opposition to the Austro-Hungarian Empire within Serbia, and many Serbs in Croatia also stopped supporting Hungary, and switched their interests instead to building closer ties with the Croats.

A series of events, culminating with the assassination of the Austrian Archduke in Sarajevo (organized by a Serbian movement known as the Black Hand, without the knowledge of the Serbian king), led the entire region into the First World War (1914-1918).

During the First World War, the centre of Croatian politics was moved outside the country with the exiled Yugoslav Committee, which represented the Yugoslavian people under the Austro-Hungarian monarchy, and aimed to unify all the South Slav countries into one nation. A very important event, which somehow inspired the idea of a new South Slav nation, was an agreement between the allied forces of the Triple Entente (Britain, France and Russia) and Italy. Formulated in 1915 and known as the London Agreement, it promised a large part of the Croatian coast to Italy, provided Rome entered the war on the Allied side.

The Kingdom of Yugoslavia & Tito's Yugoslavia

At the end of the First World War, the southern Slavs – the Croats and their neighbours the Serbs and Slovenes – set up their own state. On 1 December 1918 this unification was officially announced in Belgrade and the new Kingdom of Serbs, Croats and Slovenes was formed. The only person to oppose the unification was Stjepan Radić, leader of the Croatian Peasants' Party, who said to the Croatian delegation before their journey to Belgrade, "Do not rush yourselves like geese in the fog."

The basic problem with the unification was that it was done unconditionally, leaving Croatia with little state autonomy. The unification came about not only due to the aspiration of South Slavic intellectuals from within the country, but also through the interest of France and Britain to disable

German influence and the Bolshevik ideal. Meanwhile, under the Treaty of Rapallo, the Triple Entente awarded Italy the region of Istria, the islands of Cres, Lošinj, Lastovo and Palagruža, the city of Zadar and part of Slovenia, as promised in the London Agreement.

In 1921, on St Vitus Day (28 June), parliament voted for a constitution that was centralistic, and as such could not satisfy the Croats, who were determined to keep some sort of autonomy. The Croatian Peasants' Party opposed the move and tried to obtain the support of several Western European countries, but they approved the politics of Belgrade.

Thus in 1927, the Croatian Peasant's Party, lead by Radić, together with the Independent Democratic Party, lead by Svetozar Pribičević, formed a political coalition named the Peasants' Democratic Coalition. Svetozar Pribičević was a Serbian politician from Croatia who initially supported Yugoslavian centralism, and was one of the people responsible for the unconditional unification. However, he was later disheartened and changed his views. Realizing that there was a danger that the Serbs in Croatia might unite with the Croats, extremist politicians from Belgrade shot at members of the Croatian Peasants' Party in parliament on 20 June 1928. Two members of the party were killed and Stjepan Radić later died of the wounds he had received.

King Aleksandar used the assassination to dismiss the parliament on 6 January 1929, to abolish the constitution and set up a royal dictatorship. In the same year, he changed the country's name to the Kingdom of Yugoslavia, meaning the 'Kingdom of the South Slavs', and divided it into nine governmental regions. The use of the terms Croat, Serb and Slovene, together with their national flags, was prohibited. Exception was made for the Serbian flag, on the grounds that it was also the flag of the Serbian Orthodox Church. In 1931, the king announced the new constitution of the Kingdom of Yugoslavia, without a parliamentary vote.

By this time, around 90% of all higher governmental official were Serbs, and out of 165

Tito's birthplace, Kumrovec.

generals, 161 were Serbs and only two were Croats. Out of reaction to the regime, the Bosnian-Croat Ante Pavelić founded the Ustaša movement, which stood for military action against the Kingdom of Yugoslavia, and was supported by extremists in Italy and Hungary. On 9 October 1934, members of this movement assassinated King Aleksandar in Marseille while he was on an official visit to France. After Aleksandar's death, Duke Pavle Karadjordjević was installed as a regent to lead the country in the name of the underage king, Peter.

Even though Duke Pavle was strongly opposed to the Germans, the kingdom was surrounded by Axis Powers, and he therefore felt he had no choice but to join them. In reply to a message from the American president, Franklin Roosevelt, that Yugoslavia should not approach the Germans, the duke said: "It's easy for you big nations a long way away to tell the smaller ones what to do." Two days later, on 27 March 1941, a military putsch took place in Belgrade, organized and paid for with 100,000 pounds in gold by the British secret services.

Once the regency had been removed from power, a new government, led by General Dušan Šimović, was formed. Already on 6 April 1941, Germany and Italy attacked the kingdom. On

10 April, in Zagreb, the Independent State of Croatia (NDH) was proclaimed, with Ante Pavelić as leader. Croatia's independence was at first met with high hopes by the majority of Croats, but when the government gave a large part of the coast to Italy, and began persecuting Serbs, Jews and Gypsies, this support suddenly vanished. The country was divided into two spheres: the south was governed by Italians, and the north by Germans.

As a reaction, the Partisan movement was founded and as the terror enforced by the Italians, Germans and the government increased, so the number of partisans rose. Even though the movement was mainly organized by Communists, members of the Croatian Peasants' Party also participated. The leader of the outlawed Communist Party, Josip Broz, now became the organizer of the largest anti-fascist movement in occupied Europe.

On 8 September 1943, Italy capitulated, and it was decided that both the Treaty of Rapallo from 1920 and the Treaty of Rome from 1941, through which Italy had taken possession of much of the Croatian coast, should be abolished.

Initially, the Allied forces only acknowledged the Yugoslav royal government in exile, based in

London, but later the British were the first to help the partisans, having been persuaded by Winston Churchill, who even sent his son as a military agent to Tito. That was how the British established a strong military base on the island of Vis, which for some time was the capital of liberated Yugoslavia. It was on Vis, on 14 June 1944, that the first meeting between Tito and Šubašić, the representative of the Yugoslav government in exile, took place. In early 1945, there was a conference in Yalta, where the well-known division of interests in a liberated Europe was agreed between Stalin and Churchill. Their interests in Yugoslavia were divided 50-50.

Germany capitulated on 9 May 1945, bringing about the end of the Independent State of Croatia. Together with the military retreat, many pro-Ustaša civilians also tried to leave the country, frightened of possible revenge attacks. When they reached Austria, they were turned back by the British army, and regardless of whether they were soldiers or civilians, they were handed over to the partisans and killed on the field of Bleiburg.

The true number of war casualties remains unknown. After the Second World War, the Yugoslavian government sent a report (for obtaining war reparations) to an international committee in which they stated that 1,700,000 people had been killed. But many people believe that the real number was around 1,000,000. Estimates regarding how many people died in the infamous concentration camp of Jasenovac vary from 60,000 to 700,000.

The Federal People's Republic of Yugoslavia was proclaimed on 29 November 1945, organized as a federal and socialist country of people with equal rights. It was made up of six republics (Slovenia, Croatia, Serbia, Montenegro, Macedonia, and Bosnia and Herzegovina), and unlike the other countries of Eastern Europe, did not acknowledge Stalin as holding absolute power, as the Yugoslav partisans had liberated the country from the Germans by themselves.

Yugoslavia now found itself acting as a barrier between the Eastern and Western blocks. Placing itself midway between the Communist East and the Capitalist West, it set up the so-called self-management organizations, in which firms were managed by the workers themselves through a workers' council, which had the power to determine production, to decide on the distribution of profit and to build homes for their workers.

Post-war reconstruction was rapid and optimistic. Increased industrialization brought about mass migration from rural areas to the cities, and modern high-rise suburbs sprung up. Public health and education were well funded, and living standards rose significantly. Tourism began developing along the Adriatic coast in the 1960s, bringing with it foreign currency. All this was conducted under the ideal of 'Brotherhood and Unity', a motto Tito coined to stress the importance of holding the country together and suppressing individual nationalist aspirations.

However, the richer republics (Croatia and Slovenia) soon began to object to having to pay hefty taxes to Belgrade for investment in the less-developed parts of the country. This, plus the fact that national feelings could not be openly expressed, gradually lead to a silent discontent that culminated in the so-called 'Croatian Spring' of 1971. Those who participated demanded greater autonomy for Croatia, greater cultural freedom, and for the foreign currencies received from tourism and earned by Croats working abroad to stay in the republic. By the end of 1971 Tito decided that it had all gone too far and the movement was suppressed. However, some results were gained in 1973 when a new constitution was introduced by which the individual republics' sovereignty was strengthened and their right to eventual independence was acknowledged.

On 4 May 1980, Josip Broz Tito, the persona who had held Yugoslavia together for almost four decades, died in Ljubljana. The respect he had gained abroad was illustrated by the extraordinary line up of world statesmen who attended his funeral, said to have been the largest gathering of its kind in history. Due to his policy of non-alignment and skilful manoeuvres between the

MINE MINES

NE PRILAZITE
NA OVOM PODRUČJU JE VELIKA
OPASNOST OD MINA

Landmines warning sign.

Croatian flag.

East and West, Yugoslavia had gained greater importance and more loans than a country of such proportions and economic development objectively deserved. Tito left behind the proposal of a rotating presidency, whereby each republic would take a turn at leading the country for one year. But as only a charismatic persona such as Tito himself could hold so many different interests and people on one leash, future problems were in store.

The war of independence

In the late 1980s, the appearance of Albanian nationalism in Kosovo gave a good excuse for the programme for a Greater Serbia. Having seized the presidency in Serbia, in 1988 Slobodan Milošević deposed the Communist leaders of Vojvodina, Kosovo and Montenegro, and in 1989 he made amendments to the Serbian constitution, thereby eliminating the autonomy of the provinces of Vojvodina and Kosovo.

The year 1989 saw the fall of the Berlin Wall and the demise of Communist regimes throughout the countries of Eastern Europe, followed the

disintegration of the USSR. Attempts by the Croatian economist Ante Marković and the Reformed Communists to save Yugoslavia seemed destined to fail from the start, mainly because of Milošević. In spring 1990, the Croatian Democratic Union (HDZ), lead by Franjo Tudjman, won the elections in Croatia on a nationalist manifesto. The Assembly met for the first time on 30 May 1990, and Tudjman was elected president. However, in August, Serbs in Knin began rebelling against the Croatian state, fearing that they would be marginalized by its nationalist agenda.

During the first months of 1991, the presidents of the six republics of Yugoslavia conducted negotiations about the governmental structure of Yugoslavia. Croatia and Slovenia wanted a confederation, while Milošević insisted on a firm federation. In May 1991, a referendum for independence and sovereignty was held in Croatia, with 93% of those who attended voting in favour (turn out was 82%).

At the end of June, the Yugoslavian People's Army (JNA) was sent in to Slovenia, but fighting there lasted just a few days as the country was not a target of Milošević's expansionism, having no significant Serbian minority. However, the war then transferred to Croatia, where Milošević was eager to defend the 600,000 strong Serbian community, who were mainly concentrated in the old *Krajina* (military border) zones. Local Serbs worked together with the JNA, who were confronted by poorly armed Croatian policemen and voluntary soldiers. Much of the former *Krajina* came under Serb control in the so-called Log Revolution (trees were felled and placed across roads to block access to the region), and the Republic of the Serbian Krajina was declared, effectively cutting off one-third of the country. Basically the Serbs said that if the Croats could claim independence from Belgrade, then they wanted independence from Zagreb.

Serbian TV, Milošević's main propaganda tool, predicted the resurgence of the Independent State of Croatia (NDH), spreading fear among Serbs of a return to the Second World War-style persecution. Likewise, Croatian TV broadcast horrific stories of Serbian barbarianism and the evils of Communism. The seeds of ethnic hatred had been sown and it became increasingly impossible to distinguish the truth from the lies.

Since negotiations with the mediation of the EU proved unsuccessful, the Croatian parliament broke off all relations with Yugoslavia on 8 October 1991. Also in October, the JNA and Montenegran forces placed Dubrovnik under a six-month siege, and in November, after heroic resistance by the Croats, the Serbs managed to take Vukovar in eastern Slavonia in the bloodiest and cruellest fighting the war would see.

Members of the EU, with much persuasion from Germany and the Vatican, recognized Croatia's independence on 15 January 1992. The JNA left Serb-occupied territories, which remained, however, in the hands of the self-proclaimed Republic of the Serbian Krajina. In March 1992 UN peacekeepers were sent in to oversee the situation. Isolated incidents of ethnic violence continued, but all out fighting had stopped. On 22 May 1992 Croatia became a member of the United Nations.

Under President Clinton, the US began sending in American military advisors to train the Croatian army. In early May 1995, with American blessing, in the military operation Blijesak (Lightning), Croatian forces attacked a Serb-held enclave in western Slavonia. The Serbs were forced to evacuate the region, giving the Croatian army a victory and considerably reducing the Croatian territory controlled by the Serbs.

Then, in August, with the military operation Oluja (Storm), Serb-held areas of North Dalmatia and Lika were liberated. The fall of the Republic of the Serbian Krajina was officially announced when Croatian soldiers hoisted the red and white flag above Knin Fortress. A mass exodus of Serbian families ensued, with most fleeing to neighbouring Bosnia and to Serbia-proper.

Through the Erdut Agreement, the area of eastern Slavonia with Vukovar and Baranja was placed under UN control, until being reintegrated into Croatian territory in January 1998.

Once hostilities were over, it was time to pick up the pieces. Despite having delivered the country its long-desired independence, Tudjman and the ruling HDZ party rapidly lost popularity. The international community accused the Croatian state of interfering with Bosnia (Tudjman had set up an embarrassing allegiance with Bosnian Croats), media manipulation, an appalling human rights record, and the failure to comply with The Hague over war crimes. During the war, Tudjman's upholding of conservative values such as the family, the church and the nation had been enough to keep many people happy.

But after several years of peace, it became apparent that the entire national economy had been undermined, and that nothing would improve until there was a complete change in policy. A new elite class had emerged – those close to the HDZ who had been awarded hefty slices of state property for their loyalty, and those who had made fast money out of black market dealings during the war. The rest of society remained impoverished, unemployment was rife, and even those who had jobs seldom saw their monthly pay cheque on time. *(This section was researched and written by Domagoj Mijan.)*

Art & architecture

Osijek's Church of St Peter and St Paul is one of the very few to have stained-glass windows in Croatia.

Painting & sculpture

The first individual artists to have been recorded in the history of Croatian art were sculptors working in Romanesque style during the 13th century: Master Radovan, who completed the magnificent main portal of Trogir Cathedral, and Andrea Buvina, who carved the well-preserved wooden doors to Split Cathedral. Then, during the 15th century, with the dawn of the Renaissance, some important artists combined the skills of architecture and sculpture, notably Juraj Dalmatinac, who was responsible for the 74 heads cut in stone that make up the freize on the exterior of Šibenik Cathedral, and his pupil Andrea Aleši, who completed the delicately carved baptistry in the same building.

The 15th century also saw the first notable Croatian movement of painters. In the wealthy and culturally advanced city of Dubrovnik, a group of painters inspired by Italian Gothic art and the

Byzantine tradition became known as the Dubrovnik School. Unfortunately, few of their works have been preserved – mainly due to the destructive earthquake of 1667 – but Blaž Jurjev Trogiranin (also known as Blasius Pictor) from Trogir and Lovro Dobričević from Kotor (present-day Montenegro) can be singled out. They produced a wealth of icons and ornate polyptychs featuring religious scenes, both for Catholic and Orthodox churches, using rich blues, greens and reds, often against a golden background. Today you can see examples of Trogiranin's work in Korčula Town – a polyptych *Our Lady with Saints* in the Abbey Treasury and a polyptych *Our Lady the Co-redeemer* in the Church of All Saints. Several outstanding pieces by Dobričević are on display in the Dominican Monastery in Dubrovnik.

The country's most noted 19th-century painter is Vlaho Bukovac (1855-1922). Born in Cavtat, he studied in Paris and also spent some time in England, where he executed portraits of various aristocratic families, into which he was received as a friend and guest; his *Potiphar's Wife* was exhibited in the Royal Academy of London. From 1903 to 1922 he was a professor at the Academy of Art in Prague. The house were he was born in Cavtat has been turned into a gallery displaying a collection of his paintings and drawings.

Split's greatest painter is generally acknowledged to be Emanuel Vidović (1870-1953). He studied in Venice then moved back to Split, where he would work outdoors, making colourful sketches, then return to his studio to rework his impressions on large canvasses, often producing dark, hazy paintings with a slightly haunting atmosphere. The Vidović Gallery in Split displays almost 70 of his paintings, donated to the city by his family.

For many people, Croatia's most outstanding 20th-century artist is Edo Murtić (1921-2005). Born in Velika Pisanica near Bjelovar in inland Croatia, he grew up in Zagreb where he also studied art. During the Second World War he designed posters and illustrated books connected to the Partisan liberation movement. After the war he visited New York, where he met American abstract expressionists such as Jackson Pollock, and completed a cycle of paintings called Impressions of America. During the 1960s and 1970s he was one of the masters of European abstract art, painting vast canvasses with mighty bold strokes and daring colours. In the 1980s his works became less abstract, featuring recognizable Mediterranean landscapes. He has paintings in the Tate Gallery in London and MOMA in New York.

Croatia's best-known and most prolific 20th-century sculptor has to be Ivan Meštrović (1883-1962). Born into a peasant family from the Dalmatian hinterland, he was sent to work with a stonecutter in Split, where he showed considerable skill and was thus sent to study at the Art Academy in Vienna, financed by a Viennese mine owner. Although he did not like his professor, he had great respect for the noted Austrian architect Otto Wagner, who also taught there, and soon became influenced by the Vienna Secession movement. In Vienna he also met Rodin, who inspired him to travel in Italy and France, and then to settle in Paris, where he became internationally renowned. He then spent several years in Rome, mixing with members of the Italian Futurist movement, such as Ungaretti and de Chirico. In 1911 he won first prize at an international exhibition in Rome, where critics hailed him as the best sculptor since the Renaissance.

During the First World War he spent some time in England where he staged a one-man exhibition at London's Victoria and Albert Museum. After the First World War he returned to his homeland, taking a house in Zagreb – which is now open to the public as the Meštrović Atelier – and designing a villa in Split, today the Meštrović Gallery. However, at the beginning of the Second World War he was imprisoned by the fascist Ustaše, and it was only through the intervention of his friends in Italy, including the Pope, that he managed to leave the country. He spent the rest of his life in the USA, but upon his death his body was returned to Croatia where he was buried in the family mausoleum as he had requested. Today he has pieces in stone, bronze and wood on show in the Tate Gallery in London and the Uffizi in Florence. In several Croatian towns you can see bronze statues of important local cultural figures, such as Grgur Ninski and Marko Marulić in Split and Juraj Dalmatinac in Šibenik, which he created as public works. In the US his best-known outdoor piece is *Equestrian Indians* in Grant Park, Chicago.

Architecture

Classical

The finest remaining buildings from Roman times can be seen in the cities of Pula and Split. In the former, the oldest significant monument is a first-century BC triumphal arch, known as the Arch of the Sergi. It was built to celebrate the role of three high-ranking military officers from the Sergi family at the Battle of Actium in 31 BC; upon their return home they would have led their triumphant soldiers through the arch into the walled city. Made up of a single arch flanked with slender columns with Corinthian capitals, it is ornamented with base reliefs of dolphins, a sphinx and a griffon, and an eagle struggling with a snake. Originally it would have been topped with statues of the three generals. Italian Renaissance architects Palladio and Michelangelo were obviously suitably impressed by it, as both sketched it on their travels. Close by, the present-day main square was once the forum and, of the principal public buildings that stood here, the first-century AD Temple of Augustus remains intact. Typically designed to be viewed from the front, it is elevated on a high base with steps leading up to an open portico supported by six tall columns. Located outside the former walls, Pula's best-known Roman building is the colossal first-century AD amphitheatre, which was built to host gladiator fights and could accommodate up to 22,000 spectators, making it the sixth largest surviving Roman amphitheatre in the world.

Moving south down the coast, Split grew up within the 25-m-high walls of a unique third-century palace, commissioned by Emperor Diocletian as a retirement residence. Combining the qualities of a Roman garrison and an imperial villa, this vast structure is based on a rectangular ground plan measuring 215 m by 180 m, and contains various individual monuments such as an octagonal mausoleum (now the cathedral) and a classical temple dedicated to Jupiter (now a baptistery). British and French architects and artists first acknowledged its magnificence during the 18th century when many visited it as part of the Grand Tour; it is said to have inspired the Scottish architect Robert Adam in some of his finest neoclassical projects upon his return to the UK.

Six kilometres inland from Split, the archaeological site of Salona was once the largest Roman urban centre in Croatia, with an estimated population of 60,000 in the third century AD. Sadly it was devastated in the seventh century; today only the ruins remain.

During the sixth century the coastal region came under Byzantine rule. Architecturally, the Byzantine Empire is best known for its magnificent Christian basilicas, and the most outstanding example in Croatia is Euphrasius Basilica in Poreč. Built under the rule of Emperor Justinian (AD 483-565), during the same period as Hagia Sophia in Constantinople (present-day Istanbul), this complex comprises a central atrium, with an octagonal baptistery to one side, and opposite it the basilica itself, where the central aisle focuses on a main apse decorated with splendid golden mosaics.

Pre-Romanesque

The Croats arrived in the region in the seventh century and gradually began taking on the Christian faith. Between the ninth and 11th centuries about 150 small pre-Romanesque churches, often referred to as early Croatian churches, were built, mainly along the coast. Byzantine influence is apparent in their geometric massing, though they tend towards minimum decoration, limited to finely carved stonework ornamented with plait-design motifs reminiscent of Celtic art. The most perfect example is the tiny ninth-century Holy Cross in Nin, based on the plan of a Greek cross, while the largest and most imposing is the monumental ninth-century rotonda St Donat's in Zadar, based on a circular ground plan with three semi-circular apses. You can see an excellent collection of early Croatian church stonework in the Croatian Museum of Archaeological Monuments in Split.

Romanesque

The 12th century saw the dawn of the Romanesque age, which was marked by imposing cathedrals, generally made up of triple naves with semi-circular apses, and ornate façades featuring blind arches. The most beautiful – the Cathedral of St Anastasia and the Church of St Chrysogonus – are in Zadar, though other notables examples include the Cathedral of Our Lady of the Assumption in Krk Town, the Church of St Mary the Great (which was a cathedral until 1828) in Rab Town, and the portal of the Cathedral of St Lawrence in Trogir, which was carved by the outstanding Dalmatian sculptor Master Radovan in the early 13th century. Unfortunately, Croatia's two most important Romanesque cathedrals were destroyed – the one in Zagreb by the Tartars in 1242, and the one in Dubrovnik by the 1667 earthquake (subsequently rebuilt in later styles).

Venetian Gothic

When Venice began colonizing the east Adriatic coast, it brought with it the so-called Venetian Gothic style, characterized by the pointed arch and rib vaulting. The style is apparent in 15th- and 16th-century churches and houses in Istria and Dalmatia, such as the finely carved portal of Korčula Cathedral by Bonino from Milan, and the triple pointed-arch windows of the Čipko Palace in Trogir by Andrea Aleši. It is often seen mixed with more severe Renaissance elements, most notably in the work of Juraj Dalmatinac on Šibenik Cathedral (see below), hence the term Gothic-Renaissance.

Renaissance

The Renaissance, which started in Italy, marked a revival of Roman civilization, not just in art and architecture but in an entire set of values. The movement is normally said to have dawned in Croatia in 1441, when Juraj Dalmatinac, a builder from Zadar who had trained for a short time in Venice, began work on Šibenik Cathedral (although he did not live to see it completed; the later work was carried out by two of his pupils, Nikola Firentinac and Andrija Aleši). Dalmatinac also drew up the urban plan for Pag Town in 1443, and worked on other noted projects, such as the Chapel of St Anastasius in Split Cathedral and Minceta Fortress in Dubrovnik. You can see a 20th-century statue of Dalmatinac, by Ivan Meštrović, in front of Šibenik Cathedral.

The Renaissance continued developing along the coast, in areas that were not under the Turks, until the end of the 16th century. During this period many towns were fortified with defensive walls and towers, the best examples being Dubrovnik, Korčula and Hvar.

Increased wealth, plus the ideals of Renaissance philosophy, lead to the construction of more sophisticated houses, with refined details such as carved doors and window frames, balconies with balustrades, stone washbasins, decorated fireplaces and built-in cupboards. People became interested in the relationship between man and nature; houses were set in gardens with arcaded walkways, fountains and stone benches, the best examples being Tvrdalj in Stari Grad on the island of Hvar and Trsteno Arboretum near Dubrovnik, both from the 16th century.

Baroque

Regarded as a symbol of Western civilization, and therefore the antithesis of Ottoman culture, the baroque style flourished in northern Croatia during the late 17th and 18th centuries. The Jesuits, who played an important part in reinforcing the Roman Catholic faith in areas threatened by the Turks, were responsible for introducing the grandiose, curvilinear baroque style to the region. As the Turks were gradually pushed out, many buildings were constructed, reconstructed or extended in baroque style.

Today, the best-preserved baroque town centre is in Varaždin; tragically Vukovar, formerly regarded as the finest baroque town in Croatia, was all but devastated during the war of independence during the 1990s. Other notable examples can be found in Osijek (the 18th-century Tvrđa complex) and in Dubrovnik (the Cathedral from 1671 and the Jesuit Church from 1725, both designed by Italian architects during reconstruction following the earthquake of 1667).

Eclectic

During the 19th century, eclectic design – the revival and reinterpretation of past styles – was popular throughout Europe. In Zagreb, the buildings of Donji Grad, constructed when the region was under Austro-Hungary, mix various elements from classical, Gothic and baroque periods. The most prolific architect in north Croatia at this time was Herman Bolle (1845-1926). Born in Koln, Germany, he participated in the construction of about 140 buildings in Croatia, including Zagreb Cathedral, Mirogoj Cemetery and the Museum of Arts and Crafts, all in Zagreb.

Vienna Secession

By the close of the 19th century, artists and architects in various parts of Europe were rebelling against the decadence of eclectic buildings and the pomp and formality of older styles, and searching instead for more pure and functional forms. In German-speaking countries this trend was known as Jugendstil, and in France as art nouveau. In 1897 in Vienna, a group of visual artists founded a movement, which became known as the Vienna Secession. The architects involved strove to give simple geometric forms to their buildings, while working in close collaboration with artists, who provided discreet, elegant details such as frescoes and mosaics. The best examples of this style in Croatia, which was still part of the Austro-Hungarian Empire at the time, are Villa Santa Maria, Villa Frappart and Villa Magnolia, all designed by the Austrian architect Carl Seidl and found in Lovran, close to Opatija. In Osijek, Europska Avenue is lined with fine Viennese Secessionist buildings by local architects.

Modernism

There are very few examples of quality modernist architecture in Croatia, though the ideals of the modern movement were held dear by the Socialist state during the second half of the 20th century. The resulting buildings are primarily high-rise apartment blocks, most of which are light and airy with large balconies, and vast hotel complexes that have sprung up along the coast, which are rather impersonal but functional and comfortable.

Modern apartment building.

Croatia today

Parliament building, Zagreb.

Politics

After the war of independence both Tudjman and Milošević dodged justice: Tudjman died, after a long illness, in December 1999, and Milošević passed away in March 2006, before The Hague was able to pass sentence on either of them.

After Tudjman's death, the HDZ immediately set about trying to organize a convincing election campaign, but the Croatian public had already lost faith. At the elections in January 2000 a new centre-left six-party coalition won and former Communists Ivica Račan and Stipe Mesić were sworn in as Croatia's prime minister and president. However, early elections in November 2003 saw the HDZ back in power, the party having apparently dispelled its nationalist, authoritarian image to become a mainstream conservative movement. Ivo Sanader thus replaced Račan as prime minister.

The new government promised to steer the country towards the European Union and encourage national reconciliation. However, despite much-improved relations with Serbia, and the fact that the Independent Democratic Serbian Party (SDSS), which aims to facilitate the return of refugees, formed a part of Sanader's coalition government, by 2007 only 125,000 of the 250,000 displaced Croatian Serbs had returned to register in Croatia, and most of these were elderly people from rural villages, or people who had registered but were not actually living in Croatia. This slow progress is attributed to problems over property (many Serb homes were destroyed or occupied by other people during the war), unemployment and fear of discrimination.

Another major stumbling block, up until late 2005, was Croatia's failure to hand over indicted war criminals to the Criminal Tribunal for the Former Yugoslavia (ICTY) in The Hague. The key to Croatia commencing EU accession negotiations was the capture of General Ante Gotovina (indicted for crimes during and after Operation Storm in 1995, but considered by extreme Croatians nationalists to be a hero). In December 2005, Gotovina was arrested in Spain and handed over to The Hague. In 2005 and 2006, President Mesić of Croatia and President Tadić of Serbia exchanged official visits in a bid to improve relations between the two countries.

Sanader's government was narrowly re-elected in November 2007. In July 2009, he resigned unexpectedly, and was replaced by Croatia's first female prime minister, Jadranka Kosor. In November 2009, Jadranka Kosor and her Slovenian counterpart Borut Pahor signed an agreement ending Slovenia's blockade of Croatia's EU accession. Slovenia, which was the first former Yugoslav state to join the EU in 2004, had been blocking Zagreb's progress due to land and maritime border disputes, which still need to be resolved.

Mesić remained president until January 2010, when his maximum two five-year terms in office came to an end. Following a tense presidential

Political carnival decoration.

campaign, the Croatian people voted Josip Josipović as their new President.

Josipović, a left-wing law professor and classical music composer, promised to fight corruption and bring the country into the European Union. His victory was welcomed by Serbian President Boris Tadić, and he is expected to improve Croatia's relations with the other counties of former Yugoslavia. Croatia now hopes to enter the EU in January 2012.

Economy

The war and its after effects had a devastating effect on the Croatian economy, especially in the industrial sector. Shipbuilding and maritime transport, in which former Yugoslavia held the third position in the world economy (and which were mainly concentrated along the Croatian coast), faced a sharp decline. Some 35,000 Croatian sailors now work on foreign ships.

Privatization began in earnest after the war, though it is still not complete. Most steel companies and shipyards are still under state ownership, although the financial sector has been completely privatized and 90% of banks are now owned by foreign investors.

When the kuna was introduced as the national currency in 1994, the stability of the kuna-German deutschmark exchange rate was maintained; now stability is monitored against the euro.

The Croatian trade deficit is constantly growing, though it is being compensated for in part by money transfers from Croats living abroad, sailors working for foreign companies, and by income from tourism: 80% of deposits in Croatian banks are in euro.

Sector by sector, the Croatian GDP is composed of agriculture and fisheries 7%, industry 32% and services 61% (2009). In 2009 the GDP growth rate stood at 5.2% and the GDP per capita at US$17,600, exceeding that of many of the Eastern European countries that became EU members in 2004. The strongest Croatian companies, such as pharmaceutical company PLIVA and the food processor PODRAVKA, are present on the world market.

However, the costs of the state represents a major burden on the economy. The war and its after effects led to a drastic rise in unemployment. In 1980 the unemployment rate was 5.5%; in 1989 it

Shipbuilding, Split.

was 8%; in the following years it rose as high as 22%, though by 2007 it had dropped to 11.8%. By 2009 it had risen again to 16.1%, reflecting the general global economic crisis.

The biggest potential lies in the tourism and travel sector, which in 2009 was employing 26.3% of the working population. According to the World Travel and Tourism Council (WTTC), the contribution of travel and tourism to Croatia's GDP is expected to rise from 24.8% (US$14,481 million) in 2010 to 29.4% in 2020. The introduction of the euro has made Croatia more attractive to EU citizens: such clean sea cannot be found anywhere else in Europe, and Croatia is probably the safest destination on the Mediterranean. Many hotels have been privatized and upgraded to offer high-class accommodation and luxurious extras such as wellness centres.

Croatia's greatest resource is its well-preserved natural environment. The decline of the industrial sector as a result of the war meant that an ecologically clean country became even cleaner.

The high proportion of fertile land per capita gives the country the potential of producing large quantities of healthy food. Land and property prices are still lower than in most EU countries, though they have risen significantly since 2000 due to the interest shown by second-home buyers from abroad. Croatia obtains a large share of its power supply from hydroelectric power plants, and could potentially provide for its energy needs from renewable sources such as wind and sun. Drinking water is abundant and tap water is drinkable throughout the country.

Two new motorways, linking Zagreb and Split, and Zagreb and Rijeka, opened in summer 2005. In October 2007 construction work began on the new Pelješac Bridge, intended to improve connections to South Dalmatia. When completed, this 2.4-km cable-stayed bridge will span the channel between Komarna on the mainland to Rosčica Glavica on Pelješac. Unfortunately, building work has fallen behind schedule so that it looks unlikely to open before 2015.

Nature & environment

Dinaric Alps.

Landscapes & geography

Croatia is a boomerang-shaped country with a total surface area of 56,690 sq km, making it about three-quarters the size of Scotland. It sits on the east coast of the Adriatic and serves as the main gateway from the Mediterranean to Eastern Europe. It has 1778 km of indented mainland coastline and more than 1000 islands and islets, of which only 67 are inhabited.

The territory is made of flat plains, low mountains, the mainland coast and offshore islands, and can be broken down into three regions: the Pannonian Basin, the Dinaric Mountains and the Adriatic coast.

Pannonian Basin

The gently undulating hills and flat plains between the River Drava to the north (forming a natural border with Hungary), the River Danube to the east (border with Serbia) and the River Sava to the south (border with Bosnia and Herzegovina) were known as Pannonia, which was later renamed Slavonia. This is a region of fertile agricultural land, producing wheat, corn, sugar beet and sunflowers, with lush pastures and vineyards on the hills to the north. Moving west towards Zagreb, the Peri-Pannonian area is made up of low hills and pastures suitable for livestock, which gradually gives way to industry as you approach the capital.

Dinaric Mountains

The Dinaric Alps extend 640 km along the east coast of the Adriatic Sea from the River Isonzo in northeast Italy to north Albania. A belt running from northwest to southeast, they mark the natural border between the west of Bosnia and Herzegovina and Croatia, and form a barrier to travel from the coast to the interior, as there are no natural passes. They are composed of limestone and dolomite, easily eroded sedimentary rocks that give rise to karst forms such as sinkholes and caves. The region is sparsely populated and supports scanty cereal production, some orchards and vineyards, livestock breeding and dairy farming. The highest peak, also called Dinara, reaches 1831 m.

Adriatic coast

The partially submerged western slopes of the Dinaric Alps form the bays, gulfs, inlets and offshore islands along the Croatian coast. The coast extends from the northwest to the southeast, following the basic extension of the Dinaric system. Between Rijeka (Kvarner) and Šibenik (Central Dalmatia), the islands run parallel to the coast, and are separated by channels, interlinked by straits. Southeast from here, between Split and Dubrovnik, the islands of Čiovo, Šolta, Hvar, Brač, Korčula, Vis, Lastovo and Mljet extend from the west to the east. The largest island is Krk; other islands include Cres, Brač, Hvar, Pag and Korčula. The coastal area may be further divided into the northern (Istria and Kvarner) and southern (Dalmatia) parts.

Wildlife & vegetation

Croatia's contrasting geographic regions afford a variety of natural vegetation. Approximately 35% of the country is forested. The common oak predominates in the hills on the northern edge of the Pannonian Basin, while the forests and grasslands of the eastern part have been largely felled and turned into arable land, the one exception

National parks

The richest and most fascinating areas of natural beauty have been designated national parks. To enter them, visitors are required to pay an entry fee, which goes towards their upkeep. Each park has an information office providing maps and a basic introduction to the area's flora and fauna. Three of the national parks (Kornati, Brijuni and Mljet) are on islands, two centre on systems of waterfalls (Plitvice and Krka) and the others are mountainous.
National park websites:
Brijuni brijuni.hr
Kornati kornati.hr
Krka npkrka.hr
Mljet np-mljet.hr
Paklenice paklenica.hr
Plitvice np-plitvicka-jezera.hr
Risnjak risnjak.hr

being the wetlands of Kopački Rit, which have been preserved as a nature park. The Dinaric Mountains are quite barren, though lower altitudes of up to 1200 m support dispersed forests of beech and fir, while specimens of spruce, sycamore and elm can be found in the same belt. The area along the Adriatic coast and the islands are covered with sub-Mediterranean and Mediterranean vegetation. Evergreen forests of holm oak and Aleppo pine, as well as macchia, are typical of the coastal belt and the islands. Some of the islands, notably Pag and the Kornati, display karst features and are relatively barren, but for feather grass and sage.

There are some 380 protected animal species in Croatia, the largest being the brown bear, the wild boar and the wolf, all of which are sighted in Risnjak, Paklenica and Plitvice national parks. The deer, wildcat and lynx are also present in Risnjak, while the otter is sometimes spotted in Plitvice. The seaward slopes of the Dinaric Mountains, notably Velebit and Biokovo, are populated by mouflon and chamois. Birds of prey such as Eurasion griffon vultures and peregrine falcons can be found in seaward-facing cliffs and gorges, while wading birds such as storks and herons are seasonal visitors to the inland wetlands of Kopački Rit and Lošinjsko Polje nature parks. Whales and dolphins swim in the Adriatic.

Festivals & events

Traditional dance, Cavtat.

January

Nova Godina (1st)

Croats celebrate the arrival of New Year with open-air concerts and fireworks in all the big cities – in Zagreb locals head for the main square, Trg Bana Jelačića; in Rijeka they gather on the Korzo; in Split on the Riva (seafront promenade) and in Dubrovnik on Placa in the old town.

February

Sveti Vlaho (3rd)

In Dubrovnik, the life of Saint Blaise, the city's patron, is celebrated with a religious procession around the old town; the saint's remains, in the form of relics, take pride of place. During the time of the republic, those prisoners who did not present a threat to public safety were released on this day to participate in the festivities.

Karneval (around Shrove Tuesday)

In the days leading up to Lent, many towns and villages in Croatia celebrate carnival. The biggest celebrations take place in Rijeka (ri-karneval.com.hr). The main event is the International Carnival Parade, held on the Sunday before Shrove Tuesday and attracting over 100,000 spectators and several thousand participants in costumes and masks. Young men dress up as *zvončari* (clothed in a sheepskin cape, a grotesque animal mask with horns, and a large iron bell tied around the waist). Traditionally, their role is to chase away the forces of evil and invite the coming of spring and new life. In Lastovo Town, on the island of Lastovo, on Shrove Tuesday locals make a straw figurine, known as Poklad, who is tied to a rope and hoisted up and down the hill in the centre of town three times, with fireworks attached to his boots. He is put on a donkey and taken to the square in front of the parish church where he is burnt.

In Split, carnival is known as *maškare*. On the evening of Shrove Tuesday, locals take part in a costume procession, culminating in the burning of *Krnjo* (an effigy symbolizing the past year's evils) on the seafront.

to create a floating stage, with piers and mooring spaces accommodating several hundred luxurious sailing boats and speedboats. Sailing, scuba-diving and windsurfing equipment is also on display. The event attracts thousands of visitors from countries all over the world.

Dani Šparoga

The Asparagus Festival in Lovran, near Rijeka, is one of several food festivals staged here, with a dozen or so of the town's restaurants preparing dishes made from local seasonal delicacy. The event closes with the making of a giant omelette.

Sveti Križ (night before Good Friday)

On the island of Hvar, the Carrying of the Holy Cross is an all-night procession connecting the six villages of Jelsa, Pitve, Vrisnik, Svirče, Vrbanj and Vrboska. Activity begins in the late evening, when groups set out from each parish church, led by a much-honoured young man carrying a large wooden crucifix. The parties pass through each of the other villages in turn, to return to their respective churches for sunrise on Good Friday morning.

March

Festival Dokumentarnog Rock Filma
dorf-vk.com.

The unconventional Festival of Documentary Film brings together both film and music lovers, showcasing documentaries about modern music idols. It's held in Vinkovak near Osijek in Inland Croatia. In 2010 it was expanded to take place in Zagreb and Rijeka as well.

April

Croatia Boat Show
croatiaboatshow.com.

Held in Split, this one-week boat show sees the city's seafront promenade extended over the water

May

Sudamje (7th)

In Split, the bones of St Domnius, the city's patron saint, are on display in the cathedral, and a festival takes place on the Riva (seafront), with stands selling handmade wooden objects and basketry. It is a local public holiday.

Festival Hrvatske Tamburaške Glazbe

Held in Osijek in Slavonia (inland Croatia), the Croatian Tambura Music Festival is a one-week folk music festival celebrating the *tambura*, a long-necked lute popular in Eastern and Southern Europe. Some 30 *tambura* groups participate, hailing from Croatia, Slovenia, Serbia and Austria.

All Saints celebrations, Mirogoj cemetery, Zagreb.

June

Plitvički Maraton (first Sunday)
Plitvice's marathon takes competitors through the forests and around the lakes of the national park.

Dani Trešanja
In Lovran, the Cherry Festival sees these tasty little red fruits consumed in large quantities in local restaurant and cafes. The festival closes with the sampling of a 5-m cherry strudel.

Hartera Festival (mid-June)
hartera.com.
This two-day rock, indie-electro and dance music festival is held in a former-paper factory in Rijeka. The 2009 event saw the London-based dance punk band the Klaxons and the Norwegian electronic band Royksopp performing.

Motovun Film Festival (late June)
motovunfilmfestival.com.
This five-day international festival of avant-garde cinema, founded in 1999, takes place in the medieval hilltown of Motovun.

Libertas Film Festival (late June to early July)
libertasfilmfestival.com.
This international film festival takes place in Dubrovnik's old town. Past guests include Woody Harrelson, Owen Wilson, Nick Nolte and Kevin Spacey.

July & August

Garden Festival (early July)
watchthegardengrow.eu.
This open-air music festival runs over two weekends and is staged at Barbarella's Disco by the sea in Petrčane. It was launched by Zadar's Garden Club in 2006. The 2009 line-up included live acts and DJs including Gilles Peterson, Norman Jay, Greg Wilson, Todd Terje, Lindstrom, Overproof Sound System and Stuart Patterson.

Dubrovačke Ljetne Igre
(mid-July to mid-August)
dubrovnik-festival.hr.
The international Dubrovnik Summer Festival hosts drama, ballet, concerts and opera at open-air venues in the old town.

Zagrebačke Ljetne Večeri
(mid-July to mid-August)
kdz.hr.
Zagreb Summer Evening sees performances by Croatian and foreign orchestras and soloists.

Ethnoambient Salona (late-July)
ethnoambient.net.
Held on the Salona archaeological site near Split, this three-day open-air event attracts musicians from as far afield as Scotland, Portugal and Greece.

Medjunarodna Smotra Folklora (late July)
msf.hr.
In Zagreb, the five-day International Folklore Festival is a celebration of music and dance with performers from Croatia and other southeast European countries dressed in folk costumes.

Pula Festival Igranog Filma (late July)
pulafilmfestival.hr.
The Pula Film Festival is a two-week competitive event held in Pula's Roman Arena and at Kaštel. It features films from both Croatia and abroad.

Rapska Fjera (late-July)
fjera.hr.
Rab Tournament is a three-day event held in Rab Town to record the defence of the town by knights with crossbows in 1364. Locals dress in medieval costume, streets are lit by torches, there's music and demonstrations of traditional skills such as coin minting, grape treading and flour milling.

Seasplash Reggae Festival (late July)
seasplash.net.
This four-day reggae festival is held on the beach at Veli Vrh near Pula.

About the region

Soundwave (late July)
soundwavecroatia.com.
This is one of several dance festivals staged at Barbarella's Disco in Petrčane near Zadar. Summer 2009 saw London-based hip hop DJ Yoda and British soul singer Alice Russell performing.

Glazbene večeri u Sv Donatu (July and August)
kuz.hr.
In Zadar, the Musical Evenings in St Donat's see medieval, Renaissance and baroque music concerts staged inside the churches of St Donat, St Chrysogonus, St Michael, St Simeon and also the Franciscan Monastery.

Festival Dalmatinskih Klapa (July and August)
fdk.hr.
In Omis, the three-week Dalmatian Klapa Festival aims to preserve this form of harmony singing and promote new songs. It now attracts about 80 groups comprising more than a 1000 singers. Performances are held at open-air locations around town and inside the parish church.

Histria Festival (July and August)
histriafestival.com.
This festivals sees live concerts in Pula's Roman Arena, starring international musicians from the worlds of rock and classical music.

Koncerti u Eufraziani (July and August)
concertsinbazilika.com.
In Poreč, sacral and secular music concerts are held in the Basilica of St Euphrasius.

Splitsko Ljeto (July and August)
splitsko-ljeto.hr.
The Split Summer Festival hosts opera, theatre and dance at open-air venues within the walls of Diocletian's Roman Palace.

Jazz u Lapidarju (July and August)
jazzinlap.com.
Jazz in Lapidarium is a jazz festival held in the courtyard of Poreč Town Museum, attracting classical and contemporary performers.

Grisia (early August)
Held in Rovinj's old town, this is a vast open-air art exhibition.

Electric Elephant Festival (late August)
electricelephant.co.uk.
This three-day festival is staged at Barbarella's Disco by the sea in Petrčane near Zadar. It was set up by the team behind Manchester's Electric Chair Club in 2008. The 2009 line-up included Post-rock and electronic musician Kieran Hebden (aka Four Tet) and London DJ Andrew Weatherall.

Faros Marathon (last weekend of August)
Held in Stari Grad on the island of Hvar, this swimming competition sees competitors from as far afield as France and Russia swim 16 km, from town to the end of the bay and back again. In 2008, 20 men and 13 women competed in the race, representing 16 different countries.

September

Stop Making Sense Festival (early September)
sms-2010.com.
Dubbing itself as 'three days and nights of musical anarchy by the sea', this music and dance festival takes place at Barbarella's in Petrčane near Zadar. The 2010 line-up features South African DJ team Sud Electronic and Franco-Brazilian electronic funk band Favela Chic.

Outlook Festival (mid-September)
outlookfestival.com.
On Zrče beach in Novalja on the island of Pag, this three-day event showcases reggae, dub and dance music, attracting thousands of clubbers from all over Europe.

Burning the boats on St Nicholas' day, Komiza.

Varaždinske Barokne Večeri (two weeks from late September to early October) *vbv.hr.*
The Varaždin Baroque Evenings attract international musicians who give baroque music concerts in the cathedral and the Varaždin theatre auditorium. It's hailed as one of Croatia's most important cultural events.

Marunada (late September to early October)
The Chestnut Festival is held in Lovran with local eateries and cafés serving cakes and sweets.

October

Zagreb Maraton (second Sunday)
zagreb-marathon.com.
The Zagreb marathon.

November

Martinje (11th)
In inland Croatia, St Martin's Day is a big event throughout Zagorje, when the ritual blessing of the season's young wine is accompanied by copious festivities until the early hours. It's also celebrated in Zagreb with a big marquee on the main square selling the new season's wine.

December

Sveti Nikola (6th)
St Nicholas, the patron saint of sailors, fishermen and travellers, is honoured with the ceremonial burning of a fishing boat in front of St Nicholas' Church in Komiža on the island of Vis.

Sleeping

Palace Hotel, Hvar.

Along the coast, private accommodation, either in a rented room or apartment, is the best choice in terms of cost, facilities and insight into the way the locals live. However, if you feel like splashing out and being pampered here and there, the hotels listed in this guide have been selected for their authentic atmosphere and central location. There aren't any websites listing private accommodation, but local tourist offices often have details and their websites are listed throughout the book.

Hotels

Croatian tourism dates back to the late-19th century when the region was under Austro-Hungary, and so along the coast you'll find a number of Vienna Secession-style hotels built for the Central European aristocracy of the time, the best examples being in Opatija.

During the tourist boom of the 1970s and 1980s, many of the older hotels were neglected in favour of large modern complexes, which sprang up in popular resorts such as Poreč, Rovinj, Bol, Hvar Town, Korčula Town and Dubrovnik. Although they tend to be vast and somewhat impersonal, these socialist-era hotels are equipped with excellent sports facilities, generally overlook the sea and are discreetly hidden by careful landscaping, a short walk from the centre of town. Over the last few years, some have been totally refurbished and have introduced chic minimalist design and wellness centres, bringing them into the luxury market.

The third and most recent breed of hotel are the small, private, family-run establishments, often in refurbished town houses, which have opened over the last decade and are now united under the **National Association of Small and Family Hotels**. For a full list, check out the website, omh.hr.

All hotels are officially graded by the Ministry of Tourism into five categories: five-star, luxury; four-star, de luxe; three-star, first class; two-star,

moderate; and one-star, budget. Classified hotels are listed by the Croatian National Tourist Board (croatia.hr) under their respective regions.

When referring to price lists, you will find that some hotels list half board and full board only. Simple 'bed and breakfast' works out only very slightly cheaper than half board, but is recommended as, by and large, hotel restaurants lack atmosphere, and the standard of the food unfortunately reflects the savings made in order to be able to offer cheap package deals. You are far better off eating out in local restaurants.

Last but not least, if you are staying on the coast it is well worth asking for a room with a sea view (most of which have balconies); it may cost a little more, but makes all the difference when you wake up in the morning.

Private accommodation

Along the coast you will find a plethora of families offering *sobe* (rooms) and *apartmani* (apartments) for rent, usually with en suite bathrooms and simple self-catering facilities provided. These can be in anything from quaint, old stone cottages with gardens to modern concrete-block three-storey houses with spacious balconies. Hosts are generally welcoming and hospitable, and many visitors find a place they like and then return each summer. Local tourist offices and travel agents have lists of recognized establishments and can arrange bookings for you. In busy areas, you'll also find people waiting for travellers at the ferry ports and bus stations, and offering rooms by word of mouth, but in this case you're not guaranteed to find the best standards.

Prices vary enormously depending on location, season and facilities provided, but you can expect to pay anything from 150-250Kn per person per day for a double room with an en suite bathroom, and anything from 400-1200Kn per day for a four-person apartment with a kitchen and dining area. Note that there is normally a 30% surcharge for stays of less than three nights.

Lighthouses

Another novel and highly popular form of accommodation is the lighthouse. Along the Croatian coast, there are now 11 carefully restored lighthouses with apartments to rent on a weekly basis. Nine of these are on islands (you will be taken there and brought back by boat), and three on peninsulas along the mainland coast. In Istria, these include Savudrija (Umag), Rt Zub (Novigrad), Sv Ivan (Rovinj) and Porer (Pula), while in Dalmatia there are Prišnjak (Murter), Sv Petar (Makarska), Palagruža (Vis), Pločica (VelaLuka), Sušac (Lastovo), Struga (Lastovo) and Sv Andrija (Elafiti).

Most lighthouses have one or two apartments sleeping anything from two to eight people, and several are still home to a resident lighthouse keeper. However, you can be sure of extreme isolation and minimum contact with the outside world, as most of them are located on lonely islets far out to sea. Each apartment has electricity, running water, TV and a fully equipped kitchen. Bed linen and blankets are provided, but be sure to take a week's provisions as there will be no chance of shopping once you are there, unless you come to a special arrangement with local fishermen or the lighthouse keeper.

Prices vary greatly depending on the size of the apartment, location and season, but as an indicator the cost of renting a four-person apartment in the lighthouse of Sv Ivan, near Rovinj, are as follows: July to August €129 per day; June and September €99 per day; and during the rest of the year €79 per day. However, as this has become a hugely popular alternative, be sure to book several months in advance.

For further details contact **Adriatica Net** (Heinzelova 62a, Zagreb, T01-241 5611, adriatica.net) who have an online booking service.

Porer lighthouse, Istria.

About the region

A British-based operator specializing in quality private villas and apartments for holiday rentals in top Croatian resorts is **Croatian Villas Ltd** (Wood Green Business Centre, 5 Clarendon Rd, Wood Green, London N22 6XJ, T020-8888 6655, croatianvillas.com).

Robinson accommodation

So-called 'Robinson Crusoe' style accommodation started out on the Kornati islands, though it is gradually spreading to other isolated locations. As the term implies, this type of accommodation consists of a simple stone cottage, basically furnished and offering minimum modern comforts: gas lighting and water from a well. The beauty of these cottages lies in their detachment from the rest of the world – they are normally found on small unpopulated islands with no regular ferry links to the mainland, no shops and no cars. They are generally for rent on a weekly basis, and transport to them is arranged by the agencies responsible for letting them. For Croatian agencies specializing in these cottages, see page 173.

The British-based operator **Croatia for Travellers** (63 Therberton St, London N1 0QY, T020-7226 4460, croatiafortravellers.co.uk) can also book a cottage for you.

Agrotourism

An increasingly popular accomodation option is so-called agrotourism: farmhouses offering overnight accommodation and home cooking. This is a great solution for families with young children, as exploring the farm and getting to know the animals is guaranteed to go down well with kids. To date, the idea has only really taken off in Istria, but the potential is enormous.

Most of these establishments are off the beaten track (you normally need a car to reach them) and offer bed and breakfast deals in simply furnished rooms with en suite bathrooms. Many also have a restaurant area, often done out in rustic style, serving authentic local dishes (generally far superior to the food served in commercial restaurants), along with their own wine, cheese and olive oil. Some of the larger centres also offer a range of sporting activities such as horse riding and mountain biking.

Prices vary greatly depending on the type of room, the location and season, but expect to pay anything from 180-320Kn per person per day for a double room (with an en suite bathroom) with breakfast in August.

For a list of farms and rural homes offering overnight accommodation and meals throughout the country, visit seoski-turizam.net (in Croatian with some texts also in English), and in Istria check out istra.com/agroturizam.

Camping

The sunny, dry climate and unspoilt nature make Croatia an ideal place for camping. Of at least 130 registered campsites, about 90% are on the mainland coast or on the islands, many backed by pinewoods overlooking the sea. Most operate from early May to early October, are well run and offer basic facilities such as showers and toilets and a small bar, while the larger ones may include restaurants and extensive sports facilities, such as scuba-diving courses and mountain bike rentals. The most developed regions in terms of capacity and facilities provided are Istria and Kvarner, while Dalmatia is in many ways more attractive thanks to its rugged, untamed natural beauty. As in other European countries, camping outside of designated areas is prohibited.

For further information contact **Kamping Udruženje Hrvatske** (Croatian Camping Union, 8 Marta 1, Poreč, T052-451324, camping.hr). Their excellent website lists all official campsites, complete with contact details, facilities and prices. Naturist campsites are also listed and marked 'FKK'.

The Croatian climate is ideal for camping.

Naturist camps

Naked bathing was first pioneered in Croatia in the early 20th century and Europe's first naturist campground opened here in 1953. Today there are 20 naturist campsites, almost all along the coast and on the islands, attracting visitors from Germany, Austria, the Netherlands, Italy and Slovenia, as well as other countries around the world. Europe's largest naturist camp, Koversada, is in Istria, and can provide accommodation for up to 7000 visitors.

For more information about naturism in Croatia, including a list of naturist camps with comments from people who have stayed at them, check out the **Croatia Naturally** website, cronatur.com. For some of the best nudist beaches, see page 198.

Youth hostels

There are youth hostels in Pula, Rijeka, Punat and Krk (both on the island of Krk), Veli Lošinj (on the island of Lošinj), Zadar and Dubrovnik. The Zagreb hostel is currently undergoing renovation, but some rooms are still available to visitors. These provide basic but comfortable dormitory-style accommodation (expect to pay around 120Kn per person per night), and some offer the option of half or full board. For information about hostels contact **Hrvatski Ferijalni i Hostelski Savez** (Croatian Youth Hostel Association, Savska 5, 10000 Zagreb, T01-482 9294, hfhs.hr).

Eating & drinking

Barbecued sardines.

C roatian cuisine can be divided into two main groups: Mediterranean along the coast and Continental in the inland regions. That said, each region has its own particular specialities reflecting its geography, history and culture. Croatia's highly complex past is clearly evident in its cooking, which displays the traces left by centuries of occupation by three foreign empires: the Venetians brought pasta and risotto to the coast; Austro-Hungary introduced paprika-flavoured goulash and strudel inland; and the Ottoman Turks bequeathed the region with *sarma* (stuffed sauerkraut rolls) and baklava.

What to eat

Dalmatia

Along the Dalmatian coast, simple, honest fish and seafood dishes top the menu. All ingredients are fresh and seasonal, so there's little attention paid to fussy preparation. The classic favourite is fresh fish, barbecued and served with olive oil and lemon, plus *blitva sa krumpirom* (swiss chard and potatoes with garlic and olive oil) as a side dish. Likewise, shellfish such as *kucice* (clams) and *škampi* (shrimps) are flashed over a hot flame with garlic, white wine and parsley, a method known as *na buzaru*, which cooks the seafood to a turn and produces a delicious rich sauce to mop up with bread. Worth mentioning here is that some of the best shellfish, notably *ostrige* (oysters) and *dagnje* (mussels), can be found in Ston on Pelješac Peninsula in South Dalmatia.

In summer, a popular and refreshing starter is *salata of hobotnice* (octopus salad) made from octopus, boiled potatoes, onion and parsley, dressed with olive oil and vinegar. Venetian influence is apparent in the abundance of risottos, the most popular being *crni rižot* (black risotto) made from cuttlefish ink, as well as *rižot frutti di mare* (seafood risotto), normally combining mussels, clams and prawns, and *rižot sa škampima* (shrimp risotto) invariably served with a splash of cream at the end. Pasta dishes are also served with a variety of seafood sauces, though the pasta is often overcooked by Italian standards. Another classic Dalmatian dish is *brodet*, a hearty mixed fish stew made with onions and tomatoes, and normally served with polenta. On the island of Hvar a local version of *brodet* is *gregada*, made with onions, potatoes and fresh herbs but no tomato. When it comes to meat dishes, locals rave about *dalmatinski pršut*, smoked dried ham on a par with Italian prosciutto. It's normally served as an appetizer on a platter together with *paški sir* (sheep's cheese from the island of Pag) and a few olives. Meats such as steak, sausages and home-made burgers are invariably prepared on a charcoal fire and served with chips and a side salad (lettuce, cucumber and tomato). Another classic Dalmatian dish, brought to the area by the Venetians, is *pasticada*, beef stewed in sweet wine and served with *njoki* (gnocchi).

Lamb has a cult following throughout the Balkans, and in Croatia you'll see many roadside restaurants serving *janjetina* – whole lamb roast on a spit – especially in inland Dalmatia. A special mention also needs to be given to the *peka*, a metal dome dating back to Illyrian times. Food is placed in a terracotta pot and covered entirely with a *peka*, which in turn is buried below white embers. Delicious casseroles of either octopus, veal or lamb can be prepared using this long, slow cooking method, though most restaurants that offer it stipulate that you should order a day in advance. Desserts are limited, the standard offering being *palacinke* (pancakes), served either *sa orasima* (with walnuts), *sa marmeladom* (with jam) or *sa cokoladom* (with chocolate). In Dubrovnik, look out for *rožata*, similar to crème caramel.

If you visit the island of Vis, *pogača* makes a perfect snack – similar to Italian focaccia (from which it takes its name), it consists of a light bread base filled with tomato, onion and anchovy; you can buy it in several local bakeries.

Istria

Besides the aforementioned, in Istria you can expect slightly more adventurous dishes with extra care given to presentation, probably due to the Italian influence. Look out for the regional speciality, *tartufi* (truffles), usually served with pasta or steak, and risotto and pasta dishes *mare monti*, literally meaning 'sea and mountains', which combine shellfish and mushrooms. The best oysters and mussels are to be found in Limski Kanal, between Rovinj and Poreč. On the meat front, Istrians prepare delicious *srnetina* (venison) stew, normally served with *njoki* (gnocchi) or *fuži*, a local form of pasta. As in Dalmatia, rich casseroles can be prepared under a *peka*, but in Istria it's known as a *cirepnja*. Regarding side dishes, you'll find delicious, colourful salads combining mixed leaves such as *rukola* (rocket) and *radicchio*.

Inland Croatia

Moving inland, food is generally heavier, with lard or dripping used in place of olive oil for frying and roasting. The Zagreb area, and especially Zagorje, is known for *štrukli*, dumplings filled with curd cheese, which can either be boiled or baked. The most popular meats are roast turkey, duck or goose, classically served with *mlinci*, wafer thin pastries cooked in dripping. The best bread is made from maize flour rather than wheat, giving it a yellow colour and a heavier consistency.

In Slavonia, pork is used to make *kulen*, a delicious spicy salami often served as an appetizer.

About the region

Hungarian influence is apparent in meat specialities such as *gulaš* (goulash) and *fiš paprikaš* (a rich stew made from river fish), both of which are generously seasoned with hot paprika.

In Lika, the inland area between Zagreb and Dalmatia, look out for *škripavac* cheese, roast lamb and hearty peasant dishes employing *kiseli kupus* (sauerkraut), *grah* (beans) and *krumpir* (potatoes). Throughout the country you will come across Turkish-inspired dishes, which make tasty and filling snacks: *burek* (filo pastry filled with either minced meat and onions or curd cheese) and *cevapcici* (meat rissoles served in pitta bread with *ajvar* – a relish made from red peppers and aubergines). Also of Turkish origin are *sarma* (cabbage leaf rolls filled with minced meat and rice), better known as *arambašici* in Sinj, which are often eaten for special celebrations. Last but not least, baklava is a delicious syrup-drenched sweet made from filo pastry and ground walnuts.

A bottle of wine from Roki's domain, Vis.

What to drink

Coffee & tea

Meeting friends for *kava* (coffee) is something of a morning ritual. Many bars open as early as 0600, and are busy all day. While most people prepare Turkish coffee at home, cafés and bars serve Italian-style espresso and cappuccino. If you ask for *čaj* (tea) you will be given *šipak* (rosehip) served with lemon; if you want English-style tea ask for *indijski čaj sa mlijekom* (Indian tea with milk). Most cafés have tables outside, even in winter, and there is no extra charge for sitting down.

Wine

Croatian wines are little known abroad as they are exported in relatively small quantities, though some of them, such as the highly esteemed Dingač, are excellent. By and large the north produces whites and the south reds, though there are some exceptions.

Among the whites, names to look out for are: Pošip and Grk (from the island of Korčula), Vugava (island of Vis), Žlahtina (island of Krk), Malvazija (Istria), Graševina and Traminac (Slavonia). Of the reds, be sure to try: Dingač (Pelješac Peninsula), Plavac (islands of Hvar and Vis), Babič (Primošten) and Teran (Istria). Dalmatia also produces a rich sweet wine known as Prošek, similar to sherry.

To buy top wines at better prices, go direct to the producer. You will find vineyards open to the public on Pelješac Peninsula and the island of Hvar. On the island of Vis, some producers have opened shops where you can sample wine and then buy bottles to take home. In Istria, the regional tourist board has drawn up a series of wine routes with a list of producers who receive visitors, for a map check out the website, istra.com/vino .

Lower-grade wines are bottled in one-litre bottles with a metal cap, while better wines come in 0.75 litre bottles with a cork. Sometimes you will find the same label on both, but the 0.75-litre bottle will be more expensive and of much higher quality. Most bars serve wine by the glass, either by the *dec* (1 dl) or *dva deca* (2 dl). In Dalmatia, *bevanda* (half white wine, half water) is a refreshing summer drink.

Beer

Beer was introduced to Croatia under Austro-Hungary, when the Hapsburgs built the first breweries to supply their soldiers. Light-coloured lager, served well chilled, is the most common sort of beer, with popular brands being Karlovačko, Kaltenburg, Laško Zlatorog and Ožujsko. Tomislav is a stout (dark beer) brewed in Zagreb. When you buy beer by the bottle, you pay a small deposit, which you can get back upon return of the empties and display of the receipt. Imported draught Guinness is popular but tends to be about three times the price of local beer.

Spirits

Rakija, a distilled spirit usually made from a grape base, was introduced to the region by the Turks, and is normally drunk as an aperitif before eating, but can also be taken as a digestive at the end of a meal. The most popular types are: *loza* (made from grapes), *travarica* (flavoured with aromatic grasses), *šljivovica* (made from plums) and *pelinkovac* (flavoured with juniper berries and bitter herbs, similar to Italian amaro). In addition, there are various regional specialities such as biska (flavoured with mistletoe) in inland Istria and *rogoš* (flavoured with carob) on the island of Vis. Imported spirits such as whisky and gin are popular but expensive.

Eating out

For a full blown lunch or dinner, visit a *restoran* (restaurant), where you can expect formal service and a menu including a wide range of Croatian dishes. Most restaurants are open 1200-1500 and 1900-2300, and many, especially along the coast, have a large terrace for open-air dining through the summer months. For a simpler meal, try a *gostionica*, a place you can also go just to drink. There may not be a written menu, but many *gostionice* in Dalmatia serve *merenda* (a hearty cut price brunch), offer daily specials chalked up on a board, and sometimes have a set three-course meal, which works out very cheap. Service will be

less formal, but you can often land some excellent home cooking, and they tend to stay open all day, Monday to Saturday 0800-2300. The terms *konoba* (in Dalmatia) and *klet* (in Zagorje) were originally associated with places for making and storing wine, but the names are now used by many rustic-style restaurants serving local specialities. Some open in the evenings only and may stay open for late-night drinking. Most towns have a pizzeria, and some serve excellent pizza, comparable to the best in Italy. A few also offer a choice of substantial salads and a limited selection of pasta dishes.

For something sweet, call at a *slasticarnica*. Many are run by Albanians (one of former Yugoslavia's ethnic minorities) and they offer eastern goodies such as baklava (see above), along with a selection of *sladoled* (ice creams). Most are open 0800-2000, and serve coffee, tea and fruit juices, but no alcohol.

If you are travelling in inland Istria, look out for agrotourism centres, where you can expect quality local produce such as home-made cheese and wine, as well as unusual seasonal specialities such as *šparoge* (wild asparagus) in spring, and *tartufi* (truffles) and *gljive* (mushrooms) in autumn.

Eating in

If you opt for private accommodation you will probably have self-catering facilities. All cooking utensils and kitchen equipment such as pans, bowls, plates, glasses, cups and cutlery will be provided: if anything is missing ask your host and they will give you anything extra you require. Occasionally basics such as sugar, salt and pepper are provided – normally left by the people who were there before you.

You will probably also be supplied with a *džezver* – a metal coffee pot with a handle, used for preparing Turkish-style coffee, which is usually drunk here rather than instant, filter or espresso coffee. Vacuum-packed ground coffee can be bought in general stores.

Menu reader

blitva sa krumpirom Swiss chard and potatoes with garlic and olive oil, a side dish

brodet a hearty Dalmatian fish stew made with onions and tomatoes, and served with polenta

crni rižot black risotto, made from cuttlefish ink

dagnje mussels

friganje lignje fried squid

Hvarska gregada a type of brodet made on the island of Hvar, using fish, onions, potatoes and fresh herbs, but no tomato

janjetina roast lamb, normally roast whole on a spit

kobasice sausages

kućice clams

mješanja salata mixed salad, usually lettuce, cucumber and tomato

na buzaru cooked with garlic, white wine and parsley to produce a delicious rich sauce

ostrige oysters

palačinke pancakes

paški sir a hard, salty sheep's cheese from the island of Pag

pašticada s njokima beef stewed in sweet wine and served with gnocchi

pasticada beef stewed in sweet wine and served with njoki (gnocchi)

peka an ancient method of slow-cooking food (generally lamb, veal or octopus) when a terracotta pot is placed over white embers and covered by a metal dome; note that most restaurants require you to order *peka* dishes at least one day in advance

pršut smoked dried ham similar to Italian prosciutto

ražnjiči kebabs

riba na žaru barbecued fish, normally drizzled with olive oil and served with a wedge of lemon

rižot frutti di mare seafood risotto, normally combining mussels, clams and prawns

rižot sa škampima shrimp risotto, invariably served with a splash of cream at the end

salata od hobotnice octopus salad, made from octopus, boiled potatoes, onion and parsley, dressed with olive oil and vinegar

rožata a Dubrovnik speciality, similar to crème caramel

škampi shrimps

škampi na buzaru shrimps cooked in garlic, white wine and parsley to produce a delicious rich sauce

sladoled ice cream

Shopping

Croatian doll.

Croatia is hardly a shopper's paradise, a state of affairs clearly illustrated by the number of organized shopping buses to Trieste in Italy and Graz in Austria. As manufacturing industries still struggle to recover from the crisis of the 1990s, clothes and household goods are largely imported from Western Europe, and come with the predictable mark-up price.

However, the open-air fruit and vegetable markets are animated, colourful affairs, particularly in Zagreb and Split, and well worth a look around to check out local seasonal produce. If you opt for private accommodation with self-catering facilities you will find shopping for food gives closer insight into the way people live and eat. There are very few large supermarkets in the town centres (though several big foreign-owned, out-of-town supermarkets have opened since 2004), the nearest thing being Croatian-owned general stores, where you can shop for basics. But remember that fresh bread is best bought from a *pekarna* (bakery), meat from a *mesnica* (butchers) and fruit, vegetables and fish from the open-air morning market.

What to buy

Top of the list, both during your stay and when it's time to go home, should be Croatian wine and *rakija* (see Eating and drinking, page 62). Each region makes its own wines, and even though they are all available in general stores throughout the country, it is worth tasting local wines while you travel from region to region. Better still, in some areas it's possible to visit cellars for wine-tasting sessions and then buy direct from the producer. On a slightly more sober note, Croatia produces some excellent herbal teas, available freshly dried at the open-air market, or in packages in the shops; the most popular varieties are *šipak* (rosehip), *menta* (mint) and *kamilica* (camomile). Throughout Europe, olive oil varies greatly from country to country. Although Croatia is not big on

preserving olives to eat, Istrian and Dalmatian farmers produce some excellent *maslinovo ulje* (olive oil); when selecting a bottle, be sure to choose *djevičansko* (virgin), which is slightly more expensive but has a fuller flavour. And if you like truffles, look out for *tartufi* (truffles) and truffle-based products in Istria.

Other ideas for gifts include handmade lace (the best being from the island of Pag), lavender (either dried or distilled, from the island of Hvar), and an original Croatian tie (in a presentation box complete with a brief history). Look out for **Aromatica** (aromatica.hr) shops in Zagreb, Pula, Rovinj and Split, with their range of scented soaps and cosmetics made from olive oil and wild herbs.

Activities & tours

Cycling on Mljet.

Beaches & bathing

With a rugged indented coastline, countless islands and a pleasant Mediterranean climate, Croatia is a great place for sunbathing and swimming. The emerald-blue water is crystal clear and can reach temperatures of up to 27°C in summer. Bear in mind that the majority of Croatian beaches are pebbly or rocky, not sandy, so buy rubber beach shoes if you have sensitive feet. Along the coast and on the islands, 114 beaches have been awarded the Blue Flag, blueflag.org, a European eco-label indicating high environmental standards as well as good sanitary and safety facilities.

The most memorable and easily accessible beaches include Veli Plaža in Baška (island of Krk), Lopar (island of Rab), Brela (Makarska Rivijera), Zlatni Rat in Bol (island of Brač), Šunj (island of Lopud) and Saplunara (island of Mljet). Many small beaches are now equipped with sun beds and umbrellas, which you pay to hire, while the bigger, more commercial beaches, such as Veli Plaža and Zlatni Rat, also have water-sports facilities including scuba-diving, sea kayaking and wind surfing.

Beware of large modern hotels that claim to have a beach out front – in reality this is often no more than a concrete bathing area giving easy access into the water. The general rule with Croatian beaches is that the more difficult it is to reach, the more worthwhile the journey; many of the most stunning beaches are accessible only by boat.

Birdwatching

Birdwatching is still a relatively unknown pastime in Croatia, but there are some excellent opportunities for spotting rare species in beautiful surroundings.

The top sites include the wetlands of **Lonjsko Polje Nature Park**, pp-lonjsko-polje.hr, and **Kopački Rit Nature Park**, kopacki-rit.com, in inland Croatia. Both parks offer vast expanses of wetlands inhabited by herons, storks, ducks, kingfishers and woodpeckers; Lonjsko Polje is reputed to have the highest concentration of storks in Europe.

The Makarska Rivijera can get very busy in summer.

Along the coast, the top birdwatching destination is the island of Cres, noted for its Eurasion griffon vultures, as well as eagles, peregrines and buzzards. Although the birds are under special protection, the Eco-Centar Caput Insulae, supovi.hr, in Beli, organizes guided tours for small groups of enthusiasts. Likewise, **Paklenica National Park**, paklenica.hr, near Zadar is a natural habitat for various birds of prey, and birdwatching tours headed by a qualified ornothologist can be arranged through the national park office upon request.

Cycling & mountain biking

Local tourist boards have begun designating bike routes, though there is plenty of scope for further development. Mountain bikes are generally available for rent in places suitable for cycling, either from agencies that specialize in hiring bikes, mopeds and boats, or from large hotels with extensive sporting facilities.

The most organized region for cycling is Istria, though many of the Dalmatian islands also lend themselves to being explored by bike. If you are planning on taking your own bicycle, it is worth noting that on overnight ferries from Italy to Croatia bikes travel free (you just pay the passenger ticket), but some local ferries between the mainland and the islands add a small surcharge for bikes.

About the region

Snorkelling in Istria.

Croatia's most impressive dive sites include Stambedar (a sea wall with red and violet gorgonians) near the island of Hvar, Modra Splija (Blue Cave) on Biševo near the island of Vis, and Taranto (a shipwreck from 1943) near Dubrovnik.

Hiking & climbing

Croatia's unspoilt nature and varied landscapes (ranging from slopes supporting meadowland and forests ideal for gentle hiking to steep grey cliffs ideal for free climbing), plus a pleasant mild and reasonably dry climate through spring and autumn, make it a great place to explore on foot. The majority of mountains belong to the Dinaric range and, although none are over 2000 m, they require the same efforts from the climber as many much higher mountains thanks to their rugged, rocky karst landscape and sparse population. There are a number of marked trails and *planinarski dom* (mountain refuges) offering simple food and accommodation.

All official hiking paths are clearly signed at regular intervals by a red circle with a white dot in the middle, or occasionally two parallel red lines with a white line between them. The best venues for serious hiking include Medvednice Nature Park (pp-medvednica.hr) near Zagreb, Paklenica National Park (paklenica.hr) near Zadar in North Dalmatia, and Mount Biokovo behind Makarska in Central Dalmatia. The islands have been little exploited by walkers, but the potential is certainly there.

Hrvatski Planinarski Savez (Croatian Hiking Association, Kozarčeva 22, Zagreb, T01-482 4142, plsavez.hr) is an umbrella group for some 200 local walking clubs, which can supply maps and information about mountain huts throughout t he country.

Biokovo Active Holidays (Kralja P Krešimira IV 7B, T021-679655, biokovo.net) organize one-day and one-week hiking tours, exploring Mount Biokovo and the island of Brač.

The British company **Skedaddle Tours**, T0191-265 1110, skedaddle.co.uk, arrange biking tours of rural and coastal Istria staying in agrotourism farmhouses.

Diving

Along the coast you'll find some 150 diving clubs offering lessons (with multi-lingual instructors), guided tours and rental equipment. To dive in Croatia, you need to hold a valid diver's card issued by the **Hrvatski Ronilački Savez** (Croatian Diving Federation, Dalmatinska 12, Zagreb, T01-484 8765, diving-hrs.hr). These can be obtained from all recognized Croatian diving clubs and are valid for one year as of the date of issue.

Naturism

Organized naturist bathing began on the island of Rab in the early 20th century, but the real naturist expansion started in the 1960s when the first naturist camps opened in Istria and Dalmatia, making Croatia the first country in Europe to commercialize naked bathing. An estimated 15% of all tourists to Croatia are naturists.

There are about 30 official naturist resorts and beaches, marked 'FKK' (from the German *freikörperkultur* meaning 'free body culture'), as well as countless unofficial naturist beaches, usually found in more secluded areas. For a region by region listing, check out the Croatia Naturally website at cronatur.com.

The following British companies arrange naturist holidays in Croatia: **Dune Leisure** (2 Market Pl, Great Dunmow, Essex CM6 1AT, T0870-751 8866, awaywithdune.co.uk); **Peng Travel** (86 Station Rd, Gidea Park, Romford, Essex RM2 6DB, T0845-345 8345 (in UK) or T+44-1708- 471832 (from outside the UK), pengtravel.co.uk).

Rafting

Of all the so-called extreme sports that have emerged over the last decade, whitewater rafting is probably the most accessible to complete beginners. The best rivers for rafting in Croatia are the Zrmanja in the Velebit mountains in North Dalmatia, and the Cetina near Omiš in Central Dalmatia.

Upon arrival, you'll be given a lifejacket, helmet and an oar, and board a raft for six to eight people, led by a guide. Most tours involve a series of light to moderate rapids and last around three hours. You should also take a towel and a dry set of clothing to change into afterwards.

Generalturist (Branimirova obala 1, Zadar, T023-318997, generalturist.com) and **Zara Adventure** (Danijela Farlattija 7, Zadar, T023-342368, zara-adventure.hr) can organize rafting on the River Zrmanje.

Rafting in Krka National Park.

About the region

Active Holidays (Knezova Kačića bb, Omiš, T021-863015, activeholidays-croatia.com) and Adventure Dalmatia (Matije Gupca 26, Split, T021-540642, adventuredalmatia.com) arrange rafting on the River Cetina.

Sailing

With so many islands, deep, clean sea and moderate winds, Croatia is a sailor's paradise. Some 50 fully equipped modern marinas line the coast all the way from Umag in the north to Dubrovnik in the south, while temporary mooring facilities are available along the seafront in most coastal towns and villages, and there are plenty of deserted bays, ideal for dropping anchor and bathing in total solitude.

Croatia is perfect for first-time sailors as the islands run parallel with and close to the mainland coast, affording easy line-of-sight navigation and island-hopping in protected waters. The most crowded period is July and August, when sailing enthusiasts from all over Europe flock to the Adriatic, and resorts, such as Hvar Town, are inundated with yachts and yachters. The mid-season periods of May to June and September to October are more peaceful, and the weather still fairly reliable.

There are over 140 charter companies in Croatia, operating tens of thousands of sailing boats and motorboats of all sizes. Most companies rent yachts on a weekly basis from 1700 Saturday to 0900 the following Saturday. When you charter a yacht this can be bareboat (meaning you are alone) or with a skipper. To go bareboat you, or one of the crew, must have a sailing licence and at least two years' sailing experience. The third alternative is to sail as part of a flotilla (a group of yachts, normally between five and 10, with people of mixed levels of sailing experience, lead by a qualified expert).

If you wish to take a course in sailing, try either Adriatic Nautical Academy (ANA, Nautička 3, Bakar, Rijeka, T051-711814, anasailing.com), who run an annual sailing school Jezera on the island of Murter (Central Dalmatia), or Ultra Sailing (Uvala Baluni bb, Split, T021-398980, ultra-sailing.hr), who offer courses in Trogir near Split (Central Dalmatia).

The following British charter companies offer sailing holidays in Croatia: Activity Yachting (South View, Boxham Lane, Sidlesham, West Sussex PO20 7QF, T01243-641304, activityyachting.com); Adriatic Holidays Ltd (1 Victoria St, Oxford OX2 6BT, T01865-516577, adriaticholidaysonline.com); Nautilus Sailing (87 High St, Edenbridge, Kent TN8 5AU, T01732-867445, nautilus-yachting.com); Sail Croatia (160 Brompton Rd, London SW3 1HW, T0871-733 8686, sailcroatia.net) and Sailing Holidays Ltd (105 Mount Pleasant Rd, London NW10 3EH, T020-8459 8787, sailingholidays.co.uk).

Sea kayaking

Sea kayaking is the perfect way to explore a small cluster of islets located close to one another. In Croatia, the sport began developing round the Elafiti islands near Dubrovnik. It is now also possible to join a sea kayaking tour from Hvar Town, to paddle round the nearby Pakleni islets, and from Brela near Makarska to explore the mainland coast.

The following agencies arrange kayaking trips: Adriatic Kayak Tours (Zrinsko-frankopanska 6, Dubrovnik, T020-312770, adriatickayaktours.com); Adventure Dalmatia (Matije Gupca 26, Split, T021-540642, adventuredalmatia.com); Big Blue (Podan Glavice 2, Bol, T021-635614, big-blue-sport. hr); Biokovo Active Holidays (Kralja P Krešimira IV 7B, Makarska, T021-679655, biokovo.net); and Hvar Adventure (Obala bb, Hvar Town, T021-717813, hvaradventure.com).

Windsurfing

Croatia's top windsurfing locations are off Zlatni Rat beach in Bol on the island of Brač in Central Dalmatia, and Viganj on Pelješac Peninsula in South Dalmatia, both of which catch the maestral (wind from the northwest) through summer. Further north, the coast is less suitable for windsurfing as the main wind is the bura (wind from the northeast), which blows mainly through winter.

Windsurfing.

Big Blue (Podan Glavice 2, Bol, T021-635614, big-blue-sport.hr) offers courses at all levels from beginner to advanced and rent equipment to experienced surfers on Zlatni Rat beach on the island of Brač.

Wine tasting

Several vineyards have cellars open to the public for wine tasting and direct purchasing, while a number of chic wine boutiques stocking the country's best wines can be found in the larger resorts.

In inland Croatia, the Lovrec vineyard (see page 95), at Štrigova near Čakovec, offers wine tasting in an authentic wooden outbuilding complete with rustic furnishing.

In Istria, the tourist board have set up a network of wine routes leading to countless vineyards, wine cellars and agrotourism centres where it is possible to sample and purchase the region's red Teran and white Malvazija. For maps and contact details check out istra.com/vino.

In the Kvarner region, in Vrbnik on the island of Krk, visit Konoba Nada (see page 156) to try, and buy, their excellent dry white Vrbnička Žlahtina

Nada. They also have a vast wine cellar, just outside the town walls, offering wine-tasting sessions for large groups with a video presentation.

In Central Dalmatia, the island of Hvar is famed for its excellent reds, produced on the south side, which receives more sun, and its dry whites, produced on the cooler north side. Two vineyards of note are Podrum Plančić in Vrbanj Svirče (plancic.com) near Jelsa, and the highly esteemed but expensive Zlatan Otok, run by the Plenković family in Sveta Nedjelja (zlatanotok.hr) on the south coast. On the island of Vis, which produces the red Plavac and white Vugava, call at the wine bar Peronospora Blues (see page 222) in Vis Town to sample the owner's excellent Plavac Mali, which is also available in bottles to take home.

In South Dalmatia, the best reds come from Pelješac Peninsula and the best whites from the island of Korčula. On Pelješac, several vineyards heave their cellars open to the public for wine tasting (see page 245).

The Croatian travel agency Atlas (Vukovarska 19, Dubrovnik, T020-442222, atlas-croatia.com) runs an eight-day Wine and Gourmet Tour, travelling from Zagreb to Dubrovnik by coach.

Advantage Croatia

F or a country of only four million, Croatia has scored outstanding success in international sporting events. Before the country's break up in 1991, Yugoslavia was a force to be reckoned with in sports such as football, basketball, handball and water polo, all of which remain favourite team games in Croatia today.

Athletics

In 2007 and 2009, Blanka Vlašić from Split was the World Champion female high jumper. Although she had been favourite to win the gold medal at the Beijing 2008 Olympics, she ended up with silver. With a personal best of 2.08 m, many believe she will eventually topple the world record of 2.09 m.

Football

As in most countries, football is the most popular spectator sport. During the late 1990s the Croatian national team was extremely strong, with players including Davor Šuker and Zvonimir Boban. They reached the quarter-final in the European Championship in 1996, and coming third in the World Cup in France in 1998. The team fared less well in the 2002 World Cup and the 2004 European Championship. They secured a place at the World Cup in 2006, impressively beating Sweden and Bulgaria to finish top of the European qualifying Group 8, undefeated and with eight wins out of 10 matches. In 2007, they once again finished top of their group in the Euro 2008 qualifiers, knocking England out on the way. The current national team is made up mainly of youngsters, and that includes the charismatic

coach, Slaven Bilić. Sporting an earring and known for his love of rock music, he is the youngest national team manager in the world. As a player, he spent time with West Ham United and Everton, and several English Premier teams have shown interest in taking him on as their coach. New names to look out for on the Croatian team include Brazilian-born striker, Eduardo da Silva and Tottenham Hotspur's Luka Modrić.

Skiing

Alpine skier Janica Kostelić is considered one of the greatest female skiers of all time. She was the World Cup overall champion in 2001, 2003 and 2006, and won a total of four gold medals at the 2002 and 2006 Winter Olympics. Her younger brother, Ivica, won a silver medal in the slalom at the 2010 Winter Olympics in Vancouver.

Tennis

Croatia's best known sportsman is probably tennis player Goran Ivanišević, who ranked second in the world in 1992 and won the much-coveted Wimbledon tournament in summer 2001. It seems he has inspired a whole new generation of players, with Croatia taking the bronze in the Men's Doubles at the Athens 2004 Olympics, represented by Ivan Ljubičić and Mario Ančić. Croatia then went on to win the international Davis Cup in 2005, thanks to Ljubičić, Ančić, Ivo Karlović and Goran Ivanišević (who came out of retirement to make up the national team, though he did not play). In 2009, the International Tennis Federation ranked Croatia as number five in the World Group – the team was made up of Marin Čilić, Ivo Karlović, Ivan Dodig and Antonio Veić.

Contents

79 Introduction
80 Zagreb & around
82 *Map: Zagreb*
90 North of Zagreb
96 East of Zagreb
100 Great days out:
    Plitvice Lakes
102 Listings:
102 Sleeping
104 Eating & drinking
157 Entertainment
157 Activities & tours

Zagreb & inland Croatia

Ban Jelačić, Main Square, Zagreb.

Introduction

This is another world from the open seascapes and sun-soaked medieval stone towns of the coast. Inland Croatia is flatter, damper and infinitely more Central European. Nowhere is the Hapsburgian influence felt more strongly than in Zagreb, the country's economic, political and cultural capital. North from here, the rolling hills of Zagorje offer vineyards and rural villages, as well as several proud castles. North of Zagorje, close to the Hungarian border, Varaždin is noted for its well-preserved baroque old town.

East of Zagreb, the flat, fertile plains of Slavonia extend to the border with Serbia. The main town here is Osijek, built on the south bank of the River Drava and worth visiting to see Tvrđa, a complex of 18th-century buildings erected by the Austrians to defend the region from the Turks. Close by, Kopački Rit Nature Park is a vast wetland supporting protected birds such as storks and herons.

South of Zagreb, on the road to Dalmatia, lies Plitvice Lakes National Park, a paradise of emerald-green lakes and thundering waterfalls set amid a dense forest.

What to see in...

...one day
Explore Zagreb's hilltop Upper Town, visiting the cathedral, the Meštrović Atelier and Lotrščak Tower, before browsing the stalls of Dolac open-air market. Visit the Museum of Modern Art in the Lower Town in the afternoon. Round off the day with a romantic dinner at Prasac.

...a weekend or more
Drive through the vineyards of Zagorje to visit the Staro Selo in Kumrovec (Tito's birthplace) and the castles of Veliki Tabor and Trakošćan, having lunch at Grešna Gorica en route.

Plitvice waterfall.

Zagreb & around

Mitteleuropean-style capital, Zagreb, is often overlooked as a tourist destination. However, as Croatia's economic and administrative centre, and home to one in four Croats, it's certainly worth devoting a few days to the city if you want to understand what (or who) makes the nation tick.

The city centre is composed of two main areas, the hilltop Gornji Grad (Upper Town) and the lower-lying Donji Grad (Lower Town), which meet at Trg Bana Jelačića, the main square. Medieval Gornji Grad, home to the cathedral and the Croatian Parliament, is reminiscent of old Prague, thanks to its romantic, winding, cobbled streets, red-tiled rooftops and church spires. In contrast, Donji Grad, where you'll find the museums, theatre and university, was laid out on a strict grid system during the 19th century and is made up of grandiose Hapsburgian buildings interspersed between a series of green squares linked by tree-lined boulevards. Beyond the city centre lie the standard suburbs of high-rise apartment blocks, constructed during the latter half of the 20th century.

Most of the buildings still manage to carry off their proud Austro-Hungarian image pretty well. Unfortunately, high living costs, low wages and mass unemployment are still a harsh reality for locals, but visitors can spend a pleasant enough few days exploring the city's museums, parks and churches.

Trg Bana Jelačića

Map: Zagreb, D3/4, p82.

Lying between Gornji Grad and Donji Grad, Ban Jelačića is the capital's main square. A vast paved space, it's closed to cars but plays the role of the city centre's main tram intersection, making it an important public meeting place and providing the surrounding cafés with a steady influx of customers. Buildings lining the square date from 1827 onwards, and include several fine examples of Vienna Secessionist architecture. In the centre of the square stands a proud bronze equestrian statue of 19th-century Croatia viceroy, Ban Jelačić.

Gornji Grad

Dolac

Dolac bb.
Mon-Fri 0700-1600, Sat-Sun 0700-1200.
Map: Zagreb, D3, p82.

On the northern edge of the main square, Dolac has been Zagreb's main market since 1930. Arranged on two levels, it's a colourful and entertaining affair, with farmers from the surrounding countryside setting up stalls of fruit and vegetables on a raised piazza, while meats and dairy products are sold in an indoor area below. Behind the fruit and vegetable section, you'll find people selling handmade items such as lace, hats and jewellery, and to each side of the piazza a conglomeration of snack bars serving cheap eats.

Essentials

❶ Getting around All the main sights are in the city centre, within walking distance of one another, unless otherwise stated.

❷ Bus station The bus station is at Avenija M Držića 4, a 15-minute walk from the main square, T060-313333, akz.hr. See also Getting around by bus, page 272.

❸ Train station The train station is at Trg Kralja Tomislava 12, a 10-minute walk from the main square, T060-333444, hznet.hr. See also Getting around by train, page 272.

❹ ATM Cash machines are plentiful and are available at Trg Bana Jelačića (the main square), in the train station and at the bus station.

⊕ Hospital Draškovićeva 19, T01-469 7000.

✚ Pharmacy Each pharmacy is marked by a glowing green cross. There are 24-hour pharmacies at Trg Bana Jelačića 2, T01-481 6159, and Ilica 301, T01-375 0321.

❺ Post office The main post office is at Branimirova 4, next to the train station, and stays open 24 hours. The central post office is at Jurišićeva 4, close to the main square, Monday-Friday 0700-2100, Saturday 0700-1400.

❻ Tourist information The main Tourist Information Centre (TIC) is on the main square at Trg Bana Jelačića 11, T01-481 4051, zagreb touristinfo.hr. Close to the train station, the Zagreb Tourist Guide Association at Trg Nikole Šubića Zrinskog 20/3, T01-481 7022, offers guided city tours.

Flower seller at Dolac open-air market.

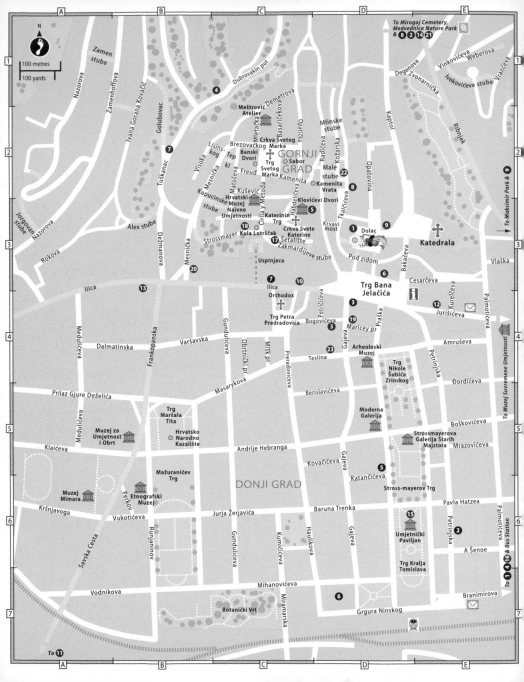

Zagreb listings

① Sleeping
1 Arcotel Allegra Zagreb *Branimirova 29* **E7**
2 Best Western Hotel Astoria *Petrinjska 71* **E6**
3 Hotel Dubrovnik *Gajeva 1* **D4**
4 Hotel Fala *II Trnjanske ledine 18* **E7**
5 Hotel Palace *Strossmayerov Trg 10* **D5**
6 Hotel Regent Esplanade *Mihanovićeva 1* **D7**
7 Jagerhorn *Ilica 14* **C3**
8 Tomislavov Dom *Sljemenska cesta bb* **D1**
9 Vila Tina *Bukovačka Cesta 213* **E2**

① Eating & drinking
1 Amfora *Dolac 2* **D3**
2 Baltazar *Nova Ves 4* **D1**
3 Bulldog *Bogovićeva 6* **D4**
4 Dubravkin Put *Dubrovakin put bb* **C1**
5 Gallery Klovićevi Dvori museum café *Jezuitski trg 4* **C3**
6 Gradska Kavana *Trg Bana Jelačiča 10* **D3**
7 Hemingway Bar *Tuškanac 1* **B2**
8 Ivica i Marica *Tkalčićeva 70* **D2**
9 Kaptolska Klet *Kaptol 5* **D3**
10 Maraschino *Margaretska 1* **C3**
11 Medvedgrad Pivnica *Ilica 49* **A7**
12 Mimice *Jurišićeva 21* **E4**
13 Nova *Ilica 72* **B3**
14 Okrugljak *Mlinovi 28* **E1**
15 Paviljon *Trg kralja Tomislava 22* **E6**
16 People's Lounge *Hektorovićeva 2* **E7**
17 Pod Gričkim Topom *Za kmardijeve stube 5* **C3**
18 Prasac *Vranicanijeva 6* **C3**
19 Restoran Boban *Gajeva 9* **D4**
20 Stari Fijaker *Mesnička 6* **B3**
21 Stari Puntijar *Gračanka cesta 65* **D1**
22 Sunčani Sat *Tkalčićeva 27* **D2**
23 Vinodol *Nikole Tesle 10* **D4**

Zagreb cathedral.

Katedrala

Kaptol 31.
Daily 0800-2000.
Map: Zagreb, E3, p82.

Zagreb's cathedral dates back to the 12th century, though much of the original building was destroyed by the Tartars in 1242. While reconstruction and extension work took place between the 13th and 16th centuries, this in turn was badly damaged by the 1880 earthquake, thus the neo-Gothic façade and twin steeples we see today were designed by an Austrian architect, Herman Bolle. Inside, the north wall bears an inscription of the Ten Commandments in 12th-century Glagolitic script (see page 127) and, nearby, a touching relief by Ivan Meštrović portrays the late Archbishop Alojzije Stepinac kneeling before Christ, and marks the controversial bishop's final resting place.

Tkalčićeva

Map: Zagreb, D2/3, p82.

Once a brook forming the boundary between Kaptol and Gradec, in 1898 the channel was filled in to form a cobbled street. Today it's a pretty pedestrian zone lined with 19th-century town houses, most of which host popular street-level café-bars and informal restaurants with open-air seating; it's Zagrebian students' favourite spot for morning coffee, a cheap lunch or an early-evening drink, and is perfect for people-watching.

St Mark's Church.

Kamenita Vrata

Map: Zagreb, C/D2, p82.

The so-called Stone Gate was once one of four entrances into the walled town of Gradec. In 1731, after a devastating fire had consumed the surrounding wooden buildings, a painting of the Virgin Mary was found in the ashes, remarkably undamaged. The Stone Gate was reconstructed and became regarded as a place of miracles. Today locals come here to pray and pay tribute to the Virgin: there's a delightful shrine adorned with flickering candles and the walls are hung with small plaques saying *Hvala* (thank you), so it obviously works.

Trg Svetog Marka

Map: Zagreb, C2, p82.

Saint Mark's Square was once the centre of Zagrebian political, cultural and commercial life. A daily market used to be held here, and it was the main public meeting place until Ban Jelačić Square took over the role during the 19th century. The centrepiece is the 13th-century St Mark's Church, noted for its red-, white- and blue-tiled roof, which was added during reconstruction in 1880 and depicts the coats of arms for Zagreb (on the right) and the Kingdom of Croatia, Dalmatia and Slavonia (on the left). During the Middle Ages, a pole of shame was erected in front of the church, where local lawbreakers were punished with a public whipping. Facing the main entrance to the church stands the Sabor (Croatian Parliament), housed within a neoclassical building completed in 1910.

Meštrović Atelier

Mletačka 8, T01-485 1123, mestrovic.hr.
Tue-Fri 1000-1800, Sat-Sun 1000-1400, 20Kn.
Map: Zagreb, C2, p82.

For many, the Meštrović Atelier is one of Zagreb's most charming attractions. During the 1920s, the Dalmatian sculptor Ivan Meštrović (see page 190) refurbished this 17th-century building to serve as a home and studio. Dividing his time between Zagreb and Split, he lived and worked here on and off until fleeing the country during the Second World War. When he died in 1962 it was turned into a memorial museum with a beautifully presented exhibition of his sculptures and drawings.

Hrvatski Muzej Naivne Umjetnosti

Čirila i metoda 3, T01-485 1911, hmnu.org.
Tue-Fri 1000-1800, Sat-Sun 1000-1300, 20Kn.
Map: Zagreb, C2/3, p82.

You may not consider Croatian Naïve art aesthetically pleasing, but it certainly is unusual. During the 1930s, a group of farmers from the village of Hlebine in Slavonia took up painting (with no previous tuition), and the canvasses on display here in the Croatian Naïve Art Museum show what they produced. Several of the artists, most notably Ivan Generalić, went on to receive international recognition.

Crkva Svete Katerine

Katerinin Trg.
Daily 0800-2000.
Map: Zagreb, C3, p82.

Built for the Jesuit order between 1620 and 1632, the baroque St Catherine's Church was modelled on Giacomo da Vignola's Il Gesu in Rome. The vaulted ceilings are encrusted with sugary pink and white stuccowork, and there's a clever 18th-century illusionist fresco above the main altar.

Klovičevi Dvori

Jezuitski Trg 4, T01-485 1926, galerijaklovic.hr.
Tue-Sun 1100-1900, 40Kn.
Map: Zagreb, C3, p82.

Most major international exhibitions are staged in this former Jesuit College, dating back to the 17th-century, which was reconstructed in 1982 to form a large art gallery. There isn't a permanent collection. Temporary exhibitions have included

St Lotrščak Tower.

Marc Chagall, '2000 years of Nigerian Art' and 'Jewels of Ottoman Art from the Topkapi Museum'. During the Zagreb Summer Festival, concerts are staged in the internal courtyard. The museum café makes an ideal stopping point for weary legs.

Kula Lotrščak

Strossmayer Šetalište 9.
Apr-Oct Tue-Sun 1100-1900, 10Kn.
Map: Zagreb, C3, p82.

On Strossmayer Promenade, a pleasant walkway following the line of Gradec's former south-facing wall and offering stunning views over the city rooftops, Lotrščak Tower is part of the 13th-century fortification system. It now houses a gallery, and it is possible to climb to the top for dramatic views across the city to Novi Zagreb, on the south side of the River Sava. Each day at noon, a small (but extremely loud) cannon is fired from the top of the tower, in memory of the times when it was used to warn off the possibility of an Ottoman attack.

Muzej Mimara.

Uspinjača

Strossmayer Šetalište.
Daily 0630-2400, 4Kn.
Map: Zagreb, C3, p82.

Zagreb's tiny funicular railway connects Gornji
Grad and Donji Grad. Built in 1891, it ran on steam
until 1934 and makes an amusing way to descend
40 m to Tomićeva, just off Ilica. From here it's just a
five-minute walk back to Trg Bana Jelačića, the
main square.

Donji Grad

Muzej za Umjetnost i Obrt

Trg Maršala Tita 10, T01-488 2111, muo.hr.
Tue-Wed and Fri-Sat 1000-1900, Thu 1000-2200,
Sun 1000-1400, 30Kn.
Map: Zagreb, B5, p82.

The Arts and Crafts Museum is housed in a light and
airy purpose-built 19th-century structure. The
visitor-friendly exhibition space displays a vast
collection of furniture, laid out in chronological

order and illustrating how Croatian design has been
influenced by Austrian and Italian tastes, from the
baroque period up to the modern movement.

Muzej Mimara

Rooseveltov trg 4, T01-482 8100.
Tue-Wed, Fri-Sat 1000-1700, Thu 1000-1900,
Sun 1000-1400, 40Kn.
Map: Zagreb, A6, p82.

Roosevelt Trg is dominated by the renowned
Mimara Museum, housed within a neo-
Renaissance former grammar school building. This
phenomenal private collection was donated to the
city by Ante Topić-Mimara when he died in 1987.
On display are canvases attributed to old masters
such as Raphael, Rembrandt and Rubens, as well
as more modern paintings by Manet, Degas and
Renoir (though whether all these pieces are
genuine remains a matter of controversy). The
collection also includes an astounding hoard of
ancient Egyptian glassware, Chinese porcelain and
Persian carpets – all well worth seeing but of little
relevance to Croatian culture.

Etnografski Muzej

Mažuranićev trg 14, T01-482 6220, emz.hr.
Tue-Thu 1000-1800, Fri-Sun 1000-1300,
15Kn (free Thu).
Map: Zagreb, B6, p82.

Zagreb's Ethnographic Museum is well worth a visit
if you're interested in traditional folk costumes – the
variety of colours, materials and styles on display
illustrates the cultural diversity of Croatia's
contrasting inland and coastal regions. The lace
from the island of Pag and the gold embroidered
scarves from Slavonia are particularly worth seeing.
There's also a section devoted to artefacts from the
South Pacific, Asia and Africa, collected by
19th-century Croatian explorers and travellers.

Botanički Vrt

Trg M Marulića 9a, T01-484 4002.
Jun-Aug Mon-Tue 0900-1430, Wed-Sun
0900-1900, Apr-May and Sep-Oct Mon-Tue
0900-1430, Wed-Sun 0900-1800, free.
Map: Zagreb, B/C7, p82.

Founded in 1889 as research grounds for the
Faculty of Botany at Zagreb University, the
Botanical Gardens are small but well kept, and offer
a welcome retreat from the bustle of the city. The
main section is an arboretum, arranged informally
in the style of an English garden, beside two ponds
with water lilies and an ornamental bridge.

Umjetnički Paviljon

*Trg Kralja Tomislava 22, T01-484 1070,
umjetnicki-paviljon.hr.*
Mon-Sat 1100-1900, Sun 1000-1300, 20Kn
(free Mon).
Map: Zagreb, D/E6, p82.

The charming Art Pavilion was originally built to
celebrate '1000 years of Hungarian Culture' in
Budapest in 1896. It was then dismantled and
reassembled here, under the initiative of the
Croatian artist Vlaho Bukovac. Today it is used
for temporary art exhibitions.

Moderna Galerija

*Andrije Hebranga 1, T01-604 1055,
moderna-galerija.hr.*
Tue-Fri 1000-1800, Sat-Sun 1000-1300, 30Kn.
Map: Zagreb, D5, p82.

Refreshingly colourful and thought-provoking, the
Modern Art Gallery exhibits paintings, sculpture,
posters, instillations and videos, created by
Croatian artists during the 19th and 20th centuries.
It's highly recommended for anyone interested in
modern art, but should not be confused with
Zagreb's new Museum of Contemporary Art, which
covers works from 1950 up to the present day.

Strossmayerova Galerija Starih Majstora

*Trg Nikole Šubića Zrinskog 11, T01-489 5117,
hazu.hr.*
Tue 1000-1900, Wed-Fri 1000-1600, Sat-Sun
1000-1300, 10Kn.
Map: Zagreb, D/E5, p82.

Housed in a proud 19th-century building, the
Strossmayer Gallery of Old Masters was founded in
1884. The collection has expanded gradually over
the last 130 years and now includes many notable
canvases by Venetian Renaissance and baroque
painters such as Bellini and Carpaccio, and Dutch
masters Brueghel and Van Dyck. Worth a special
mention is a small *Mary Magdalene* by El Greco.

Arheološki Muzej

Trg Nikole Šubića Zrinskog 19, T01-487 3101, amz.hr.
Tue-Wed and Fri 1000-1700, Thu 1000-2000,
Sat-Sun 1000-1300, 20Kn.
Map: Zagreb, D4, p82.

The Archaeological Museum exhibits finds from
prehistoric times up to the Tartar invasion. Its most
unusual piece is the so-called Zagreb Mummy – a
female mummy, brought here from Egypt in the
19th century. Wrapped in linen baring the longest
known text written in mysterious and little-
understood Etruscan characters (thought to date
from 250 BC).

Maksimir Park.

East of the city centre

Maksimir Park

Maksimirska cesta, 3 km east of the city centre, park-maksimir.hr.
Open sunrise to sunset.
Trams No 11 and 12 (direction Dubrava) from Trg Bana Jelačića, the main square.

Zagreb's biggest park, Maksimir, is a green expanse animated by joggers, lovers and families with kids. Founded as a city garden in 1784, Maksimir claims to be the first public park in southeast Europe. During the 19th century it was extended and the English-style landscaping with lawns, woods, tree-lined avenues, artificial lakes and romantic follies were added. Today there's also a small zoo. Opposite the park stands Dinamo Football Stadium, home ground to the city football team and the main venue for international matches played in Croatia.

North of the city centre

Mirogoj Cemetery

Mirogoj 10, 2 km northeast of city centre.
Apr-Sep 0600-2000, Oct-Mar 0800-1800.
Bus No 106 from Kaptol, opposite the cathedral.

Mirogoj Cemetery dates back to 1876. The west side of the cemetery is enclosed within a protective wall sheltering a neo-Renaissance arcade, while the monumental main entrance is crowned with a copper cupola. Over the decades citizens of varying religious and political persuasion have been laid to rest here, as can be seen by the stylistic range of tombs: the elongated pentagonal Muslim headstones, the Orthodox stones bearing Cyrillic script, the Jewish with the six-point star, the Socialists with the five-point red star and, of course, the majority, Catholics.

Medvednica Nature Park

Nature Park office, Bliznec bb, T01-458 6317, pp-medvednica.hr.
Trams No 8 and 14 from the main square to the last stop (terminal) Mihaljevac. The cable car is temporarily out of use (a new system is planned for the future but no dates are set), in the meantime, buses operate from Mihaljevac to Tomislavov Dom, a 5-min walk from Sljeme, the highest peak.

Just north of Zagreb – in fact the city's suburbs extend on to the lower slopes – Medvednica mountain is a popular hiking destination for the people of Zagreb, especially on Sundays, when

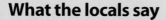

What the locals say

If you have a whole day to spend in Zagreb, this might be your ideal itinerary. Get rid of morning lethargy with an Italian coffee in cinema-music bar **Kino Gric** (Jurisiceva 6), where you can sit in red cinema chairs, enjoying the interior by a well-known Croatian artist. (Pick up a movie schedule, too – you might return in the evening, to watch a cool European art film.) Then stretch your legs with a walk around the **'green horse-shoe'**, a chain of eight city parks in the form of a horse-shoe in the Lower Town, to experience Zagreb's atmosphere and people. You can pick up a map and get details of the walk from the TIC on the main square.

At noon, I recommend you go to **Lotrscak Tower**. The canon fires at 1200 prompt to split the day in half and if there are tourists unaware of this, you might witness some comic situations. Explore the Upper Town, and when hunger calls, head to **Dolac Market**. Beside the covered fish market is a lovely small bistro called Amfora. It's always packed with locals, but it's worth trying to grab a table. For €5-6 you can eat fresh fish and sip budget Croatian wines.

From Dolac, go down to **Jelacic Square**, continue along **Gajeva Street**, turn right onto **Bogoviceva Street** to arrive at **Preradovic Square**. Stop for coffee here – it's another vibrant location in town with lots of positive energy. You might like to finish the day with a beer in your hand and music in your ears. There are two urban music clubs, **Gjuro 2** (downtown), or **Močvara** (a little off the beaten track).

Mladen Čar, Funky Zagreb.

local hikers flock here, decked in appropriate walking gear and armed with a picnic lunch.

Medvednica was declared a nature park in 1981, with walking paths winding their way across the slopes, 64% of which are covered with deciduous and coniferous woods of oak, beech, chestnut and fir. The park is at its prettiest in spring, when the woodland paths are dense with wild flowers, and in autumn, when the trees take on golden and russet hues. In winter there are basic skiing facilities.

The highest peak, Sljeme (1033 m), which is crowned by a TV tower and a small chapel, was for many years served by a cable car, which now defunct. However, it lies just a five-minute walk from Tomislavov Dom, where the bus drops hikers. On a fine day it's possible to see Zagreb to the south, Zagorje to the north and the Slovenian Alps to the west from this fine vantage point.

Tip...

If you can hold out till the homeward journey, there are a number of good traditional restaurants on the road between the national park and the capital.

Medvednica (named after the bears, *medvjedi*, which once populated its slopes) is ideal for picnicking, with several designated areas equipped with tables and benches.

South of the city centre

Muzej suvremene umjetnosti

Avenija Dubrovnik 11, Novi Zagreb, T01-605 2700; msu.hr.
Tue-Sun 1100-1900, Thu 1100-2200, 30Kn (free entry first Wed of each month). Tram 6 from train station in centre, tram 7 from bus station.

The light and airy glass-and-steel Museum of Contemporary Art opened in December 2009, after many years of delays. On display are some 600 works by Croatian and foreign artists, created between 1950 and the present. Expect paintings, drawings, posters, sculpture, film and video, and some new media art. Facilities include a café, restaurant and library. It is a 30-minute tram ride from the city centre – the trek is well worth the time for anyone interested in contemporary art.

North of Zagreb

Northwest of Zagreb, lies the rural area of Zagorje. The scenery is calm and enchanting: rolling hillsides are planted with vineyards and orchards, and narrow country roads meander through a succession of villages of red-brick cottages and open-sided wooden barns filled with maize. Zagorjians are renowned for their drinking habits, and there is a local song that says "there is no man from Zagorje who can produce as much wine as his friends can drink", or words to that effect. Indeed, St Martin's Day on 11 November is a big event throughout the region, when the ritual blessing of the season's young wine is accompanied by copious festivities until the early hours.

Public transport is slow and sporadic, but if you have a car and are prepared to devote an entire day to Zagorje, you can visit an open-air ethnological museum in Kumrovec, and the medieval hilltop castles of Veliki Tabor and Trakošćan.

Close to the Hungarian border and easily reached by public transport from Zagreb, the neighbouring provincial towns of Varaždin and Čakovec are both presided over by 16th-century castles, open to the public as museums; they make a comfortable day trip from the capital.

Essentials

ⓘ Tourist information The Zagreb County Tourist Office at Preradovićeva 42, T01-487 3665, tzzz.hr, provides information about destinations in Zagorje. Varaždin has a town tourist office at Ivana Padovca 3, T042-201005, tourism-varazdin.hr. Čakovec has a town tourist office at Ilvana Padovca 3, T042-201005, tourism-cakovec.hr.

Kumrovec, Staro Selo

40 km from Zagreb, T049-225836, mdc.hr.
Apr-Sep 0900-1900, Oct-Mar 0900-1600, 20Kn.

The sleepy village of Kumrovec sits on the east bank of the River Sutla. It was here that the late Yugoslav President, Josip Broz Tito was born in 1892. Tito's home and a huddle of some 20 19th-century thatched cottages and wooden farm buildings in the old quarter have been turned into an open-air ethnological museum, known as Staro Selo (Old Village). Set amid orchards, with a stream animated by ducks, it offers a lifelike reconstruction of 19th-century Zagorje rural life. Tito's childhood home, which was the first brick house in the village, built in 1860, was turned into a small memorial museum in 1953. The furniture inside is just as it would have been when Tito was a child, and there's a small room displaying letters and gifts sent to the Yugoslav leader by foreign allies. In the garden stands an imposing bronze statue (an occasional target for local vandals) of the man himself, created by Antun Augustinčić in 1948.

Reconstruction of the surrounding buildings started in 1977, so that today you can see a blacksmith's shop, a potter's studio, a candlemaker's workshop and a kitchen, where demonstrations are laid on by respective craftsmen at weekends.

Josip Broz Tito's birthplace.

Veliki Tabor

Desinić (15 km north of Kumrovec),
T049-343963, veliki-tabor.hr.
May-Sep daily 1000-1800,
Oct-Apr daily 1000-1500, 20Kn.

Sitting on a hill close to the small village of Desinić the lofty ochre-coloured castle of Veliki Tabor is quite impressive seen from a distance. Closer inspection reveals a medieval structure with high-pitched terracotta roofs, which has been carefully restored and was reopened in autumn 2007. Close by, an informal farm restaurant serves delicious, reasonably priced local goodies.

Although some people believe that Veliki Tabor stands on the site of a second-century Roman fortress, the main pentagonal form of the castle dates back to the 12th century when it was the property of the Counts of Celje (in present-day Slovenia). In the 16th century the castle passed to the Ratkaj family, who added four side towers as protection against the Turks and enhanced the courtyard with three levels of open-arched galleries. During the Second World War, Franciscan nuns used the building as an orphanage to host 80 children who had lost their families, after which the castle became state property.

Veliki Tabor and the unfortunate Veronika

According to hearsay, during the 15th century, Freidrich, the son of Count Herman II Celjski, who resided in the castle at the time, fell in love with a pretty peasant girl, named Veronika, from the nearby village of Desinić. Deeming the fair maiden unworthy of his son, the count prohibited the affair, prompting the two young lovers to run away together. Count Herman sent his soldiers in hot pursuit: Freidrich was captured and locked up in a tower in the castle and Veronika was tried for witchcraft – she had, after all, enchanted the young man. When judges found Veronika innocent, the enraged count had her drowned and her body bricked up in a wall in the castle. Strangely, during renovation work in 1982, a woman's skull was found here. It is now on show in the castle chapel on the first floor and is said to be the last trace of the unfortunate Veronika. However, some say that Veronika's ghost can still be seen and heard wandering through the castle at night.

Veliki Tabor.

Tito

The seventh of 15 children, Josip Broz was born on 7 May 1892, in Kumrovec (then part of Austria-Hungary), to a Slovenian mother and a Croatian blacksmith father. Although he only attended school between the ages of seven and 12, he was to become one of the 20th century's most extraordinary leaders.

During the First World War he served with the Austrian army in Russia and was wounded and taken prisoner – a turn of events he used to his advantage, learning Russian and discovering the ideals of the Bolshevik movement. He returned to his homeland (by this time the Kingdom of the Serbs, Croats and Slovenes) in 1920 and joined the Communist Party. After a series of arrests and a stint in prison he went to work for the Balkan sector of Comintern in Moscow. In 1937 he returned home and became Secretary General of the Yugoslavian Communist Party.

When Germany attacked Yugoslavia in 1941, Tito formed the Partisan resistance movement, fighting the German Nazis and their allies, the Croatian Ustaše, as well another anti-fascist group, the pro-royalist Serbian Chetniks, who were initially backed by the British. In 1944, however, the allied forces switched their backing to the Partisans and, at the end of the Second World War, Tito set up the new Yugoslav government, based on Communist ideology.

After a series of disagreements over foreign policy, Tito broke with Stalin in 1948 and began to govern Yugoslavia along socialist lines, decentralizing the economy and setting up workers' self-management organizations. This gained him considerable favours from the West, which began giving Yugoslavia loans. When Stalin died in 1953, Tito forged good relations with Kruschev, making Yugoslavia a 'midway country' between the Communist USSR and the capitalist West. In the 1960s he founded the Non-Aligned Nations together with leaders of African and Asian countries.

Undoubtedly a colourful character, he had four wives and a penchant for Scotch whisky, Cuban cigars and fast cars – the collection he left behind includes a 1960 Rolls Royce Phantom and several Mercedes limousines. His circle of friends included Elizabeth Taylor and Richard Burton. At 1505 on May 4 1980, sirens sounded throughout Yugoslavia. Tito was dead. The entire country came to a standstill. His funeral, in Belgrade, was attended by representatives from over 125 countries. On his deathbed, he prophetically described himself as the last of the Yugoslavs.

Trakošćan

Trakošćan (36 km north of Veliki Tabor and 40 km south of Varaždin), T042-796422, trakoscan.hr. Apr-Oct 0900-1800, Nov-Mar 0900-1600, 30Kn.

Trakošćan is one of the most visited castles in Croatia and probably the most popular sight in Zagorje. A white fairy-tale fortress complete with turrets and a drawbridge, it stands on a small hill overlooking a lake, and is undoubtedly at its most magical at night, when it is floodlit.

The first castle on this site was built in the 13th century as an observation point above the Bednja Valley. It then passed on to various feudal lords, until being presented to the Drašković family, as a thank you for their dedication in defending the region against the Ottoman Turks in the late 16th century. Over the following 200 years various defence towers and a drawbridge were added, until the castle fell into disuse (the Turks long since gone). However, in the mid-19th century the Romanticist movement became fashionable among Central European aristocracy, and Vice-Marshall Juraj Drašković had the building restructured in neo-Gothic style and turned into a sumptuous country residence. He also landscaped the surrounding parkland, and created an artificial lake and a mixed forest of beech and fir. After the Second World War, the Drašković family moved to Austria and the property was nationalized and opened to the public in 1953.

On the first floor you can visit the luxurious wood-panelled living quarters, complete with late 19th-century furniture and solemn family portraits, while the bedrooms, furnished in baroque style, are on the second floor. There is also an arms collection on display, consisting of rifles, pistols and Turkish weapons from between the 15th and 19th centuries.

Tip...

The grounds at Trakošćan are especially pretty in spring and autumn.

Around the region

Lying 77 km northeast of Zagreb, Varaždin, with its 18th-century baroque churches and town houses, makes a manageable day trip from the capital. The main attraction is Stari Grad, a well-preserved 16th-century castle surrounded by grassy ramparts, now housing a museum. The best time to visit Varaždin is in autumn, when the trees take on russet hues complementing the pink and ochre façades. If you're lucky, you'll also catch the renowned Varaždin Baroque Evenings music festival, staged late September to early October.

Stari Grad

Strossmayerovo Šetalište 7, T042-658754.
Apr-Sep Tue-Sun 1000-1800, Oct-Mar Tue-Fri 1000-1700, Sat-Sun 1000-1300, 20Kn.

Just a five-minute walk from the centre stands Varaždin's top attraction, the castle, surrounded by lofty fortifications and ringed by a moat (now unfortunately empty). There's been a castle on the site for over 800 years, but the building's present appearance dates largely from the 16th century, when the existing structure was heavily reinforced against the possibility of a Turkish attack. The main entrance is an imposing gatehouse with a central tower and a wooden drawbridge, which leads into an internal courtyard ringed with three levels of open-arched galleries, designed by the Italian architect Domenico dell'Allio in the 1560s.

In 1925 the castle was given to the town and it now houses the Town Museum, displaying a collection of period furniture, with individual rooms devoted to particular epochs, following on one from another in chronological order.

Katedrala

Pavlinska ulica, just off Trg Kralja Tomislava (the main square).
Open 0800-1200 and 1600-1800.

Officially taking on the title of cathedral in 1997, when Varaždin became the seat of a diocese, this was the first baroque building in town. It dates back to the mid-17th century, when the style was brought here by Jesuit monks. Inside, the richly gilded main altar fills the central nave and bears paintings of the Virgin. The space is said to have exceptional acoustic qualities, and during the Varaždin Baroque Evenings music festival, concerts are held here.

Čakovec is a proud though rather uninspiring provincial town 82 km northeast of Zagreb. It centres on Trg Kralja Tomislava, the main square, a pleasant pedestrian area surrounded by two-storey pastel-coloured baroque town houses with steep-sloping tiled roofs. Throughout the rest of the country, Čakovec is known for its castle, textile industry and hard-working citizens – indeed, it's a world away from the *fjaka* (easy-going laziness combined with an appreciation of all things good in life) of Dalmatia.

On the main road to Hungary, it is hardly a big tourist destination. However, the castle, *medjimurska pita* (a delicious pie made of poppy seeds, cream cheese and walnuts, unique to the area) and the region's excellent white wines make it worth a half-day visit.

Tip...

Čakovec is just 15 km northeast of its neighbour and arch-rival, Varaždin, so the two can be easily combined as a day trip from the capital.

Stari Grad, the castle at Varaždin.

Čakovečki Dvor

Trg Republike 5, T040-313499.
Tue-Fri 1000-1500, Sat Sun 1000-1300, 15Kn.

On the edge of Čakovec, set amid carefully tended parkland, stands the castle complex. A generous section of the old 16th-century walls, complete with three semicircular bastions, is still standing, though the original Renaissance castle was devastated by an earthquake in 1738. The 'New Castle', as it stands today, is a four-storey baroque structure, based on a quadrangular ground plan with an inner courtyard, built by the Czech Counts of Althan during the 18th century. From 1855 to 1870 part of the complex was used as a sugar factory, and during the Second World War the northern wing was badly damaged.

However, post-war restoration work saw the castle return to its former glory, and the Muzej Medjimurja (Museum of Medjimurje) opened here in 1954. Inside, you'll find an Ethnographic Department, with a fine display of local costumes on the first floor and an Archaeological Department and Art Gallery, with a collection of paintings by 20th-century artists who were born, lived or worked in the region, on the second floor. The ground floor is devoted to heavy stone pieces, tombstones and sculpture, from the first to 20th centuries.

Lovrec Vineyard

Sv Urban 133, Štrigova, T040-830171.
Open daily for wine tasting, but better to telephone first to arrange a time.

A pleasant drive 20 km northwest of Čakovec, through undulating countryside planted with vineyards, brings you to the sleepy village of Štrigova, close to the Slovenian border.

Here the Lovrec family run a small, high-quality vineyard, producing a variety of award-winning white wines: Chardonnay, Pinot, Rizling, Graševina, Sauvignon and Trminac. In an authentic wooden outbuilding, complete with rustic furnishing, you can take part in an amusing and informative wine-tasting session (available in Croatian, Slovenian, English and German). Expect to sample six different wines, ranging from dry to sweet, accompanied by home-made bread, local cheese and salami. At the end, it is possible to buy wine to take home.

East of Zagreb

Seldom visited by tourists, other than those arriving from Serbia, the flat fertile plains of Slavonia spent several centuries under the Turks until they were reclaimed by the Hapsburgs. Up until the Second World War a sizeable German minority lived here and, still today, there are many Hungarian families. The largest town in the region is Osijek, built on the River Drava, while nearby war-torn Vukovar presides over the River Danube. Birdwatching enthusiast will enjoy exploring the wetlands of Lonjsko Polje and Kopački Rit, both nature parks. The region is known throughout Croatia for its excellent *kulen* (spicy salami) and *fiš paprikaš* (fish stew flavoured with paprika).

Osijek.

Essentials

❶ Tourist information Osijek town tourist office is at Županijska 2, T031-203755, tzosijek.hr. There's also a Tourist Information Centre (TIC) in **Tvrđa**, T031-210120. **Vukovar** town tourist office is at JJStrossmayera 15, T032-442889, turizamvukovar.hr.

Lonjsko Polje Nature Park

Nature park information centre, Čigoć 26, Čigoć, T044-715115, pp-lonjsko-polje.hr.
Daily 0800-1600, 25Kn.

This vast area of wetland and oak woods, 82 km southeast of Zagreb, is renowned for its storks, which come here to nest between April and October, then spend the rest of the year in South Africa. The main entrance to the nature park is in Čigoć, which is noted for its lovely Posavina-style wooden houses, complete with finely carved balconies and thatched roofs.

Declared a nature park in 1990, Lonjsko Polje is one of largest wetlands in Europe, displaying a landscape typical of large parts of Central Europe 150 years ago, before the advent of modern land-drainage systems. Each year in spring, as the surrounding rivers swell, the oak woods and meadows of the river basin flood, providing a perfect natural habitat for some 240 bird species. While the best known visitors to the park are storks – some 600 couples, the highest concentration of storks in Europe – other endangered species such as herons, egrets, cormorants and eagles can also be spotted. The marshy meadows and woods of ash, willow and poplar host more than 10,000 ducks through winter. Other indigenous species include the Turopolje pig, which feeds on freshwater mussels and acorns, the semi-wild Posavac horse, wild boar, deer, otters, beavers and wild cats.

It is recommended that visitors to the park wear hiking boots, long-sleeved shirts and long-legged trousers (because of mosquitoes), a sun hat and insect repellent. A bottle of drinking water is also a good idea.

Osijek & around

Lying 280 km east of Zagreb, Osijek is the largest town in the flat fertile region of Slavonia. The town can be divided into Gornji Grad (Upper Town), the main commercial centre, Donji Grad (Lower Town), a residential area, and Tvrđa, a picturesque 18th-century quarter originally built by as a military barracks. Strung along the south bank of the River Drava, the three distinct parts of town are interspersed by tree-lined avenues and green parks, giving it an airy and relaxed feel. The main attraction is Tvrđa. A pleasant 2-km waterside walkway, known to locals as the *promenada*, leads along the south bank from Gornji Grad to Tvrđa, while a pedestrian suspension bridge connects Gornji Grad to Copacabana, the 'town beach', where bathing is possible through summer. You can probably cover Osijek in a day, after which you might visit the nearby Kopački Rit Nature Park.

Tvrđa

Work on Tvrđa began in 1712, when the Austrians set about constructing a large army barracks surrounded by eight bastions linked by defensive walls (now only partly visible). Besides military and public buildings, civilian town houses were erected within the complex, along with several fine churches and monasteries, which cared for the centre's spiritual welfare as well as providing schools and a printing press.

Osijek Town Council has put forward Tvrđa as a candidate to be a UNESCO World Heritage Site, and there are plans to restore many of the old buildings and turn them over to educational and cultural institutions.

Tip...

Tvrđa is especially lovely at night, when the cobbled streets are lamplit and a number of popular bars and cafés, plus a handful of excellent little restaurants attract the local student community.

Kopački Rit Nature Park.

Today Tvrđa is something of an open-air museum, looking now much as it would have done in the 18th century. The complex centres on a main square, Trg Sv Trojstvo, lined by ochre-coloured baroque buildings with steep-pitched tile roofs, one of which houses the **Museum of Slavonia** displaying finds from Mursa (the Roman name for the earliest settlement on this site).

Kopački Rit Nature Park

Nature park information centre: Petefi Šandora 5, Bilje, T031-752320, kopacki-rit.com. Daily 0900-1700, 10Kn.

Located 12 km northeast of Osijek, Kopački Rit Nature Park is a vast expanse of marshland prized for its wealth of rare birds. Situated between the River Drava and the River Danube, the park is part of Baranja, a region of flat, fertile agricultural land, which until the war for independence hosted a mixed farming community of Croats, Serbs and Hungarians. It was taken by the Serb military at the beginning of the war in 1991, was designated a UN-protected zone from 1992 to 1996, and then came under UN transitional administration until it was incorporated into Croatia in January 1998.

Said to be one of the largest and most beautiful wetlands in Europe, the park's waters, flora and fauna attract experts and scientists from far afield, as well as curious day trippers. Around 260 bird species nest here, including geese, ducks, herons, storks, coot, gulls, terns, kingfishers and woodpeckers, and in spring and autumn many other migratory species use the area as a temporary shelter. The waters are abundant in fish – which is why so many birds are attracted to

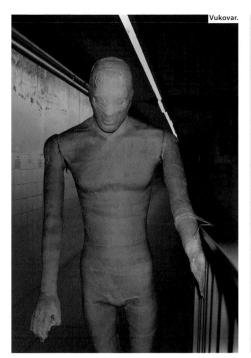

Vukovar.

Casualties of war

Some people say the war started and ended in Vukovar. When Croatia claimed independence, Serbs from the surrounding villages were adamant that they would rather remain part of Yugoslavia. A group of Croatian activists (among them members of Tudjman's HDZ ruling party) provoked the situation by firing three rockets at the Serb-populated village of Borovo Selo. Tensions escalated and the situation soon ran out of control. By 1 August 1991 Vukovar lay under siege, surrounded by Yugoslav army reinforcements and Serb irregulars. On 19 November 1991, the town fell, by this time devastated, buildings lying in rubble and the streets lined with corpses. Some 264 patients and medical staff were taken from Vukovar hospital and transported to Ovčara, 10 km southeast of town, where they were killed and buried in a mass grave. Of those who remained, the women and children were spared, but many of the men disappeared and have never been found. Vukovar officially came back under Croatian administration in January 1998 and a lengthy reconstruction programme was initiated in the hope that former residents, both Croats and Serbs, would return. The process of rebuilding and reintegration is slow and will take many years to complete. Nowhere else in the country are the physical and psychological traumas caused by the war so apparent.

the park – including pike, tench, bream, carp, catfish and perch, while the surrounding oak woods host deer, wild boar, wild cats, pine martens, stone martens and weasels. Some of the willow lined ponds are home to otters. A group 'zoological reserve' tour is available and includes transport through the wetland by boat (60Kn), while real enthusiasts might prefer to take part in a six-hour guided birdwatching tour (1000Kn).

Vukovar

Some 35 km southeast of Osijek, on the west bank of the River Danube, which forms a natural border with Serbia, Vukovar was once a prosperous market town famed for its elegant 18th-century baroque architecture. Since 1991, it has become better known as an image of the suffering and devastation caused by the war of independence. Many who fled at this time remain in other parts of Croatia or abroad. An eerie silence pervades in a town still divided between Croats and Serbs. There is little in the way of sightseeing, though the **Ovčara Memorial Centre** and the **War Victims Memorial Cemetery** serve as a poignant reminder of the atrocity of war (see box, above).

Tip...

It is recommended that visitors to the park wear light waterproof sports shoes, long-sleeved shirts and long-legged trousers (because of mosquitoes), plus insect repellent. A bottle of drinking water is also a good idea.

Plitvice Lakes

South of Zagreb, the inland road to Dalmatia takes you through the rural area of Lika. Before the war of independence, many Serbian families lived here – most fled during the hostilities, but some are slowly returning now. The main sight here is Plitvice Lakes National Park, well worth a stop for its spectacular waterfalls. South from here, Dalmatia beckons with its dramatically stunning mountains, sea and islands.

About 128 km southwest of Zagreb lies Croatia's most popular inland destination, Plitvice Lakes National Park. Encompassing 16 emerald-green lakes, connected by a series of spectacular waterfalls and stretching 8 km in length, it more than warrants a stop and even an overnight stay. The surrounding slopes are covered with forests of beech and fir, and the entire park is criss-crossed by a series of marked paths and wooden bridges. The lakes are rich in trout (fishing is prohibited), while the surrounding forests are home to foxes and badgers, as well as seldom-sighted lynx, wolves and bears. Birdwatchers should look out for woodpeckers and herons, plus rare species such as grey eagles and peregrine falcons. Owls are plentiful, though rarely seen in daylight hours.

The best way to explore the lakes is to begin at Entrance 2 then take the national park bus to **Labudovac Falls**, where the water from Proščansko Jezero, the highest of the lakes (639 m above sea level) begins a spectacular journey,

cascading down through a succession of smaller basins to reach the park's largest lake, **Jezero Kozjak**. The stretch from Labudovac Falls to Jezero Kozjak is comfortably completed on foot, after which you can ride a national park boat the length of the lake, then follow a series of wooden bridges and walkways over and around a number of smaller pools to arrive at the park's largest and most spectacular waterfall, **Veliki Slap**, where water thunders down to the lowest lake, **Kaluderovac** (503 m). You are now just a 10-minute walk from Entrance 1, from where the national park bus shuttles visitors back to Entrance 2. This entire circuit takes about four hours. A map and information about alternative routes are available from the national park office.

Karst features

Making up part of a karst landscape, the lakes and falls of Plitvice have developed over the last 10,000 years, and the process is continuing today. Such features are formed when limestone rock, consisting of calcium carbonate ($CaCO_3$), dissolves in water, which then becomes super-saturated and deposits the $CaCO_3$ in the form of microcrystals. In the case of Plitvice, the deposits have built up to make rapids and travertine barriers that form the waterfalls.

National park information office
Entrance 2, Plitvička Jezera, T053-751014, np-plitvicka-jezera.hr.
Daily Jun-Aug 0700-2000, Apr-May and Sep-Oct 0800-1800, Nov-Mar 0900-1600; Apr-Oct 110Kn, Nov-Mar 70Kn.

Sleeping

Hotel Regent Esplanade €€€€
Mihanovićeva 1, T01-456 6666, regenthotels.com.
Map: Zagreb, D7, p82.
Standing next to Zagreb train station, this five-star hotel was built in 1925 for passengers travelling on the Orient Express. Exuding old-fashioned charm, it has an elegant art deco interior with a marble lobby, and 209 rooms and suites, each with a marble bathroom with a bathtub and drench shower. Facilities include two restaurants and a sauna and gym.

Arcotel Allegra Zagreb €€€
Branimirova 29; T01 4696000; arcotel.cc.
Map: Zagreb, E7, p82.
A five-minute walk from the train station and a 15-minute walk from the main square, this Design hotel has a funky pop interior. The 151 rooms and four business suites are bright and spacious, and equipped with DVD player, flat-screen TV and Wi-Fi. The Radicchio restaurant serves a generous buffet breakfast, plus Mediterranean and Austrian specialities at lunch and dinner. There's also a wellness area, with sauna, jacuzzi, massage and gym.

Best Western Hotel Astoria €€€
Petrinjska 71; T01 4808900; bestwestern.com.
Map: Zagreb, E6, p82.

Built in 1932, this 100-room hotel was fully refurbished in 2005. Conveniently located in a side street between the train station and the main square, it's popular with tourists and business visitors. The rooms may be rather small and lacking in atmosphere, but they are comfortable and have free Wi-Fi. You can expect friendly, helpful staff, a plentiful breakfast spread and reasonable prices.

Hotel Dubrovnik €€€
Gajeva 1, T01-487 3555, hotel-dubrovnik.hr.
Map: Zagreb, D4, p82.
Ideally located, just off Trg Bana Jelačića, the main square, this hotel makes a perfect base for exploring Zagreb's cultural attractions, cafés, restaurants and shops. Its 258 rooms and eight suites are a little dated, but clean and comfortable and have free Wi-Fi. Ask for a room with a view of the main square or the cathedral.

Hotel Palace €€€
Strossmayerov Trg 10, T01-492 0530, palace.hr.
Map: Zagreb, D5, p82.
Overlooking a leafy square, between the train station and Trg Bana Jelačića, this Secessionist building was converted to become the city's first hotel in 1907. Besides old-world elegance, it offers 126 fairly basic rooms, plus a pleasant street-level Viennese-style café.

Jagerhorn €€
Ilica 14, T01-483 3877, jaegerhorn.hr.
Map: Zagreb, C3, p82.
Tucked away in a passageway off Ilica, 100 m west of the main square, Jaegerhorn dates back to 1827, making it the capital's oldest-running hotel. Under renovation through 2010, while still operating, it is gradually being upgraded to an atmospheric three-star hotel. Expect a cosy lounge furnished with antiques, a garden café, and 13 rooms.

Tomislavov Dom €€
Sljemenska cesta bb, T01-456 0400, hotel-tomislavovdom.com.
Map: Zagreb, D1, p82.
North of Zagreb, and located on the top of Mount Medvednica, this Yugoslav-era hotel is set amid woodland and makes a superb base for keen hikers. Renovated in 2006, it offers 42 basic but comfortable rooms, each with a shower but no bathtub, plus a café, a restaurant, a wellness centre with an indoor pool, gym and sauna, and conference facilities.

Vila Tina €€
Bukovačka Cesta 213, T01-244 5204, vilatina.com.hr.
Map: Zagreb, E2, p82.
North of the city centre, close to Maksimir Park, a 20-minute tram ride from the main square, this delightful family-run hotel comprises 25 tastefully furnished

rooms, adorned with extras such as fresh fruit and flowers. There's an excellent restaurant with outdoor seating on a summer terrace, plus a small indoor pool, solarium, sauna and gym.

Hotel Fala €
Il Trnjanske ledine 18, T01-611 1062, hotel-fala-zg.hr.
Map: Zagreb, E7, p82.
A 15-minute walk south of the train station brings you to this small family-run hotel, operated by welcoming staff and offering good value for money. The 13 rooms are basic and a bit small and outdated, but all have TV and minibar. There's a cheerful breakfast room with a pine floor and blue details, and guests can use the internet in the reception.

Hotel Varaždin €€
Kolodvorska 19, Varaždin, T042-290720, hotelvarazdin.com.
Opposite the train station, this hotel offers 27 basic but comfortable rooms, each with an en suite bathroom with a massage shower. The interior is shiny and new, as it opened in summer 2007, while the hotel restaurant occupies a restored brick vaulted cellar.

Hotel Aurora €
Franje Punčeca 2, Čakovec, T040-310700, hotelaurora-ck.com.
In a yellow and blue post-modern building just 300 m from the town centre, this small hotel offers 10 cosy guest rooms. There's also a bar where they serve breakfast, with outdoor tables on a pleasant terrace, plus a small gym, sauna and massage.

Hotel Lav €€€
JJ Strossmayera 18, Vukovar, T032-445100, hotel-lav.hr.
Reopened after reconstruction in 2005, this four-star hotel dates back to 1840, and has the unenviable record of having been destroyed three times by war. There are 38 rooms and four suites, all with satellite TV and WLAN internet – the best ones overlook the River Dunav. It is a short walk from the centre; there is a restaurant and café.

Waldinger Hotel €€€
Županijska 8, Osijek, T031-250450, waldinger.hr.
This elegant Secessionist building, dating from 1904, is in the centre, just a few doors down from the tourist office. The 14 rooms and two suites each have satellite TV, minibar, safe deposit, and internet connection, and most also have jacuzzi. Facilities include a fitness studio and sauna. Excellent value for money.

Agroturizam Crvendać €
Biljske Satnije 5, Kopački Rit Nature Park, T031-750264, crvendac.com.
Set in a garden in Bilje (5 km north of Osijek), on the edge of Kopački Rit. The three guest rooms (with TV and air conditioning) share a bathroom. Breakfast is served in a conservatory overlooking the garden and there are bikes to rent.

Hotel Osijek €
Šamačka 4, Osijek, T031-230333, hotelosijek.hr.
This high-rise concrete block stands just a five-minute walk from the main square, overlooking the river. The 147 rooms and suites are spacious, smart and modern, and all have free Wi-Fi and slick bathrooms. There's also a restaurant, three cafés, a wellness centre (sauna, jacuzzi and gym) and beauty centre (hairdressing, facials, manicure and massage).

Tradicije Čigoč €
Cigoc 7a, Lonjsko Polje Nature Park, T044-715124, tradicije-cigoc.hr.
This carefully restored 180-year-old family house comes complete with storks nesting on the roof. There are six guest rooms furnished with old-fashioned wooden beds, each with shower, TV and air conditioning. Expect bikes for hire, a hearty breakfast spread and an adjoining restaurant (see Eating, page 107).

Eating & drinking

Plitvice Lakes National Park

Hotel Jezero €€
Plitvička Jezera bb, T053-751400, np-plitvicka-jezera.hr.
This three-star hotel, a mountain lodge built on high ground overlooking the lakes, close to Entrance 2, offers the park's most upmarket accommodation. The 222 rooms and seven suites are comfortable but dated, but the best ones afford stunning views over the lakes. Facilities include a massage pool, sauna, gym and tennis court. Be aware that its often crowded with tour groups and some say the food is disappointing.

Obitelj Krizmanić €
Rastovača 15, T053-758028, plitvickajezera.info.
Just a 10-minute walk from Entrance 1 and the area's best restaurant, Lička Kuća (see Eating, page 107), this slightly rustic house offers six rooms and self-catering apartments, plus a bungalow. Facilities include internet, laundry and a kids' play area.

Sobe San Korana €
San Korana 15, T053-774140, sankorana.com.
In the small peaceful village of Korana, next to the River Korana and 3 km from the national park, this traditional stone-and-wood house offers comfortable rooms and a warm welcome.

Zagreb

Gornji Grad
Dubravkin Put €€€
Dubrovakin put bb, T01-483 4975, dubravkin-put.com.
Daily lunch and dinner.
Map: Zagreb, C1, p82.
Considered by many to be the best fish restaurant in town, Dubravkin Put comprises a light and airy dining room, plus outdoor seating on a leafy terrace. The house speciality is *brodet* (fish stew) prepared with fresh herbs. You'll find it in Tuškanac Park, a 10-minute walk north from the main square.

Prasac €€€
Vranicanijeva 6, T01-485 1411, prasac.hr.
Mon-Sat lunch and dinner, closed Sun.
Map: Zagreb, C3, p82.
In an old stone cottage close Lotrščak Tower, cosy gastro-pub Prasac (which means 'pig') can seat only 18 guests, including two at the bar. Owner-cook Dino Galvagno keeps the menu small and changes it often, turning out creative cuisine based on locally sourced ingredients. Portions are small but the food exquisite. Reservations recommended.

Baltazar €€€-€€
Nova Ves 4, T01-466 6999, restoran-baltazar.hr.
Mon-Sat lunch and dinner, closed Sun.
Map: Zagreb, D1, p82.
Located north of the cathedral, Baltazar specializes in classic Balkan dishes such as *ražnjići* (mixed grilled meat), *čevapčići* (kebabs) and *zapečeni grah* (oven-baked beans). In summer there are tables outside in a pretty courtyard.

Ivica i Marica €€€-€€
Tkalčićeva 70, T01-482 8999.
Daily lunch and dinner.
Map: Zagreb, D2, p82.
This cosy eatery offers an old-fashioned interior, homely Croatian cooking and waiters dressed in folk costumes. Favourites include *rezanci sa tartufima* (pasta with truffles) and *govedja pisanica sa umakom od zelenog papra* (fillet steak with green pepper sauce). The adjoining cake shop is under the same management.

Kaptolska Klet €€€-€€
Kaptol 5, T01-481 4838, kaptolska-klet.hr.
Daily lunch and dinner.
Map: Zagreb, D3, p82.
Opposite the cathedral, this popular rustic eatery offers extensive seating both indoors and out, hence its popularity with tour groups. The menu features reasonably priced, hearty local dishes such as *purica sa mlincima* (turkey with savoury pastries) and *zagorski štrukli* (baked cheese dumplings).

Pod Gričkim Topom €€€-€€
Za kmardijeve stube 5,
T01-483 3607.
Daily lunch and dinner.
Map: Zagreb, C3, p82.
This small, homely restaurant has stunning views over the city's rooftops. Dalmatian fish dishes predominate: try the *ligne na žaru* (barbecued squid). In summer guests sit out on a flower-decked terrace, while in winter the homely dining room, compete with sepia photographs, comes into use.

Amfora €
Dolac 2, 01-481 6455.
Open daily for lunch only.
Map: Zagreb, D3, p82.
You'll find this cheap and informal seafood eatery next door to the covered fish market, overlooking the fruit and vegetable stalls on Dolac. The kitchen serves platters of grilled sardines, fried whitebait and squid, plus simple side salads and carafes of house wine. There's seating for just 30 diners.

Cafés & bars
Gallery Klovičevi Dvori museum café
Jezuitski trg 4.
Map: Zagreb, C3, p82.
If you're doing a round of the museums in Gornji Grad, this café offers a peaceful, cultural ambience.

Hemingway Bar
Tuškanac 1, T098 980 5000,
hemingway.hr.
Map: Zagreb, B2, p82.
Near Saloon (see Clubs, page 108), one of Zagreb's most sophisticated nightspots, Hemingway is a pricey, chic cocktail bar, popular with local yuppies. It also serves up Italian-inspired cuisine.

Sunčani Sat
Tklačićeva 27.
Map: Zagreb, D2, p82.
Pedestrian-only Tklačićeva is lined with informal café-bars popular with students. Suncani Sat has tables and comfy wicker chairs outside, and is as good as any.

Donji Grad
Paviljon €€€
Trg kralja Tomislava 22, T01-481 3066, restaurant-paviljon.com.
Mon-Sat lunch and dinner, closed Sun.
Map: Zagreb, E6, p82.
This refined restaurant is located in the charming 19th-century Art Pavilion, close to the train station. Choose from delights such as smoked tuna carpaccio served with parmesan, pine nuts and rocket, or turkey fillet with home-made green gnocchi.

Stari Fijaker €€€-€€
Mesnička 6, T01-483 3829.
Daily lunch and dinner.
Map: Zagreb, B3, p82.

Located a five-minute walk along Ilica from the main square, Stari Fijaker serves up traditional Zagrebian fare such as roast meats and *zagorski štrukli* (baked cheese dumplings) in an old-fashioned dining room with wooden panelled walls and crisp white table linens.

Vinodol €€€-€€
Nikole Tesle 10, T01-481 1472, vinodol-zg.hr.
Daily lunch and dinner.
Map: Zagreb, D4, p82.
A good choice for meat lovers, the specialities are roast lamb, and veal cutlets stuffed with spinach and parmesan. The dining room occupies a vaulted brick cellar with polished wooden floors, and there's outdoor seating on a large summer terrace, with whole lamb turning on a spit.

Nova €€
Ilica 72, T01-481 0059, novarestoran.com.hr.
Mon-Sat lunch and dinner, closed Sun.
Map: Zagreb, B3, p82.
On first-floor level, this modern vegetarian restaurant has a slick, cream and beige minimalist interior and wooden floors. The menu includes a good range of macrobiotic and vegan dishes, made mainly from organic and wholegrain ingredients. David Byrne, Shakira and Duran Duran have eaten here.

Medvedgrad Pivnica €€-€
Ilica 49, T01-484 6922,
pivnica-medvedgrad.hr.
Daily 1200-2400.
Map: Zagreb, A7, p82.
A popular microbrewery and
beer hall, serving five brands of
its own beer, plus generous
portions of roast meats, goulash,
beans and sausage, pizzas and a
range of colourful salads.

Restoran Boban €€-€
Gajeva 9, T01-481 1557, boban.hr.
Daily lunch and dinner.
Map: Zagreb, D4, p82.
Owned by Zvonimir Boban
(captain of the Croatian football
team during the 1998 World
Cup), this popular restaurant
occupies a vaulted brick cellar
just off the main square. It
specializes in Italian food and is
best known for its pasta dishes.
Be prepared to queue.

Mimice €
Jurišićeva 21, T01-481 4524.
Mon-Sat lunch and dinner,
closed Sun.
Map: Zagreb, E4, p82.
Just a couple of miles' walk east
of the main square, this eatery
serves fried *srdele* (sardines) and
papaline (sprats).

Cafés & bars
Bulldog
Bogovićeva 6, T01-400 2070,
bulldog-zagreb.com.
Map: Zagreb, D4, p82.
Very popular with both young
Croatians and English-speaking

visitors, this large pub is just a
five-minute walk from the main
square. Through summer tables
spill onto the pedestrian area out
front. Occasional live music.

Gradska Kavana
Trg Bana Jelačića 10.
Map: Zagreb, D3, p82.
Among the largest and most
popular cafés on the main
square, with an open-air front
terrace in summer, and outdoor
heaters also making it possible to
sit outside through much of
spring and autumn. A favourite
spot for morning coffee.

Maraschino
Margaretska 1, T01-481 2612.
Map: Zagreb, C3, p82.
Just off the main square, this bar
looks ordinary enough from
street level. But descend to the
basement for one of the hippest
venues in town, with retro tables
and chairs, chandeliers, kitsch
wallpaper and funky music.

People's Lounge
Hektorovićeva 2, T01-604 0525,
people.hr.
Map: Zagreb, E7, p82.
This chic lounge bar and
restaurant has an elegant interior
with sofas, scatter cushions and
modern art. Popular with smart,
moneyed Zagrebians, it serves
excellent cocktails as well as a
tempting range of eats including
Croatian, Italian and Southeast
Asian dishes.

North of the city centre
Okrugljak €€€
Mlinovi 28, T01-467 4112,
okrugljak.hr.
Daily lunch and dinner.
Map: Zagreb, E1, p82.
Expensive but worth it, this
renowned eatery offers
authentic Croatian cuisine, on
the road north from Zagreb to
Medvednica Nature Park. In a
wooden-beamed dining room
and a courtyard garden, expect
dishes such as *punjena pisanica
Okrugljak* (pork fillet stuffed with
cream cheese and prosciutto)
and *biftek na rukoli* (rump steak
with rocket).

Stari Puntijar €€€-€€
Gračanka cesta 65, T01-467 5500.
Daily lunch and dinner.
Map: Zagreb, D1, p82.
On the road between Zagreb
and Medvednica Nature Park,
this charming restaurant is well
known for its 19th-century
Zagreb dishes such as *podolac*
(ox) medallions in cream and
saffron, *zagorski štruki* (baked
cheese dumplings), *orehnjača*
(walnut loaf) and *makovnjača*
(poppy seed cake).

North of Zagreb
Mala Hiža €€€
Mačkovec 107, T040-341101.
4 km north of Čakovec.
Daily lunch and dinner.
This is one of the best places to
eat in the area. Antique furniture
and an open fireplace set a

homely atmosphere, while guests tuck into large platters of roast meats, along with local specialities such as fresh curd cheese and boiled ham. There's live music on Friday and Saturday evenings.

Restoran Zlatna Guska €€€-€€

J Habdelića 4, Varaždin, T042-213393, zlatna-guska.com.
Daily lunch and dinner.
Set in a vaulted cellar space, the 'Golden Goose' is relaxed during the day and romantic at night. They do delicious chicken and mushroom filled pancakes, and there's a help-yourself salad bar and excellent house wine.

Grešna Gorica €€-€

Desinić, Veliki Tabor, T049-343001, gresna-gorica.com.
Daily lunch and dinner.
This rustic eatery serves up Zagorje dishes such as *zagorski štrukli* (baked cheese dumplings) and *pura s mlincima* (turkey with savoury pastries). Everything is made from local produce supplied by neighbouring farms. From the garden there's a good view of Veliki Tabor.

East of Zagreb

Restoran Muller €€€

Trg Jure Križanića 9, Osijek, T031-204770.
Mon-Sat lunch and dinner, closed Sun.

In a restored baroque building in the romantic Tvrđa area, this restaurant serves Slavonian, Dalmatian and international dishes – try the local *smudj* (pike) followed by *palačinke* (pancakes).

Restoran Kod Varge €€

Kralaja Zvonimira 37a, Bilje, Kopački Rit Nature Park, T031-750031.
Daily lunch and dinner.
Just outside the nature park in Bilje, Kod Varge is known for tasty fish dishes and home-made sausage. The house speciality is *šaran s kajmakom i krumpirom* (carp with sour cream and potatoes).

Slavonska Kuća €€

Kamila Firingera 26, Osijek, T031-369955.
Daily lunch and dinner.
Within the Tvrđa complex, this cosy, rustic eatery specializes in traditional local dishes. Try the *riblja kobasica*, a type of sausage made from smoked fish, as an unusual starter, followed by the house speciality *riblji paprikaš* (fish stew with paprika), which comes to the table in a large bowl with a ladle.

Tri Vrske €€

Parobrodska 3, Vukovar, T032-441788.
Daily lunch and dinner.
Accessed across a footbridge, this charming informal riverside restaurant is one of the few places that managed to keep

functioning during the war. Freshwater fish tops the menu, with local dishes such as *riblji paprikaš* (fish stew with paprika) and smoked carp highly recommended.

Tradicije Čigoč €€-€

Cigoc 7a, Lonjsko Polje Nature Park, T044-715124, tradicije-cigoc.hr.
Daily lunch and dinner.
The Barić family restored this 180-year-old house and opened a small restaurant seating 50 diners at 11 long oak tables. Expect local favourites such as *gulaš* (Hungarian goulash), home-made bread and local cheeses. Most of the produce is their own. They also have rooms to rent (see Sleeping, page 103).

Plitvice Lakes National Park

Lička Kuća €€

Plitvička Jezera bb, T053-751024.
Closed Nov-Apr.
Opposite Entrance 1, this large, highly regarded restaurant is done out in rustic style with heavy wooden tables and benches. The menu features traditional Lika dishes such as *lička juha* (soup made from lamb's innards and vegetables) and *teletina ispod peke* (veal prepared under a *peka*).

Entertainment

Shopping

Zagreb

Clubs
Aquarius
Matije Ljubeka bb, T01-364 0231, aquarius.hr.
Tue-Sun, closed Mon.
Overlooking Lake Jarun, 4 km from city centre. Zagreb's top club for dance, commercial and techno, plus occasional concerts by popular Croatian bands.

BP Jazz Club
Nikole Tesle 7, Donji Grad, T01-481 4444, bpclub.hr.
Mon-Sat 1000-0100, Sun 1700-0100.
This friendly jazz club located in a basement can get very crowded when there are live concerts.

Gallery
Matije Ljubeka bb, T099-444 2444 (mob), gallery.hr.
Mon-Sat, closed Sun.
Overlooking Lake Jarun, 4 km from the city centre, Gallery is close to Aquarius, which it now rivals in the 'cool' stakes. House and techno music predominate at weekends, though you'll also hear R'n'B during the week.

Gjuro 2
Medveščak 2, Gornji Grad, T01-462 9226, gjuro2.hr.
Tue-Sat 2200-0400.
Young professionals with an alternative streak meet up here to drink and dance. Wednesday is R'n'B night, Thursday is for over 24s, and Saturday is devoted to house music.

Močvara
Trnjanski Nasip bb, Donji Grad, T01-615 9668, mochvara.hr.
Mon-Thu 1200-0200, Fri-Sun 1200-0400.
A very popular alternative youth club, located on the banks of the River Sava. Founded in 1999 by a cultural association that wanted a venue for off-beat Croatian and foreign music and drama.

Saloon
Tuškanac 1a, Gornji Grad, T01-481 0733, saloon.hr.
Fri and Sat 2200-0400.
This is the place to be seen if you want to hit the gossip magazines. Friday night sees hits from the 80s and 90s, while Saturday is dedicated to Croatian music. In summer the crowds spill out onto an open-air terrace. It's close to Hemingway Bar (see Cafés & bars, page 105) so you can combine the two.

Tvornica
Šubićeva 2, Donji Grad, T01-465 5007, tvornica-kulture.hr.
Coffee bar 0800-2200, Club 2200-0400 (closes earlier on weekdays).
Another alternative venue (*tvornica* means factory), attracting some of Europe's top DJs as well as staging rock concerts and theatre. Located close to the bus station.

Zagreb

Books
Algoritam
Gajeva 1, T01-488 1555.
Just off the main square, Algoritam is the best bookshop for foreign-language publications, including novels, travel guides and maps, plus computer games and DVDs.

Profil Megastore
Bogovićeva 7, T01-487 7325.
One block back from the main square, Profil is Zagreb's biggest bookshop. It extends over five levels and stocks both Croatian and foreign books (many in English), and also has a café.

Clothing
I-gle
Dežmanov prolaz 4, T01-481 3280, i-gle.com.
Set up by two local female designers, Nataša Mihaljčišin and Martina Vrdoljak-Ranilović, I-gle (which means needle) has a cult following among Croatian's socialites. Clothes in the Zagreb shop are not outrageously expensive – their designs are also stocked by Harvey Nichols in London.

Nebo
Radićeva 17, T01-483-0935.
Local design company Nebo (which means Sky) creates reasonably priced, funky, minimalist-style clothes and shoes. This is their main outlet – they have a second, smaller store in the Importanne Galerija (mall) in front of the train station.

Food & drink
Dolac
Just off the main square.
The open-air market is the best place for fresh fruit and vegetables. Down below in the covered halls you'll find meats, cheeses and several bakeries.

Vinoteka Bornstein
Kaptol 19, close to the cathedral in Gornji Grad, T01-481 2361, bornstein.hr.
A beautiful vaulted brick cellar stocked with quality Croatian wines, olive oils and truffle products; ideal as presents to take home.

Zigante Tartufi
Vlaška 7; T01-481 0358, tartufi.hr.
Shop here for an extensive range of Istrian truffle products including whole preserved black and white truffles, truffle oils and sheep's cheese with truffles.

Souvenirs
Aromatica
Vlaška 7, T01-481 1584, aromatica.hr.
Aromatica sells its own line in deliciously scented soaps, shampoos and massage oils made with herbal extracts.

Croata
Kaptol 13, close to the cathedral in Gornji Grad, T01-481 4600, croata.hr.
Croata sells original Croatian ties in presentation boxes with a history of the tie included.

Ethno Style
Stara Vlaška 6.
Opposite the cathedral, this small store sells authentic handmade Croatian regional folk costumes and lace.

Zagreb

Funky Zagreb
funky-zagreb.hr.
A small agency offering personalized private tours of Zagreb and the region, run by tourist guide Mladen Čar.

Kompas
Heinzelova 62/a, T01-455 0160, kompas-online.net.
Escorted half-day tours from Zagreb to the Castles of Zagorje, Kumrovec and Varaždin, and one-day tours to Plitvice Lakes National Park.

Contents

113 Introduction
114 Pula & around
118 Istria's west coast
124 Inland Istria
128 Listings:
128 Sleeping
131 Eating & drinking
133 Entertainment
134 Shopping
135 Activities & tours

Istria

Rovinj old town.

SCS IACOBVS SCS ANDREA SCS PETRVS EGO LVX SVM VERA SCS PAVLVS SCS IOHANES SCS FELIPPVS SCS MATTEV

SCS MAVRVS

Introduction

The large, triangular peninsula of Istria in northwest Croatia has an identity all of its own. Historically it has close ties with Italy and many towns, especially on the western side, are still bilingual. Dubbed the 'Tuscany of Croatia', its restaurants serve beautifully presented creative cuisine, farmhouses dish up local specialities and offer overnight accommodation (agrotourism), and the tourist board has set up a series of bike paths and wine roads.

Lying on the tip of the peninsula, the region's principal city and port is Pula, with a first-century Roman forum as the main square and an ancient amphitheatre dominating the skyline. Close by are the islands of Brijuni National Park, which once served as the summer residence of the late President Tito.

On the west coast, the popular resort town of Poreč is home to a splendid UNESCO-listed sixth-century basilica decorated with stunning golden Byzantine mosaics, while neighbouring Rovinj is made up of ochre- and russet-coloured houses clustered around a pretty fishing harbour, and crowned by a hilltop church.

Moving inland to the Srce Istre (Heart of Istria), narrow country roads meander through a gently rolling landscape of woodland and vineyards. In the lovely fortified hill towns of Motovun and Grožnjan you'll find a medieval ambience and some excellent gourmet eateries.

Detail from Euphrasius Basilica.

What to see in...

...one day
Spend the morning in **Poreč**, taking time to see the Byzantine mosaics in Euphrasius Basilica and having lunch at Ulixes. Move on to **Rovinj** in the afternoon – catch a taxi boat from the harbour to bathe on one of the nearby islets, then stay overnight in the romantic **old town**.

...a weekend or more
Take a tour of inland Istria – drive through undulating vineyards and forests, and try to see the hilltowns of **Motovun** and **Grožnjan**, being sure to taste the local delicacy: pungent truffles from the Mirna Valley.

Pula & around

Pula is something of an enigma. Here, magnificent ancient Roman ruins stand side by side with a declining industrial port, in a city that is Istria's administrative and economic centre. Somewhat surprisingly, it's also one of the best places in Croatia to find small, high-class, family-run hotels and chic seafood restaurants serving beautifully presented creative cuisine. With two well-equipped marinas, one directly in front of the city centre and the other at Veruda, it's a popular destination for yachters, as well as sightseers who come to visit the monumental first-century Roman amphitheatre (known as the 'Arena') and the nearby Brijuni National Park, and holidaymakers on package deals, who normally sleep in the large seaside hotels south of the centre at Verudela and Medulin.

Fishing boats at sunset.

Arena

Flavijevska ulica, T052-219028.
May-Sep daily 0800-2000, Oct-Apr daily
0900-1700, 40Kn.

Pula's top sight has to be this beautifully preserved
first-century Roman amphitheatre. Designed to
host gladiator fights and able to accommodate
22,000 spectators, way beyond the city population
of that time, it is the sixth-largest building of its
type in the world (after the Colosseum in Rome,
and the amphitheatres in Verona, Catania, Capua
and Arles). The outer walls are remarkably intact,
though through the centuries stones from the
inside have been carried off for use on other
buildings. Originally the interior would have been
encircled by tiers of stone seats, the central floor
would have been covered with sand, and a
velarium (large awning) would have been used
as a temporary roof structure, to shelter spectators
from the sun and rain.

The Arena fell into disuse in the sixth century,
when gladiator games were forbidden. During the
16th century the Venetians planned to transfer it,
stone by stone, to Venice, though fortunately a local
senator, Gabriele Emo, protested and the project
was abandoned. The building was restored in the
early 19th century by General Marmont under
Napoleon's Illyrian provinces. The underground
halls house a musty and rather disappointing
display of wooden oil presses and amphorae.

Essentials

⊖ Bus station The bus station is at Trg I. Istarske
brigade bb, T060-304090. For regional bus travel, see
page 272.
⊃ Ferry Venezia Lines, venezialines.com, operate a
catamaran from Pula to Venice, April-October.
☼ Train station Kolodvorska 7, T052-541733. For
regional train travel, see page 272.
⑤ ATM Cash machines are plentiful in Pula old town.
⊕ Hospital Zagrebačka 30, T052-376000.
✚ Pharmacy Each pharmacy is marked by a glowing
green cross. The pharmacy at Giardini 15, T052-222551,
works 24 hours.
⊃ Post office The main post office is at Danteov Trg 4,
Monday-Friday 0700-2000, Saturday 0700-1400.
❶ Tourist information Pula city tourist office at
Forum 3, T052-212987, pulainfo.hr.

Rimski Forum

Forum bb.

This vast, paved piazza has been the city's most
important public meeting space since Roman
times. It's closed to traffic and overlooked by
popular open-air cafés, the Renaissance Town Hall,
the city tourist office and the Temple of Augustus
(see page 116).

Arena at Pula.

Around the region

Kaštel.

Tip...

In summer, the central courtyard at the Kaštel is used for open-air cultural events including the Pula Film Festival and the Istra Etno Jazz Festival.

Augustov Hram

Forum bb.
Jun-Sep daily 0900-1300, 1800-2100, Oct-May by appointment.

On the north side of the Forum square, the well-preserved Roman Temple of Augustus has an open portico supported by six tall columns with Corinthian capitals. It was built in the early first century AD to celebrate the cult of Augustus, who founded the Roman Empire in 27 BC. Under Byzantine rule it was converted into a church and later used as a granary. Today it houses a lapidarium, displaying pieces of Roman sculpture.

Slavoluk Sergijevaca

Ulica Sergijevaca.

The Triumphal Arch of the Sergi was built in the first century BC to honour the local Sergi family for their role at the Battle of Actium, fought between the Roman fleet of Octavian and the Roman-Egyptian fleet of Mark Antony and Cleopatra in 31 BC. The Sergis were on the side of Octavian, who was victorious and consequently went on to become the first Roman emperor under the name of Augustus.

Next to the arch stands the house where the Irish author James Joyce (1882-1941) lived briefly during a spell in Istria.

West of the arch, Ulica Sergijevaca was the city's main street in Roman times and is now a pedestrian area lined with Pula's highest concentration of clothes shops.

Kaštel

For an impressive panorama over the city, follow Castropola street up to the hilltop Kaštel. The present fortress was built by the Venetians in 1630 and later renovated by the Austrians in 1840. It now houses the **Historical Museum of Istria** (T052-211740, Jun-Sep daily 0800-2000, Oct-May daily 0900-1700, 10Kn). However, for most the city views are more rewarding than the museum itself.

Gradska Tržnica

Narodni Trg.
Mon-Sat 0700-1330, Sun 0700-1200.

Built as a covered market in 1903, this iron-and-glass structure was revolutionary in its time. The daily fish and meat market is still held inside, while fruit and vegetable stands are set up outside, in the shade of a fine row of chestnut trees.

Brijuni National Park

The national park office is in the mainland village of Fažana (10 km northwest of Pula), opposite the ferry quay, T052-525888, brijuni.hr.

The only way to visit the national park is as part of an organized group and reservations should be made several days in advance. Tickets cost 125-210 Kn (depending on the time of year), which includes the boat ride and a tour of the grounds conducted by a professional guide. National park boats leave from Fažana and ferry visitors back and forth to the largest island, Veli Brijuni. It is possible to stay overnight (see Sleeping, page 128).

Having remained uninhabitable through the centuries due an infestation of malaria-carrying mosquitoes, in 1893 Brijuni was bought by Paul Kupelweiser, an Austrian industrial magnate. Kupelweiser employed the German scientist Robert Koch (founder of modern medical bacteriology, 1843-1910) to purge the place of the disease. Kupelweiser then set about creating a prestigious health resort: he laid out the parkland, tree-lined avenues and exotic planting, had fresh water and electricity brought to the island and built a heated seawater swimming pool. Brijuni fast

became a haven for Vienna's nobility and high society, with elite guests including Archduke Franz Ferdinand and the German writer Thomas Mann. In the 1920s, under Italian rule, a casino, polo club and tennis courts were built.

Then, after the Second World War, it became President Tito's official summer residence. He entertained countless world leaders here, as well as glamorous friends such as Richard Burton and Elizabeth Taylor.

After he died, the Brijuni archipelago, made up of 14 islands and islets, was made a national park, and the largest island, Veli Brijun, opened to the public. This low-lying island, with its beautifully tended parkland, herds of deer and strutting peacocks, makes a good day trip from Pula.

Here, visitors can see the safari park, with zebras, antelopes, llamas and elephants, many of which were given to Tito as presents from world leaders. It is a lovely place to walk, but other options are to rent a bike or an electric buggy.

There's also a museum (renovated in spring 2008) housing a photography exhibition *Tito on Brijuni* showing the great man enjoying his summer retreat with friends and colleagues.

Istria's west coast

The most-visited region of Istria is the west coast. Here, the seaside towns of Rovinj and Poreč are both well worth visiting, though they do get extremely crowded in peak season. These two highly developed resorts centre on beautifully preserved pedestrian-only old towns, the big hotel complexes of the 1970s thankfully having been built a short distance along the coast and cleverly hidden by landscaping and pine woods.

Sunset in Rovinj.

A medieval street in Rovinj town.

Essentials

⊗ **Bus station** Trg na Lokvi 6, T052-811453.
⇌ **Ferry Venezia Lines**, venezialines.com, operate a
catamaran from Rovinj to Venice (Italy), April-October.
Emilia Romagna Lines, emiliaromagnalines.it, run
a catamaran between Rovinj and Cesenatico and
Ravenna (Italy), July-September.
Ⓢ **ATM** Cash machines are plentiful in Rovinj.
⊕ **Hospital** There is a special tourist surgery at the
Ambulanta Rovinj at Istarska ulica bb, T052-813004.
✚ **Pharmacy** Each pharmacy is marked by a glowing
green cross. **Gradska Ljekarna** is at M Benussi-Cio,
T052-813589, open summer 0800-2100.
➲ **Post office** M Benussia 4, Monday-Friday
0700-2000, Saturday 0700-1400.
❶ **Tourist information** Rovinj city tourist office is at
Obala P Budicina 12, T052-811566, tzgrovinj.hr.

Rovinj & around

On Istria's west coast, 35 km northwest of Pula,
Rovinj is composed of densely packed medieval
town houses, built into a hillside and crowned by
a church and elegant bell tower. Down below,
Venetian-style coloured façades curve their way
around a pretty fishing harbour, rimmed with
open-air cafés, restaurants and ice cream parlours.
Out to sea lie a scattering of 14 small islands, while
south of town, the green expanse of Zlatni Rt Park
has tree-lined avenues and an indented shoreline
with several pebble coves for bathing. The town's
beauty and relaxed atmosphere have long made it
popular with Croatian and Italian artists, writers,
musicians and actors.

Church of St Euphemia.

Sv Eufemija

May-Sep daily 1000-1900, Oct-Apr daily 1000-1200, 1600-1900.

From the harbour, a labyrinth of steep, narrow cobbled streets run up to the hilltop Church of St Euphemia. The building gained its baroque appearance in 1736, though there had been a church here for centuries. The 61-m Venetian bell tower, topped by a gleaming bronze weather vane of St Euphemia, was erected in 1677. Euphemia, who lived in the region that is now northwest Turkey, was thrown to the lions in AD 304, during one of Emperor Diocletian's anti-Christian purges. According to legend, her remains were placed in a sixth-century marble sarcophagus, which floated out to sea from Constantinople and was washed ashore in Rovinj in AD 800. The sarcophagus in question is now kept within the church, covered by a finely embroidered gold cloth.

Kuča Batana

Obala Pina Budicina 2, T052-812593, batana.org. Jun-Sep daily 0900-1300, 1900-2200; Oct-Dec and Mar-May Tue-Sun 1000-1300, 1500-1700, 10Kn.

On the seafront promenade, overlooking the harbour, the eco-museum 'Batana House' is named after the *batana*, a traditional local fishing boat. Telling the story of Rovinj's centuries-old fishing community, it occupies two floors of a 17th-century building.

Akvarij

Obala G Paliage 5, T052-804712. Summer daily 0900-2100, winter by appointment, 15Kn.

Dating back to 1891, Rovinj's aquarium is one of the oldest in Europe. Marine species such as octopuses, poisonous scorpion fish and large turtles are on display, plus other underwater creatures such as sponges and sea anemones.

Limski Canal.

Around the region

Beaches

A short walk southeast of the old town, Zlatni Rt is a vast expanse of parkland planted with avenues of holm oaks, alpine pines, cedar and cypresses, and criss-crossed by footpaths leading down to a series of pebble coves ideal for bathing.

Other places for a dip are the nearby islets of Sv Katarina (St Catherine) and Crveni Otok (Red Island), both of which have pleasant rocky coastlines offering easy access to the water. In peak season, boats from the harbour leave every 30 minutes.

Limski Kanal

4 km north of Rovinj.

Accessible by boat, the Lim Fjord is a 12-km-long flooded canyon, edged in part by dramatic limestone cliffs rising 120 m above the water, and in part by green slopes covered with woods of holm oak, ash and pines. Underwater springs give the seawater a low salt content, making it ideal for farming oysters and mussels, and several excellent fish restaurants have opened here, taking advantage of both the locally produced oysters and mussels and the spectacular setting. Various agencies offer day trips to Lim Fjord by boat, and depart from Rovinj harbour.

Poreč

45 km northwest of Pula.

Poreč is Istria's most-visited seaside resort. The old town is quite tiny, a cluster of Venetian-style terracotta-roofed houses lying compact on a small peninsula. Founded as a Roman castrum (military camp) in the second century BC, the layout of the old town still follows the original Roman plan, though most of the present buildings date from between the 13th and 18th centuries. Here, Poreč's top attraction, the sixth-century Euphrasius Basilica, is decorated with golden Byzantine mosaics so stunning to have earned it a place on the UNESCO list of World Heritage Sites.

Café life centres on the seafront promenade overlooking the harbour, which is filled with fishing boats and water taxis that shuttle holidaymakers back and forth to beaches on the nearby islet of Sv Nikola (St Nicholas). South of the centre, Plava Laguna and Zelena Laguna make up a 6-km stretch of modern hotel complexes, cleverly hidden by landscaping and dense pinewoods.

Decumanus

Laid out by the Romans in the first century BC, Decumanus is a wide, paved street that still forms the main thoroughfare through the old town, running the length of the peninsula to Trg Marafor. Today it's lined with fine Romanesque and Gothic townhouses, several of which have been converted into boutiques and cafés at street level.

Eufrazijeva Basilica

Eufrazijeva bb.
Daily 0700-2000.

Halfway down Decumanus, a narrow side street leads to Euphrasius Basilica, a well-signed complex consisting of a magnificent sixth-century basilica, a delightful atrium, an octagonal baptistery, a 16th-century bell tower and the bishop's palace. The interior of the church is decorated with glistening golden mosaics above, behind and around the main apse, making it one of the most important Byzantine monuments on the Adriatic, comparable to San Vitale in Ravenna. Above the altar, the central mosaic depicts the Virgin and Child, with the first Bishop of Poreč, St Mauro, to their right, and Bishop Euphrasius, who was responsible for the mosaic project, on their left. In front of the apse stands a 13th-century ciborium supported by four marble columns.

Trg Marafor

On the tip of the peninsula, Trg Marafor was once the site of a small Roman forum. The ruins of two Roman temples, dedicated to Mars and Neptune, can still be seen today.

Beaches

The best beaches are on Otok Sv Nikola (St Nicholas' Island). The island can be reached by regular taxi boats, which leave the harbour every half an hour through peak season.

Inland Istria

Frequently overlooked by tourists but much loved by Croatians, inland Istria is sometimes compared to Tuscany, thanks to its undulating green landscapes and medieval, walled hill towns. This is the country's top area for agrotoursim (farms offering meals and overnight accommodation) and is at it prettiest in spring or autumn.

Many rural villages lie semi-abandoned, though it's fast becoming fashionable to have a restored stone holiday cottage in the area. The romantic fortified hilltop towns of Motovun and Grožnjan have established themselves as alternative cultural centres, the former with an annual festival of avant-garde film, the latter with its community of artists and craftsmen, plus an annual music summer school. The surrounding villages are much prized for rustic eateries serving dishes with truffles found locally in the Mirna Valley.

Motovun.

Motovun

25 km northeast of Poreč.

This beautifully preserved fortified hill town is frequently included on tours of inland Istria as a model example of local architecture. There are no outstanding buildings, but the complex as a whole is exceptionally pretty, with medieval stone houses and a Venetian loggia surrounded by defensive walls, towers and town gates. In fact, due to its remarkable beauty, Motovun is on the UNESCO 'Tentative List' for World Heritage status. It is possible to walk a complete circuit of the ramparts, offering sweeping views of the oak forests and vineyards of the Mirna Valley – an area also renowned for it truffles.

Each summer, the informal Motovun Film Festival, motovunfilmfestival.com, takes place here – it's very 'in' and is one of Croatia's most enjoyable cultural events; more than 70 films are shown in five venues, attracting 40,000 cinema buffs from all over Europe, see page 134.

Grožnjan

26 km northeast of Poreč.

This charming medieval hill town was all but abandoned until the mid-1960s, when it was rediscovered by painters, potters and sculptors, and proclaimed a 'Town of Artists'. They restored the crumbling medieval buildings, converting them into studios, workshops and galleries. Today it's a truly lovely place to visit, with partly preserved 14th-century town walls hugging a warren of narrow winding cobbled streets and old stone cottages.

Look out for the Venetian loggia adjoining the town gate, the baroque Church of Saints Mary, Vitus and Modest with a free-standing bell tower on the main square, and the tiny 16th-century Chapel of Saints Cosmas and Damian, decorated with frescoes by Ivan Lovrenčić in 1990, in front of the town gate. There are some well-marked footpaths leading to the surrounding villages, which make good walks.

Essentials

⊖ **Bus station** There are no bus stations in Motovun, Grožnjan or Hum. Private transport is recommended.
⑤ **ATM** You will find a cash machine in both Motovun and Grožnjan, but not in Hum.
❶ **Tourist information** Motovun tourist office is at Trg Josefa Ressela 1, T052-617480, tz-motovun.hr. Grožnjan tourist office is at Umberta Gorjana 3, T052-776131, tz-groznjan.hr.

Grožnjan's cobbled streets.

Truffles

The truffle is a subterranean European fungus, generally found in damp soils on or near the roots of oak trees. It can be white, brown or black, and although it grows approximately 30 cm below the soil, its scent is so strong that dogs and pigs can be trained to detect it. Fetching prices of up to €3000 per kg, the truffle is among the most expensive foodstuffs in the world: it is used in foie gras, and can also be eaten grated on pasta or steak, or made into a rich creamy sauce. Undoubtedly an acquired taste, past aficionados include Winston Churchill and Marilyn Monroe.

In Istria, about 500 registered truffle-hunters have a legal right to dig for this gnarled, tuberous fungus. However, each year between October and December an estimated 3000 people and three times as many dogs (usually a cross between a retriever and a hound) wander through Istria's forests and meadows searching for this prestigious delicacy, making it one of region's top sources of income and one of the main reasons why many people come here.

The largest truffle in the world, listed in the *Guinness Book of Records*, was unearthed in the Mirna Valley, Istria, on 2 November 1999. It was found by Giancarlo Zigante and his dog Diana, weighed 1.31 kg and measured 19.5 cm x 12.4 cm x 13.5 cm. Zigante decided not to sell it but instead prepared a dinner for 100 guests, and had the original cast in bronze. He now runs Zigante Tartufi, a small chain of shops specializing in truffles and truffle-based products (see Shopping, page 134).

Each year from May to October, Jeunesses Musicales Croatia, an international federation of young musicians, meets here for a summer school run by well-known international music professors.

And in July, the old streets are filled with the sounds of brass, woodwind and stringed instruments of varying tones and pitches, as musicians prepare for open-air evening as part of the 'Jazz is Back' festival.

Aleja Glagoljaša

Running for 7 km between Roč and Hum.

The Glagolitic Alley was built in 1977 to record the historic importance of the Glagolitic script in this region. The route is marked by 11 monuments celebrating important events and people associated with this all-but-forgotten form of writing (see box, opposite). It ends in Hum, which claims to be the smallest town in the world (population 17), and is made up of a dozen or so old stone houses and a tiny 12th-century Romanesque church. Most people come here specifically to eat at the renowned Humska Konoba (see Eating & drinking, page 133).

The monuments In Roč, at the junction for Hum, you can see the Pillar of the Čakav Parliament, a reference to Croatian self-rule and the Čakav dialect (one of three variants of the Croatian language). The second monument shows the Three-legged Table before Two Cypresses, with the trees symbolizing the apostles of the Slavs, St Cyril and St Methodius. Monument three is dedicated to the Assembly of Kliment of Ohrid – Kliment was a pupil of Cyril and Methodius, and he founded the first Slav university near Lake Ohrid.

The fourth monument, in front of the village church in Brnobici, is a lapidarium displaying Glagolitic inscriptions from various regions of former Yugoslavia, while monument five portrays Mount Učka partly hidden by clouds – in the Middle Ages it was regarded as the Croatian equivalent of Mount Olympus in Greece.

Glagolitic script

Invented by Saint Cyril (AD 827-869) from Thessaloniki (Greece), the glagolitic script was the forerunner to Cyrillic, today used in Russia, Serbia and Montenegro, Bulgaria and Ukraine.

Cyril devised the 38-letter glagolitic alphabet (based on Greek characters) upon the request of the Moravian leader to the Byzantine Emperor, who wanted a form of writing that would more closely represent the sounds of the Slavic languages. Cyril and his brother, Saint Methodius (AD 826-884), then proceeded to translate books of the New Testament and develop a Slavonic liturgy, earning themselves the title of the 'Apostles of the Slavs'.

The script was used in many churches along the Croatian Adriatic coast right up until the 19th century, though it met resistance from certain members of the clergy who favoured Latin as a way of forging closer ties with Rome. However, Croatian secular literature was traditionally written in Latin script, as the majority of the elite were educated at universities in Italy or Austro-Hungary.

The sixth monument is the Grgur Ninski Observation Point, featuring a block of stone engraved with the Glagolitic, Latin and Cyrillic alphabets. Monument seven represents the Istarski Razvod, the historic document defining Istria's borders, while monument eight is dedicated to Croatian Protestants and Heretics.

The ninth monument is a huge stone block recording the first Glagolitic missal, dating from 1483. Next, is monument ten, at the entrance to Hum. This is devoted to Resistance and Freedom over the centuries, with three stone blocks representing the three historic periods of Antiquity, the Middle Ages and the Modern Age.

The eleventh and final monument is the copper town gate of Hum, decorated with 12 medallions, each representing a month of the year and typical activities that take place at that time.

Sleeping

Pula & around

Hotel Scaletta €€
Flavijevska 26, T052-541025, hotel-scaletta.com.
Close to the Roman amphitheatre, this 12-room family-run hotel occupies a tastefully refurbished old town house. Rooms are decorated in sunny shades of ochre and green, and come with spanking new bathrooms. There's also an excellent restaurant with a summer terrace.

Stancija Negricani €€
Marčana, 16 km north of Pula, T052-391084, stancijanegricani.com.

This old stone farmhouse is set in extensive grounds with a pool in the garden. The nine guest rooms are furnished with antiques, and have internet connection, satellite TV and modern en suite bathrooms. There is a large restaurant with exposed stone walls serving home-made local specialities – guests can visit the kitchen to watch the food being prepared. Local activities include hiking, biking and horse riding.

Valsabbion €€
Pješčana uvala IX/26, T052-218033, valsabbion.hr.
Overlooking the sea in Medulin, 4 km from the centre of Pula, this small luxury hotel boasts 10 cheerful guest rooms adorned with pine furniture and primary coloured fabrics, plus fresh fruit and flowers. The gourmet restaurant has won various international awards. There's a swimming pool and gym on the top floor, and they offer beauty programmes such as facials, peeling and lazer treatments, plus massage.

Arena Apartments Pula €
Flavijevska 2, T052-506217, pula-apartments.com.
Practically next door to the Roman amphitheatre, this building has four apartments, each sleeping two to four people. Each unit has wooden floors and is nicely furnished with a kitchenette, plus air conditioning and satellite TV. Upon request, the owner, Ratko, will collect guests from the airport.

Omir €
Sergija Dobrića 6, T052-213944, hotel-omir.com.
Another small, family-run hotel close to the Roman amphitheatre, with 19 plain but comfortable guest rooms, all with modern furnishings. The adjoining hotel restaurant serves local dishes plus pizzas.

Brijuni National Park
Hotel Neptun-Istra €€€
T052-525807, brijuni.hr.
Overlooking the harbour on the island of Veli Brijuni, this big, 1970s-style hotel has 67 rooms and 22 suites. Guests can leave their cars in the guarded parking area in Fažana and have unlimited ferry travel to and from the island. There's a restaurant serving fish and meat dishes, plus a café for coffee and cakes.

Rovinj & around

Villa Angelo d'Oro €€€€
V Švalbe 38-42, T052-840502, rovinj.at.
This small, luxury hotel is hidden away in Rovinj's old town, one block back from the seafront, in the beautifully restored 17th-century Bishop's Palace. The 24 guest rooms are each individually furnished with antiques, and breakfast is served on a delightful rooftop garden terrace. Extras include a jacuzzi, sauna and solarium, plus a hotel boat at the guests' disposal.

Casa Garzotto €€€
Via Garzotto 8, T052-814255, casa-garzotto.com.
In Rovinj's old town, this small boutique hotel has four apartments, all with wooden floors, antique furniture and kitchenettes. Two also have open fires. Buffet breakfast is served in the ground floor bar. Extras include free bike hire, plus sauna and hydro-massage shower in winter. They also have four more cheaper rooms in a separate building called Baladur Pavan.

Dva Baladura €€€
Pilkovići 26/27, Kanfanar, 052-803 720, dvabaladura.hr.
In Kanfanar, 12 km east of Rovinj, this peaceful family-run hotel is made up of traditional stone buildings and has four cosy rooms and six apartments, all with slick modern bathrooms. There's a restaurant serving Istrian cuisine, a mini-wellness (sauna and massage), and a garden with an outdoor pool with hydro-massage.

Villa Valdibora €€€
Chiurca Silvana 8, Rovinj, T052-845040, valdibora.com.
In Rovinj's old town, this 17th-century villa has four two-room apartments, two studios and three double rooms, all with tile floors and wooden beamed ceilings. The apartments and studios also have well-equipped kitchenettes. There's a small gym, open to all guests.

Stancija 1904 €€
Smoljanci 2-3, Svetvinčenat, T052-560022, stancija.com.
In the rural village of Smoljanci, 24 km east of Rovinj, this peaceful agrotourism venture occupies a beautifully restored stone farmhouse sleeping up to eight, while the two adjoining apartments sleep two and four. It's set in lovely gardens with a covered terrace area for barbecues and a small playground for kids, making a

peaceful country alternative to touristy Rovinj.

Villa Marea €€
Vukovarska 8, T052-811397; villamarea.com.
Just a 10-minute walk from the old town, this modern house has two double rooms, eight studios and three apartments. The studios and apartments each come complete with a kitchenette. There's free Wi-Fi, bikes for hire and a pool.

Poreč

Hotel Hostin €€€
Rade Končara 4, T052- 408800, hostin.hr.
Set among pine woods close to the bus station, just a 10-minute walk from the marina and the old town, this smart, modern hotel is both central and peaceful. There are 39 spacious rooms, a buffet restaurant, an indoor pool, sauna and jacuzzi.

Hotel Neptune €€€
Obala M Tita 15, T052-465000, valamar.com.
Fully renovated in 2001, this early 20th-century hotel offers 143 smart guest rooms. There's a nice bar and restaurant with tables out front overlooking the seafront promenade in the old town. Some guests complain about the noise, but if it's central location you're looking for, this is it.

Filipini Hotel €€
Filipini bb, T052-463200, istra. com/filipini.
A perfect alternative to staying in the more touristy hotels in Poreč itself, this small country hotel lies 5 km out of town. Set in gardens surrounded by woodland, vineyards and olive groves, it has four rooms and four apartments, all furnished in minimalist style with some traditional elements. There's a restaurant with a terrace, two tennis courts, and bicycles to hire.

Hotel Poreč €€
Rade Končara 1, T052- 451811, hotelporec.com.
In need of refurbishment, this hotel is nonetheless conveniently located next to the bus station, just a 10-minute walk from the old town. There are 54 basic but clean rooms, a bar (which can get noisy) and an internet corner in reception.

Kaštel Pansion & Restaurant €€
Kaštelir, 7 km northeast of Poreč, T052-455310, kastel-kastelir.hr.
This small, boutique hotel occupies a lovely 18th-century building with exposed stonewalls and wooden ceilings. There are two double rooms and two split-level suites, plus an excellent restaurant serving local specialities by an open fireplace.

Eating & drinking

Inland Istria

Motovun

Bella Vista Motovun €€
Gradiziol 1, T052-681724,
apartmani-motovun.com.
In the old town, Villa Bazziaco
dates back to 1862 and has been
refurbished to provide two
four-bed apartments, each with
a living room (sofa-bed), kitchen,
bedroom and bathroom. The
owners also organize activities
such as truffle hunting, and
asparagus, grape, mushroom
and olive picking during the
respective seasons.

Hotel Kastel €€
Trg Andrea Antico 7, T052-681607,
hotel-kastel-motovun.hr.
Occupying an 18th-century
building just outside the town
walls, this peaceful old-fashioned
hotel has 29 rooms and three
apartments. There's also a
restaurant with open-air dining
on a leafy terrace throughout
summer, a wellness centre with
an indoor pool, sauna and
massage, plus an art gallery with
temporary exhibitions by local
and international artists.

Grožnjan

Hotel San Rocco €€€
Srednja ulica 2, Brtonigla, 15 km
northwest of Grožnjan,
T052-725000, san-rocco.hr.
In the small village of Brtonigla,
this small, family-run hotel was
voted the Best Small Hotel in
Croatia in 2007 and 2008. It

occupies a beautifully restored
old stone farmhouse and has 12
individually furnished guest
rooms, most with wooden
beamed ceilings. The highly
regarded hotel restaurant serves
local seasonal specialities in a
dining room with exposed
stonewalls and wooden floors.
There's also a garden with an
outdoor pool, and a small
wellness centre with an indoor
pool and sauna.

La Parenzana €€
Volpia 3, Buje, 14 km northwest
of Grožnjan and 3 km from Buje,
T052-777460, parenzana.com.hr.
This beautifully restored old
stone farmhouse has 16
comfortable guest rooms
furnished with antiques and a
large dining room with an open
fire and summer terrace.
Everything on the menu,
including the wine, is organically
produced on local farms. It is
close to the disused Parenzana
railway line, now a popular
cycling route, and they have
bikes for hire. They also arrange
occasional Istrian cookery
courses and wine-tasting tours.

Pula

Vela Nera €€€
Pješčana uvala bb, Medulin,
T052-219209, velanera.hr.
Daily lunch and dinner.
Voted the best restaurant in
Croatia on several occasions,
Vela Nera occupies a modern
concrete and glass pavilion with
a large terrace overlooking
Marina Veruda. The house
speciality is *rižoto* Vela Nera
(risotto prepared with shrimps,
peaches and champagne) but
they also do excellent pasta
dishes with lobster and truffles,
and fresh fish.

Restaurant Scaletta €€€-€€
Flavijevska 26, T052-541599.
Daily lunch and dinner.
Taking up the ground floor of
Hotel Scaletta (see Sleeping,
page 128), near the Arena, this
highly regarded restaurant
serves sophisticated dishes such
as gnocchi with salmon and
gorgonzola, and steak stuffed
with white truffles in a creamy
sauce. There's a pleasant summer
terrace just across the road.

Valsabbion €€€-€€
Pješčana uvala IX/26, Medulin,
T052-218033, valsabbion.com.
Daily lunch and dinner.
Voted Istria's top restaurant
several times over the last few
years, this was one of the first
Croatian restaurants to specialize
in 'slow food' (a concept which
began in Italy in the 1990s as a

reaction against fast food and globalization – it means making the most of local seasonal produce, giving extreme care to preparation, and then eating the food in a relaxed, unhurried manner). The menu changes daily depending on fresh produce, but you can expect beautifully presented dishes such as tagliatelli with pine nuts, and frogfish in vine leaves.

Kantina €€ €€
Campo Marzio, Flanatička 16, T052-214054.
Mon-Sat lunch and dinner, closed Sun.
Near the covered market, Kantina has a dining room in a cosy cellar, plus outdoor tables on a terrace through summer. You get a free selection of dips and nibbles while you look through the menu, which features goodies such as ravioli filled with *pršut* (prosciutto) and goats cheese, and steak with truffles.

Jupiter €
Castropola 38, T052-214333.
Daily lunch and dinner.
On the road leading up to the castle, this popular pizzeria has tables on a sunny open-air terrace through summer. There's a vast choice, but a good bet is a pizza diavola (topped with spicy salami and hot chilli peppers) and a cold draught beer.

Cvajner
Forum 2, T052-853465.
This trendy but unpretentious café has open-air seating on Pula's Forum square through summer. Inside are frescoes uncovered during restoration, modern furniture and contemporary art.

Rovinj

Monte €€€
Montalbano 75, T052-830203, monte.hr.
Open Easter-Oct daily for lunch and dinner.
In a terracotta-coloured house set in a lovely walled garden near the Church of St Euphemia, many now regard Monte as Rovinj's top restaurant. The ever-changing menu features creative cuisine prepared from locally sourced meat and seafood. To try a bit of everything, opt for the *degustacija* menu, which features two fish dishes, two meat dishes and a dessert. There's space for just 45 diners so reservations are essential.

Viking €€€
Svet Lovreč, Limski Kanal, T052-448223.
Closed Jan.
Ranked among Istria's top restaurants, this large establishment is best known for its fresh oysters, pasta with shrimps and mushrooms and barbecued fish dishes.

Enoteca Al Gastaldo €€€-€€
Iza Kasarne 14, T052-814109.
Daily for lunch and dinner.
With an open log fire, walls stacked with wine bottles, and candlelight, this is a great place to come on a cold winter night. Try the spaghetti with either truffles or lobster, accompanied by a delicious fresh salad of rocket and radicchio, then round off with a glass of local *rakija*.

Restaurant Gianino €€€-€€
A Ferri 38, T052-813402.
Open Apr-Oct Tue-Sun; Nov-Mar Fri-Sun.
In a narrow side street, just back from the harbour, Gianino has long been popular with the yachting fraternity. House specialities include tagliatelli mare-monti (pasta with shrimps and mushrooms), rigatoni with lobster and sole with truffles.

Gostionica Toni €€
Driovier 3, Rovinj, T052-815303.
Thu-Tue for lunch and dinner, closed Wed.
For good, down-to-earth, Istrian home cooking, the house specialities at this informal, centrally located eatery are *brodet od sipe s palentom* (cuttlefish stew with polenta) and *njoki s dagnjama i rokulom* (gnocchi with mussels and rocket). Besides the standard menu, they also have daily specials on a board.

Five of the best...

Places to try truffle dishes

❶ **Pod Voltom** Trg Josefa Ressela 6, Motovun, T052-681923. House speciality steak with truffles.
❷ **Restoran Vrh** Vrh 2, between Motovun and Buzet, T052-667123. House speciality fuži (Istrian pasta) with truffles.
❸ **Toklarija** Sovinjsko Polje, between Motovun and Buzet, T052-663031. House speciality tagliatelle with truffles.
❹ **Igor** Kaštel Buje, near the Slovenian border, T052-777131, restaurant-igor.com. House speciality gnocchi filled with truffles and scampi.
❺ **Zigante** Livade, Livade 7, T052-664302, zigantetartufi.com. House speciality sheep's cheese with truffles.

Veli Jože €€
Sv Križa 1, T052-815337.
Open Apr-Nov for lunch and dinner.
This highly popular, informal eatery serves old-fashioned local dishes such as *bakalar in bianco* (a pâté made from dried cod) and roast lamb with potatoes.

Cafés & bars
Vieccia Batana
Trg M Tita 8.
Rovinj's oldest and most atmospheric café stands on the main square, close to the harbour. Perfect for coffee.

Poreč

Dvi Murve €€€-€€
Grožnjanska 17, T052-434115, dvimurve.hr.
Daily lunch and dinner.
A short distance northwest of Poreč, this *konoba* (rustic-style restaurant, see page 63) is consistently ranked among the best in Istria. Expect tasty dishes

such as beefsteak Dvi Murve (steak with cream, mushroom and ham sauce), and *brancin u soli* (sea bass baked in a salt crust).

Istra €€€-€€
B Milanovića 30, Trg Slobode, T052-434636.
Daily lunch and dinner. Closed mid-Jan to mid-Mar.
Lying between the bus station and Poreč's main square, this highly regarded eatery is popular with both locals and visitors. The house specialities here are *jastog sa rezancima* (pasta with lobster), and fish prepared under a *peka*.

Ulixes €€
Decumanus 2, T052-451132.
Daily lunch and dinner.
In the old town, just off the main thoroughfare, this cosy *konoba* has a centuries-old stone-and-brick interior and a pretty courtyard garden. Come here for pasta dishes, seafood dishes, salads and excellent local wines.

Pizzeria Nono €
Zagrebačka 4, T052-453088.
Daily lunch and dinner.
Opposite Poreč's tourist office, Nono remains busy with locals throughout the year. It's much loved for its delicious pizzas baked in a brick oven, plus pasta and gnocchi dishes, steaks and colourful salads.

Inland Istria

Motovun
Pod Voltom €€€-€€
Trg Josefa Ressela 6, T052-681923.
Thu-Tue lunch and dinner. Closed Wed.
On the main square in Motovun's old town, close to the tourist office, this homely eatery has an exposed brick interior with an open fire. It's known for *fuži* (Istrian pasta) with truffles, steak with truffles, and local game dishes. In the summer they have outdoor tables with the best view in town.

Mondo Konoba €€
Trg Josefa Ressela bb, T052-681754.
This cosy *konoba* (formerly known as Barbican) serves traditional Istrian dishes with an innovative twist. It has an airy dining room with wooden tables, and serves up goodies such as pasta with truffles, steaks and colourful seasonal salads.

Entertainment

Grožnjan
Bastia €€
1 Svibnja, T052-776370.
This eatery serves up hearty dishes in a cosy dining room with an open fire. Try the tagliatelle carbonara, made with huge chunks of crisp pancetta, or a generous platter of mixed grilled meats.

Agroturizam Dešković €€-€
Kostanjica 58, 5km from Grožnjan, T052-776315.
This traditional stone cottage has a dining room with an open fireplace and red-and-white checked tablecloths. The house specialities are home-made pasta and roast veal – all the ingredients are locally sourced and the olive oil, wine and *rakija* are made by the Dešković family themselves.

Hum
Humska Konoba €€
Hum 2, T052-660005.
May-Oct daily lunch and dinner, Mar-Apr Tue-Sun, Nov-Feb Sat-Sun.
This tiny, old-fashioned *konoba* with an open fireplace has been serving typical home-made Istrian dishes since 1976. Expect *fuži* (a type of pasta) with truffles or goulash, homemade sausages, and *biska*, a local liquor made from mistletoe.

Bars & clubs
Rock Club Uljanik
Dobrilina 2, clubuljanik.hr.
Thu-Sat 2000-0500.
A thriving venue for alternative rock concerts, in a disused building overlooking the shipyard, close to the city centre. On the go since 1965.

Uliks
Trg Portarata 1.
A popular little bar looking onto the Triumphal Arch of the Sergi. It's next door to the house where James Joyce once lived, hence the life-size sculpture of the writer himself sitting outside.

Festivals & events
Histria Festival
histriafestival.com.
Jul-Aug.
Live concerts in the Roman Arena, starring international musicians from the worlds of rock and classical music.

Pula Film Festival
pulafilmfestival.hr.
Late Jul.
Founded in 1954, this two-week competitive festival is held in the Arena and at Kaštel, and features films from both Croatia and abroad.

Seasplash Reggae Festival
seasplash.net.
Late-Jul.
Four-day reggae festival on the beach at Veli Vrh near Pula, with free camping included in the price of the ticket.

Rovinj

Monvi Center
Luja Adamovića bb, T052-545117, monvicenter.com.
Stages open-air concerts, electronic music parties, and serves Mexican food.

Valentino
Sv Križa 28, T052-830 683, valentino-rovinj.com.
Apr-May 1200-2400, Jun-Sep daily 1800-0200.
Extremely popular cocktail and champagne bar by the water's edge in the old town, with cushions so you can sit on the rocks. Very romantic at sunset.

Poreč

Bars & clubs
Byblos
Zelena Laguna, T091-1133221, byblos.hr.
Disco playing predominantly house music with guest DJs from New York and London.

Festivals & events
Classical Music Festival
concertsinbazilika.com.
Sacral and secular music in the Basilica of St Euphrasius.

Shopping

Jazz in Lapidarium
jazzinlap.com.
Jul-Aug.
Jazz festival held in the courtyard of the town museum, attracting classical and contemporary performers from the international scene.

Inland Istria

Festivals & events
Motovun Film Festival
motovunfilmfestival.com.
Late-Jun.
Five-day international festival of avant-garde cinema, founded in 1999. They also organize an eco-camp with showers and toilets and regular shuttle buses to Motovun old town.

Pula

Aromatica
Laginjina 4, T052-382180, aromatica.hr.
Close to the Arch of the Sergi, this store stocks its own line in natural soaps and cosmetic products made from olive oil and scented with wild herbs.

Tržnica
Narodni Trg.
Mon-Sat 0700-1330,
Sun 0700-1200.
Pula's market combines a steel-and-glass pavilion selling meat and fish, plus a stall selling fruit and vegetables on the square.

Zigante Tartufi
Smareglina 7, T052-214855, zigantetartufi.com.
Near the market, this store specializes in truffles and truffle products from the Mirna Valley, plus Istrian olive oil and wines.

Rovinj

Aromatica
Carera 33, T052-812850, aromatica.hr.
In the old town, this store offers the same products as its sister shop in Pula, above.

Inland Istria

Zigante Tartufi
Gradiziol 8, Motovun, T052-681810, zigantetartufi.com.
Part of the Zigante chain, this is the place to purchase truffles and truffle products from the Mirna Valley, plus Istrian olive oil and wines.

Zigante Tartufi
U Gorjan 5, Grožnjan, T052-776099, zigantetartufi.com.
This shop offers the same services as the branch in Motovun, above. It also offers wine and truffle tasting.

Activities & tours

Diving
Diving Indie
Ližnjan 186a, T052-573658,
Banjole (10 km south of Pula),
divingindie.com.

Food & wine
Activa Travel
Scalierova 1, T052-215497,
activa-istra.com.
One-day wine-tasting tours,
departing from Pula.

Rovinj

Boat trips
Delfin Excursions
Zagrebačka 5, T052- 848265,
excursion-delfin.hr.
Runs daily boat trips from Rovinj
to Poreč, calling at the Lim Fjord
en route, with a seafood lunch
included.

Cycling
Vetura
Hotel Park, T052-815209,
vetura-rentacar.hr.
Rents bikes. A marked bike path
runs along the coast south of
town from the ACI Marina,
passing through Zlatni Rt, Rt Kuvi,
Veštar and Cisterna to arrive in Sv
Damijan. A map, *Bike Track Rovinj*,
is available from the tourist office.
See also istria-bike.com.

Diving
Nadi Scuba
J Dobrile 11, T052-813290,
scuba.hr.

Diving Centar Poreč
Brulo bb, T052-434606,
divingcenter-porec.com.

Poreč

Boat trips
Marco Polo
Poreč harbour, T091-2017474,
marco-polo-excursion.com.
Runs daily boat trips from Poreč
to Rovinj, calling at the Lim Fjord
en route, with a lunch included.

Vetura
Zelena Laguna, T052-451391,
vetura-rentacar.hr.
Rents bikes. Note that Poreč is
the starting point for two
well-marked bike routes: one
north to Tar (15 km round trip)
and the other south to Funtana
(47 km). Ask at the tourist office
for details and a map or check
the website, istria-bike.com.

Inland Istria

Cycling
Montona Tours
Kanal 10, T052-681970, Motovun,
montonatours.hr.
Rents bikes and help visitors
plan cycling tours of Inland
Istria, including accommodation
en route.

Food & wine
Zigante Tartufi
Livade 7, Livade, T052-664302,
zigantetartufi.com.
Arranges three-hour truffle-
hunting trips complete with
dogs in the Mirna Valley region.
Tours are possible October to
December for white truffles and
January to September for black
truffles. Lunch is included.

Contents

139 Introduction
140 Rijeka & around
144 Island of Krk
146 Island of Cres
148 Island of Lošinj
150 Island of Rab
152 Listings:
152 Sleeping
155 Eating & drinking
157 Entertainment
157 Activities & tours

Kvarner

Rab Town.

Introduction

T he Kvarner Gulf, a large deep bay sheltered by mountains of up to 1500 m, is presided over by Rijeka, a hard-working and slightly austere industrial port. Half an hour west of Rijeka is Opatija, Croatia's oldest coastal resort, packed with grandiose, Austro-Hungarian-style hotels. East of Rijeka, Risnjak National Park encompasses the rugged soaring heights of Gorski Kotar, offering dense pine forests, bracing mountain air, hiking paths and even skiing.

The largest and easiest of the islands to reach is Krk, which is linked to the mainland by bridge. Visit the Romanesque churches in Krk Town, a pretty monastery on the islet of Košljun and Vela Plaža beach at Baška.

West of Krk, Cres is a long, thin island of scanty pastures, dry stone walls and more sheep than people. The pine forests of the Tramuntana offer blissful walks and great opportunities for birdwatching.

South of Cres, and linked to it by a bridge, the island of Lošinj attracts tourists to the pretty town of Mali Lošinj, renowned for a string of 19th-century villas, each set amid a garden filled with exotic plants.

Between Lošinj and the mainland lies Rab, best known for Rab Town, a romantic medieval settlement built on a walled peninsula with four bell towers creating a distinctive skyline.

What to see in...

...a one day
A good introduction to Kvarner would be a few hours in **Rijeka** followed by a transfer to either **Opatija** or **Lovran**, old-fashioned seaside resorts where you should walk the coastal paths, indulge in a seafood dinner and stay overnight.

...a weekend or more
Escape to one of the nearby islands – **Krk** with its stunning beach at Baška is the most accessible, while **Lošinj** offers upmarket hotels in its main town, Mali Lošinj, and **Cres** renowned for its lamb, remains wonderfully wild and unexploited.

Sculpture at Opatija.

Rijeka & around

Overlooking the Kvarner Gulf, Rijeka is Croatia's largest port, with a shipyard, massive dry dock facilities, refineries and other heavy industries. Architecturally, the centre is remarkably similar to Trieste in Italy, with a grid of grandiose 18th-century Austro-Hungarian buildings on the seafront, and a sprawling suburb of high-rise apartment blocks from the 1960s. The main public meeting place is the Korzo, a pedestrian street a couple of blocks back from the port, lined with shops and open-air cafés. There are few memorable sights here, other than the lovely hilltop castle and pilgrimage church of Trsat, and the city has only a limited number of hotels – most visitors prefer to stay in the nearby seaside resorts of Opatija and Lovran. Rijeka receives national television coverage each year for the staging of Croatia's largest carnival.

Rijeka.

Korzo

A couple of blocks inland from Rijeka's Riva (seafront), this main pedestrian thoroughfare was created in the 18th century, when the city extended beyond the medieval city walls. Today, lined with clothes shops and open-air cafés, it is Rijeka's main shopping street and public meeting space. The name Korzo comes directly from the Italian, *Corso*.

Pomorski i Povijesni Muzej

Muzejski trg 1, T051-213578, ppmhp.hr.
Jun-Sep Tue-Fri 0900-2000, Sat 0900-1300;
Oct-May Tue-Fri 0900-1600, Sat 0900-1300,
10 Kn.

A 10-minute walk northeast of the centre, on the hillside facing down towards the port, the neo-Renaissance Governor's Palace houses the Maritime and History Museum. Downstairs you'll see archaeological finds, period furniture and clocks and paintings, while the second floor is devoted to local shipping, with a display of model ships, navigational instruments, anchors, charts and old photos.

Most hrvatskih branitelja

Fiumara bb.

The elegant Memorial Bridge to Croatian Soldiers crosses the Mrtvi Kanal (Dead Canal) east of the town centre. Built in 2002, its minimalist design features clean lines in metal and glass; at night, thanks to subtle lighting effects, it appears to float on the water. While most Croatian towns commissioned heroic sculptures to honour local soldiers who fell during the war of independence, Rijeka chose to build this pedestrian bridge instead, symbolizing the city's high regard for tolerance. It was designed by Studio 3LHD from Zagreb and has won various international architectural awards.

Essentials

☻ Bus station The bus station is a five-minute walk west of the city centre at Žabica 1, T060-302010, autotrans.hr. For regional bus travel, see page 272.

⊜ Ferry Jadrolinija, jadrolinija.hr, runs daily ferries from Rijeka to Cres Town (Cres) and Mali Lošinj (on Lošinj), plus a daily catamaran from Rijeka to Rab Town (Rab), which then continues to Novalja (Pag, North Dalmatia). A coastal ferry also runs several times weekly from Rijeka to Dubrovnik, stopping at Split and the Dalmatian islands of Hvar and Korčula en route.

◑ Train station The train station a 10-minute walk west of the city centre at Krešimirova 5, T060/333-4444, hznet.hr. For regional train travel, see page 272.

❺ ATM Cash machines are plentiful – in Rijeka city centre on Jadranski Trg you'll also find a cashpoint for exchanging foreign currency.

⊕ Hospital Krešimirova 42, near Rijeka train station, T051-658111.

✚ Pharmacy Each pharmacy is marked by a glowing green cross. **Ljekarna Centar**, Jadranski Trg 1 (T051-213101) and Ljekarna Korzo, Korzo 22 (T051-211036) work alternate 24-hour shifts.

✆ Post office The main post office is at Korzo 13, Monday-Saturday 0700-2100, Sunday 0700-1400.

❶ Tourist information Rijeka's walk-in Tourist Information Centre (TIC) is at Korzo 33, T051-335882, tz-rijeka.hr. Opatija's tourist office is at Vladimira Nazora 3, T051-271710, opatija-tourism.hr.

Wreath on Memorial Bridge.

Trsat.

Zvončari

Unique to the carnival in Rijeka and the surrounding villages, Zvončari are young men dressed in bizarre costumes consisting of a sheepskin slung over the shoulders, a mask of a grotesque animal head with horns, and a large iron bell tied around the waist. During the afternoons and evenings, in the week preceding Shrove Tuesday, they go from village to village and house to house in large groups, regardless of the weather, acting roguishly and making a dreadful din with their bells. Traditionally, locals offer them *fritule* (similar to small doughnuts) and wine, then see them on their way. Their purpose is to chase away the forces of evil and invite the coming of spring and new life.

Pilgrimage path to Trsat

Titov trg.

Up on the hill, 139 m above the town, stand the Church of Our Lady of Trsat and Trsat Castle. You can walk up following the pilgrimage path – a steep but worthwhile climb of over 500 steps brings you up through the dramatic Rječina Gorge. A baroque gateway marks the beginning of the stairway, which starts from Titov Trg on the left bank of the River Rječina. At the top, turn left and follow the busy road of Šetalište Joakima Rakovca uphill to arrive at Frankopanski Trg. If you don't feel up to the hike, take bus No 1 from the city centre.

Gospa Trsat

Frankopanski Trg, T051-452900.
Daily 0700-1900.

The Church of our Lady of Trsat was built to commemorate the 'Miracle of Trsat', when angels were said to have carried the house of the Virgin Mary from Nazareth and delivered it on this spot in 1291. As the story goes, it remained here for three years and was then moved (by the angels again) to Loreto, near Ancona in Italy.

Inside the church, above the altar, an icon of the Virgin Mary, sent as a present from Pope Urban V in 1367 to console the people of Trsat for

the loss of the holy house, is hung with offerings from pilgrims such as pearl necklaces and trinkets.

Next to the church, inside the Franciscan Monastery, the Chapel of Votive Gifts displays an extraordinary collection of offerings brought here by pilgrims, including a painted wooden sculpture of the Virgin and Child, countless religious portraits and even discarded crutches, proof of the Virgin's miraculous healing powers.

Trsat (Trsat Castle)

Ulica Zrinskog, T051-217714.
Jun-Sep daily 0900-2200, Oct-May daily 0900-1700.

A five-minute walk from Frankopanski Trg, Trsat Castle was built in the Middle Ages on the foundations of a Roman observation point. In 1826 the remains of the castle were bought by Laval Nugent, an eccentric Irishman who had served in the Austrian army. He had it restored in romantic style, and added a Classical Greek temple with four Doric columns brought from Pula, intended as the family mausoleum. The former dungeon now displays an exhibition tracing Trsat's history, and in summer there's an open-air café, offering views over the city and across the Kvarner Bay to the islands of Cres and Krk.

Opatija

15 km west of Rijeka.

Opatija is Croatia's longest-standing tourist resort with its old-fashioned hotels and an ageing clientele – through winter and spring at least half the guests are over 60. The seafront hotels, built largely in Viennese Secessionist style, offer neat gardens and sunny terraces where you can drink coffee and watch the world go by during the day; through summer dinner is also served outside, often accompanied by live music.

In the early 20th century, Opatija was one of Europe's most elegant and fashionable seaside destinations. Illustrious visitors included royalty and artists: Emperor Franz Josef, Wilhelm II of Germany and Prussia, the Italian opera composer Giacomo Puccini, the Irish novelist James Joyce and the American dancer Isadora Duncan all came here.

Opatija-Lovran Lungomare

Šetalište Franza Josefa.

This 12-km coastal footpath, lined with century-old oaks and cypress trees, runs from Volosko to Lovran, passing through the seaside towns of Opatija, Ičići and Ika en route. Construction began in 1885, coinciding with the opening of Opatija's first hotels. It makes a lovely walk, with plenty of places to stop for a drink or a snack on the way.

Lovran

21 km west of Rijeka.

Pretty Lovran gives onto the Kvarner gulf and is backed by the surging rocky mass of Mount Učka (1396 m). Many people prefer it to Opatija, and indeed it is more authentic, with a medieval centre, a harbour and a number of fish restaurants. On the edge of town, set amid lush gardens overlooking the seafront promenade, stand a row of elegant late 19th-century villas, several of which have been converted into luxury holiday apartments.

Lovran food festivals

Each year, Lovran organizes three gastro-food festivals, during which the town's restaurants prepare dishes based on seasonal delicacies. The Dani Šparoga (Asparagus Festival) takes place in April; Dani Trešanja (Cherry Festival) in June and Marunada (Chestnut Festival) late September to early October.

Risnjak National Park

Information centre, Bijela Vodica 48, Crni Lug, T051-836133, risnjak.hr, 30Kn.

Fifteen kilometres inland from the coast, the forested heights of Risnjak National Park make a pleasant contrast to Kvarner's seascapes. In summer the air is refreshingly cool and through winter the craggy peaks are snow-covered. Two-thirds of the park is covered with dense beech and fir while the rest supports mountain meadows.

The best place to start exploring the park is the picturesque little village of **Crni Lug** (726 m), 40 km northeast of Rijeka. Here, just a few minutes west of the park administration building, you'll find the beginning of the **Leska Educational Trail**, a 4.2-km circular route with information points in both Croatian and English. Also from Crni Lug, a well-marked hiking path leads to the highest peak, **Veliki Risnjak** (1528 m). Allow three hours each way, wear substantial walking boots and take plenty of water.

The Risnjak forests form a natural habitat for the lynx, after which the park is named (lynx in Croatian is *ris*). Other wild animals here include the brown bear, wildcat, roe deer, red deer and chamois, plus the seldom-sighted wolf and wild boar. Risnjak is home to over 50 bird species, too including the capercaillie, the largest type of European grouse.

Tip...

If you're here in winter, there's a ski centre at Platak, complete with ski lifts, a ski school, and 8 km of groomed pistes.

Island of Krk

Linked to the mainland by a 1430-m bridge, and home to Rijeka Airport, Krk is one of the most accessible of all the Croatian islands. It also happens to be the largest (38 km long and 20 km wide) and one of the most populous.

While the northwest part of the island is low lying, fertile and fairly developed, the southeast part is mountainous and in places quite barren. It's certainly not the most beautiful island on the Adriatic, but its accessibility and wealth of tourist facilities make it very popular.

The chief centre is Krk Town, which dates back to Roman times, with a 12th-century seafront castle and a cathedral. Punat, home to the largest marina on the Adriatic, is a haven for yachters, while Vrbnik is known for its excellent white wine, Vrbnička Žlahtina. The best beach, Vela Plaža is in Baška.

Krk Bridge.

Katedrala Uznesenja

Trg Sv Kvirina, Krk Town.
Daily 1000-1300, 1700-1900.

Taking on its present form during the 12th century, the Cathedral of Our Lady of the Assumption was built on the site of an early Christian basilica, which grew up over the first-century Roman baths. Ancient stone columns, topped with finely carved capitals, were incorporated into the structure, and a Gothic chapel dedicated to the wealthy Frankopan family was added in the 15th century.

Adjoining the cathedral, the 12th-century Romanesque **Church of St Quirinus** (same hours as the cathedral) is split into two levels, with a lower crypt area where prisoners sentenced to death attended a final mass before execution. The church's treasury displays works of religious art including a stunning silver-plated altarpiece depicting **Virgin Mary in Glory** (1477) made in Venice as a gift for the cathedral.

Punat & the Islet of Košljun

On Krk's southwest coast, Punat is a launching pad for visiting the nearby Islet of Košljun with its 15th-century **Franciscan Monastery** (T051-854017, Mon-Sat 0830-1200, 1500-1700, Sun 1030-1200, 20Kn boat transfer, plus 20Kn admission). Inside, a museum display includes paintings, model ships, and a collection of local folk costumes, with a set of ladies' scarves, each one indicating which village the wearer came from and her marital status. Košljun was home to one of the first European financial institutions: the Košljun Lending House, which was set up to protect the poor from usurers, and functioned between the 17th and 19th centuries.

Tip...

If you're thinking of driving to Krk, remember that there's a 30Kn toll for crossing the Krk Bridge, and that in winter, when the *bura* (northeast wind) is exceptionally strong, it is occasionally closed.

Essentials

⊖ Bus station There are regular buses from Rijeka bus station (Žabica 1, T060-302010, autotrans.hr) to Krk Town, Punat and Baška. For regional bus travel, see page 272.

⊜ Ferry station Jadrolinija, jadrolinija.hr, operates daily ferries from Valbiska (Krk) to Merag (Cres). **Linijska Nacionalna Plovidba**, lnp.hr, operates daily ferries from Valbiska (Krk) to Lopar (Rab).

⊛ ATM Cash machines are plentiful and are available in Krk Town, Punat and Baška.

❶ Tourist information There is a general **Krk Island** tourist office in Krk Town at Trg sv Kvirina 1, T051-221359, krk.hr. **Krk Town** has a tourist information office at Obala hrvatske mornarice bb, T051-220226, tz-krk. hr. **Puňat** tourist office is at Obala 72, T051-854860, tzpunat.hr. **Baška** tourist office is at Kralja Zvonimira 114, T051-856817, tz-baska.hr.

Baška

19 km southeast of Krk Town.

Baška is the oldest and best-known resort on the island. Its main attraction is **Vela Plaža**, a 1.8 km stretch of pebble and sand, one of Croatia's most spectacular beaches. However, it does get very busy, with the tourist office estimating space for 5000 bathers. If you prefer something more peaceful, take a taxi boat to any one of the succession of small, secluded bays (accessible only from the sea) west of town. Baška itself has few cultural attractions, and what was once a compact fishing village now straggles almost 3 km along the coast, due to the hotels, apartments and eateries that have sprung up over the last 35 years.

Vrbnik

10 km east of Krk Town

Vrbnik is a tiny, tightly packed medieval walled settlement, standing on the edge of a limestone cliff, 48 m above the sea. Most visitors come here specifically for the wine cellars, which stock the highly esteemed, dry, white Vrbnička Žlahtina. The best place to taste it is Nada (see Eating, page 156).

Island of Cres

Sparsely populated and little explored by the average tourist, this long, skinny, mountainous island is joined to a second island, Lošinj, by a bridge. The northern end is covered by a dense deciduous forest of beech and oak, known as the Tramunatana, which gradually gives way to meagre pastures and barren landscapes in the south. More for those in search of unspoilt nature rather than culture, Cres offers good opportunities for hiking and birdwatching (the rare Eurasion griffon vulture nests here), but little in the way of art and architecture. The islanders live primarily from sheep farming: *Creška janjetina* (Cres lamb) is especially tasty thanks to the clean pastures, rich in wild herbs such as *kadulja* (sage).

The clifftop village of Lubenica on the island of Cres.

Essentials

◎ **Bus station** For buses to and from Cres Town, contact Rijeka bus station, T060-302010, autotrans.hr. For regional bus travel, see page 272.

➋ **Ferry Jadrolinija**, jadrolinija.hr, operates daily ferries from Rijeka to Cres Town, Brestovo (Istria, mainland) to Porozina (Cres), and from Merag (Cres) to Valbiska (Krk). In summer only, a catamaran operates between Rijeka and Mali Lošinj, stopping at Cres Town en route.

➒ **ATM** Cash machines are plentiful in Cres Town.

➊ **Tourist information** Cres Town has a tourist information office at Conc 10, T051-571535, tzg-cres.hr.

Cres Town

The island's chief settlement is made up of pastel-coloured houses giving on to a broad seafront promenade, which cuts its way around a deep triangular harbour filled with small fishing boats. Fortified in the 16th century, the old town is made up of a maze of winding streets opening out onto small squares. The seafront promenade leads west of town to a stretch of coast offering a series of small coves ideal for sunbathing and swimming.

The Tramuntane & Eco-center Caput Insulae

Beli, 20 km north of Cres Town,
T051 840525, supovi.hr.
Mar-Oct daily 0900-2000, 40Kn.

In an isolated and semi-abandoned cluster of old stone cottages on the edge of the Tramuntane forests, you'll finds the Eco-center Caput Insulae. There's an informative exhibition, Biodiversity of the Archipelago of Cres and Lošinj, and a reserve for injured Eurasian griffon vultures. From here, seven eco-trails lead through the surrounding forests – it's well worth picking up an illustrated booklet at the information centre, to help you identify the trees and plants as you go. In fact Cres is one of the richest ornithological areas on the Adriatic – you can expect to see birds such as golden eagles, snake eagles, honey buzzards and, of course, griffon vultures.

Eurasian griffon vultures

The Eurasian griffon vulture is one of the world's largest flying birds, with a wingspan of up to 2.8 m, a body weight of up to 15 kg, a maximum speed of 120 kph and eyesight nine times better than a human. It feeds on animal carcasses but never attacks living animals, and has long been respected by the farmers of Cres as it prevents disease by eating the bodies of dead sheep. However, as the island has seen a gradual but continual trend of depopulation, so the number of farmers and sheep has declined, and the griffon has been left with little in the way of food.

During the 1980s, when the number of griffon vultures had dropped to less than 50, the Eco-centre Caput Insulae established several feeding sites, where they deposit carcasses of slaughtered sheep and rescue injured birds so they can be taken to the centre and treated.

Their numbers have since risen, and there are now about 70 couples nesting in colonies on the vertical cliffs on the northeast side of the island. The female lays one egg per year, and during the two-month period of incubation both parents sit on the egg. After hatching, the chick grows in the nest for four months, then spends another couple of months learning to fly with it parents, after which it leaves for several years roving, travelling as far a field as Greece, Israel and Spain. At the age of five, the griffon returns to the cliff where it was born, finds a mate and builds a nest, and then lives in the vicinity of its birthplace for up to 60 years.

However, modern-day life remains a constant threat to these spectacular birds. They occasionally chance upon carcasses of vermin that have been intentionally poisoned, they have a tendency to fly into electric cables, and young birds may even lose control of their wings and fall into the sea if disturbed by tourists during the summer season.

The Nature Conservation Act has declared the Eurasian griffon vulture a protected species. The killing or disturbing of griffon vultures, and the stealing of their eggs or chicks, are offences liable to a penalty of up to 40,000Kn. The public display of stuffed griffon vultures is also illegal.

Tip...

The eco-centre can arrange special birdwatching tours on request.

Island of Lošinj

Smaller but much more densely populated and certainly more touristy than neighbouring Cres, Lošinj is known for its mild climate, lush vegetation and the long-established resort of Mali Lošinj.

Sailing boats moored up in Mali Lošinj.

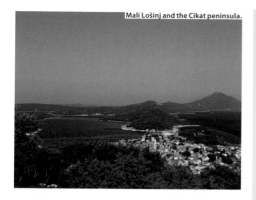

Mali Lošinj and the Cikat peninsula.

Essentials

⊖ **Bus station** For buses to and from Mali Lošinj, contact Rijeka bus station, T060-302010, autotrans.hr. For regional bus travel, see page 272.

⊃ **Ferry Jadrolinija**, jadrolinija.hr, operates daily ferries from Rijeka to Mali Lošinj and from Mali Lošinj to Zadar (North Dalmatia). In summer only, a catamaran operates between Rijeka and Mali Lošinj, stopping at Cres Town en route.

⊜ **ATM** Cash machines are plentiful in Mali Lošinj and Veli Lošinj.

❶ **Tourist information** Mali Lošinj has a tourist information office at Riva Lošinjskih Kapetana 29, T051-231884, tz-malilosinj.hr.

Mali Lošinj

At the end of a sheltered, elongated bay on the southwest coast, Mali Lošinj is the largest settlement on all the Croatian islands. Despite its name, it's far bigger than neighbouring Veli Lošinj (*mali* means small, *veli* large). Everyday life focuses on the harbour, skirted by a seafront promenade lined with cream, ochre and russet façades, many housing street-level cafés with open-air seating under colourful awnings through summer. The town's loveliest houses, set in lush gardens filled with Mediterranean planting, were built by retired sea captains during the 19th century. Through peak season the place is packed with visitors, most of whom sleep in the large, modern hotels on Čikat Peninsula, joined to the centre by a coastal path that meanders its way between the turquoise blue sea and scented pinewoods.

Mali Lošinj.

Veli Lošinj

Veli Lošinj is a little fishing town of pastel-coloured houses built around a bay. It's quieter and more authentic than its neighbour, but still has a few things worth seeing, a selection of fish restaurants and a **Marine Education Centre** (blue-world.org, Jul-Aug 0900-1300 and 1800-2200, Jun and Sep 0900-1300 and 1800-2000, May and Oct Mon-Fri 0900-1600 and Sat 0900-1400, Nov-Apr Mon-Fri 1000-1400, 10Kn), dedicated to researching a local school of bottle-nosed dolphins.

Veli Lošinj.

Island of Rab

Rab is probably the most beautiful of all the Kvarner islands. While the windswept northeast side is rocky and barren with steep cliffs plummeting down to the sea, the sheltered southwest part is gently undulating and covered with dense, green pinewoods. The main reason for coming here is to explore medieval Rab Town, an architectural treasure perched on a walled peninsula, rising high above the sea. There are also some blissful stretches of sandy beach on the northern coast at Lopar, so you can combine sightseeing with swimming and sunbathing, not to mention the excellent fish restaurants. Rab is a particularly popular destination for Germans and Hungarians, being one of the easiest islands to access from Central Europe.

Rab Town.

Essentials

➔ **Ferry Jadrolinija**, jadrolinija.hr, operates a daily catamaran from Rijeka to Rab Town, which then continues to Novalja (Pag, North Dalmatia). **Linijska Nacionalna Plovidba**, lnp.hr, operates daily ferries from Lopar (Rab) to Valbiska (Krk).

💲 **ATM** Cash machines are plentiful in Rab Town.

ℹ **Tourist information** Trg Municipium Arbe 8, T051-771111, tzg-rab.hr.

Rab Town

The old town can be divided into two parts: the medieval stone cottages of **Kaldanac** – on the tip of the peninsula – and **Varoš**, which takes up the land end of the peninsula and is made of paved streets lined with 15th- to 17th-century Gothic and Renaissance buildings. The old town has three streets (Donja Ulica, Srednja Ulica and Gornja Ulica), which run parallel to the waterfront promenade. The main cultural monuments are on **Gornja Ulica**, the upper street, and you'll find standard tourist haunts on **Srednja Ulica**, the middle street, where street artists set up their easels in peak season.

Trg Municipium Arbe

Rab's main square opens out onto the seafront, half-way along the peninsula. It's rimmed with cafés and the tourist office is also here. The main monument is the **Kneževo Dvor** (Rector's Palace), built between the 13th and 16th centuries.

Crkva Sv Marije Velike
Ivana Rabljanina.
Open 0800-1200, 1700-2000.

Standing on the highest point of the peninsula is the 12th-century Romanesque Church of St Mary the Great. The façade is made up of pink and white stone, and decorated with rows of Romanesque blind arches to each side of the main portal.

Veli Zvonik
Ivana Rabljanina.
Summer 1000-1300, 1900-2200, 20Kn.

A short distance from the Church of St Mary the Great, the free-standing, 13th-century Great Bell Tower is the tallest (25 m) and most beautiful of Rab's four campanili. You can climb to the top for views over the town and the surrounding seascapes.

Crkva Sv Justina
Gornja Ulica.
Summer 0900-1200, 1930-2200, 20Kn.

St Justine's Church houses a Museum of Sacred Art. Top exhibits are an ornate 13th-century silver-plated box containing the skull of St Christopher (the town's patron saint), and a mid-14th-century polyptych by Paolo Veneziano. The church bell tower, topped with an onion dome, dates from 1672.

Bazilika Sv Ivana Evandeliste
Gornja Ulica.
Summer 1000-1300, 1900-2200, 20Kn.

Probably originating from the early Christian era, the Basilica of St John the Evangelist, now in ruins, was abandoned in the early 19th century. Today, all that remains is the 12th-century bell tower, which was restored in 1933 and stands 20m high.

Rab Town's beaches

The most central places to swim and sunbathe are on the west side of Komrčar Park. Through summer, taxi boats shuttle visitors to and from Frkanj Peninsula, west of Rab Town, where there are plenty of rocky coves backed by woods, as well as the nudist beach of Kandarola.

Lopar Peninsula

On the northern tip of the island, the sparsely populated Lopar Peninsula boasts some of Croatia's sandiest beaches. Here you'll find the island's largest and most popular family beach, **Rajska Plaža** (Paradise Beach), a 1.5-km stretch of sand backed by restaurants and cafés. A 15-minute walk north of Rajska Plaža is the nudist beach of **Stolac**, while an even more remote nudist beach, **Sahara**, is found in the peninsula's northernmost bay.

Listings
Sleeping

Rijeka

Hotel Continental €€
Šetalište Andrije Kačića-Miošića 1,
T051-372008, jadran-hoteli.hr.
Built in 1888, the Continental is
at the foot of the pilgrimage
path up to Trsat, just south of
Titov Trg. Refurbished in 2008,
it now has 65 simple but
comfortable rooms and four
suites. There's a smart restaurant
and café, and a summer terrace.

Neboder €€
Strossmayerova 1, T051-373538,
jadran-hoteli.hr.
This 1930s modernist high-rise
building (the name means
'skyscraper') has 14 floors.
Renovated in 2007, it has 54
small but comfortable rooms,
most with a balcony and
stunning views over the city and
the sea, plus a café serving
drinks and snacks. You'll find it in
the Sušak area, just across the
river from the centre of Rijeka,
about 1 km from the port.

Around Rijeka

Hotel Balatura €€
Mali Sušik 2, Tribalj, Crikvenica,
30 km southeast of Rijeka, just
off the coastal road down to
Dalmatia, T051-455340,
hotel-balatura.hr.
Stay at this lovely ethno-hotel to
escape the masses. It occupies a
restored 300-year-old stone
manor house. It has eight rooms
and two suites, all decorated in

subtle colours with exposed
stonewalls, traditional furniture
and details such as big paintings
used to hide the flat-screen TVs.
There's also a courtyard
restaurant.

Opatija & around
Hotel Kvarner-Amalia €€€
Park 1 Maja 4, T051-710410,
liburnia.hr.
Next to the botanical garden
and Villa Angiolina, this
ochre-coloured neoclassical
building first opened its doors to
guests in 1884. It has 87 rooms
and suites, and a lovely café
terrace beside the gardens
overlooking the sea. Facilities
include indoor and outdoor
pools filled with sea water. Sauna
and massage are also available.

Villa Ariston €€
Maršala Tita 179, T051-271379,
villa-ariston.com.
This late 19th-century villa, set
in a lovely garden running down
to the seafront promenade,
attained its present appearance
during the 1920s. It has eight
luxury guest rooms and two
suites, each with parquet
flooring and antique furniture.
There's an excellent restaurant
on the ground floor, and many
non-residents come here to eat.

Ika Hotel €
Primorska 16, Ika, T051-291777,
hotel-ika.hr.
Between Opatija and Lovran, on
the seaside promenade, this

small, family-run hotel has 17
rooms and a seafood restaurant
with a terrace looking over the
water, plus a small beach.

Lovran & around
Hotel Villa Astra €€€€
Viktora Cara Emina 11,
T051-294400, lovranske-vile.com.
This Secessionist villa is set in
lush gardens overlooking the
sea. It has six beautifully
furnished suites, a restaurant
serving organic cuisine, a spa
with a flotation tank and an
outdoor heated pool with a bar.
The owners, Lovranske Vile, also
have several others in the area.

Hotel Draga di Lovrana €€€
Lovranska Draga 1, T052-294166,
dragadilovrana.hr.
High up on the slopes of Mt Učka,
7.5 km from Lovran, affording
spectacular views down onto
Kvarner Bay, this building dates
from 1910. Since 2005, it has
operated as a small hotel with
just four rooms and one luxurious
top-floor apartment (with an
open fire, jacuzzi and sauna).
On the ground floor there's a
very popular smart restaurant
serving gourmet cuisine, plus a
smaller, more informal *konoba*
(rustic-style restaurant) serving
local specialities.

Hotel Lovran €
Šetalište Maršala Tita 19/2,
T051-291222, hotel-lovran.hr.
Composed of two early
20th-century villas, joined

together by a modern reception area, this hotel is set in a lush park overlooking the sea. It has 50 rooms (most but not all with air conditioning) and three suites, a restaurant, a small wellness centre with sauna and gym, plus two tennis courts.

Risnjak National Park
Hotel Risnjak €€
Lujzinska 36, Delnice, T051-508160, hotel-risnjak.hr.
On the go since the 1930s, this hotel reopened in 2004 after a complete renovation. There are 21 rooms and one suite, a cosy restaurant and café, plus a small wellness centre. They offer a wide range of adventure sports including hiking, rafting and paragliding, and have mountain bikes to rent.

Island of Krk

Krk Town
Marina Hotel €€€
Ružmarinska 6, T052-221357, hotelikrk.hr.
Right on the seafront in the centre of Krk, Marina Hotel is close to the cathedral and dates back to 1925. Renovated in 2008, it is now an upmarket four-star hotel with just seven rooms and three suites, each with modern minimalist furniture, fabrics in shades of yellow and brown, plus a balcony and sea view. The ground-floor restaurant has a lovely waterside terrace.

Hotel Bor €€
Šetalište Dražica 5, T051-220200, hotelbor.hr.
A five-minute walk along the seafront from the old town, this hotel dates back to 1920 and was renovated in 2002. There are 18 simple but comfortable rooms and four suites, plus a front terrace with a bar-restaurant and outdoor seating below the pine trees, giving onto a rocky bathing area.

Punat & the islet of Košljun
Kanajt €€€
Kanajt 5, T051-654340, kanajt.hr.
This small hotel occupies the former 16th-century Bishop's Palace overlooking Punat marina. Renovated in 2004, it has 20 simple but comfortable rooms and two suites, all with carpets and standard 1980s furniture, plus a restaurant with a front terrace serving excellent local seafood and lamb. Popular with sailing types, it also offers a charter service.

Baška
Hotel Tamaris €€
Emila Geistlicha bb, T051-864200, baska-tamaris.com.
Overlooking Baška's fine pebble beach, this hotel has 15 spacious rooms and 15 apartments, all simply but smartly furnished. The hotel restaurant serves Mediterranean cuisine on a large sea-view terrace. It's noted for its friendly and helpful staff.

Vrbnik
Apartments Nada €€
Ulica Glavača 22, T051-857065, nada-vrbnik.hr.
These two restored houses are owned by the people who run Nada (see Eating, page 156). Apartment Božanić is located within Vrbnik's medieval town walls, and has a kitchen and living room (sofa bed) with a fireplace, a double bed on a mezzanine level, plus a barbecue and jacuzzi in the garden. Apartment Zameniljak lies just outside town, set amid dense Mediterranean planting, and has an open-plan kitchen with a beamed ceiling and fireplace, three double rooms, two bathrooms, and an outdoor jacuzzi.

Hotel Argentum €€
Supec 68, T051-857370, hotel-argentum.com.
This 10-room modern hotel is a short walk from the old town. It has a good restaurant with a terrace looking out to sea, and it makes an ideal base for a couple of days.

Island of Cres

Hotel Kimen €€
Melin I/16, Cres Town, T051-573305; hotel-kimen.com.
Refurbished in spring 2008 a 2-km walk along the coast from the centre, is Cres Town's only hotel. All the 128 basic but

Listings

comfortable rooms have a balcony, Wi-Fi and a bathroom. A wellness centre offering sauna, solarium and gym opened in summer 2009. Popular with tour groups, it arranges excursions such as a Gastro Tour, Eco Tour, Hiking and Olive Picking.

Pansion Tramontana €
Beli, T051-840519, diving-beli.com.
Close to the eco-centre and an ideal base for exploring the Tramuntane forests, this friendly family-run B&B has eight double rooms and a restaurant. The diving centre is also based here.

Island of Lošinj

Hotel Apoksiomen €€€
Riva Lošinjskih Kapetana 1, Mali Lošinj, T051-520820, apoksiomen.com.
This hotel has 25 rooms equipped with Wi-Fi and a bathroom. There's a waterfront bar-restaurant, and it's just a 15-minute walk to the beach.

Hotel Manora €€€
Nerezine, T051-237460, manora-losinj.hr.
Away from the busy tourist areas, family-run Manora is in Nerezine, 25 km north of Mali Lošinj. Located just a 10-minute walk from the harbourfront, it has 22 double rooms, plus a restaurant, and a garden with a small pool. They also arrange fishing trips.

Villa Favorita €€€
Sunčana uvala bb, Mali Lošinj, T051-520640, villafavorita.hr.
With a view of the sea and backed by pinewoods, this Secessionist building has been restored to form a small hotel with eight double rooms. There's also a bar, sauna and outdoor pool filled with sea water set in a garden.

Hotel Kredo €
Gortana 9, Čikat, T051 233595, kre-do.hr.
Overlooking the sea and backed by pinewoods in Čikat, a 15-minute walk from Mali Lošinj town centre, this villa offers nine rooms and five apartments. Expect wooden floors, simple but tasteful furnishing, plus a smart kitchenette in the self-catering units. There's a waterside bar-restaurant, a mini wellness centre, plus bikes for hire and boat transfers to nearby beaches.

Hotel & Restaurant Televrin €
Obala nerezinskih pomoraca, Nerezine; T051-237121, televrin.com.
In the yellow former town hall building dating from 1910, on Nerezine harbourfront, this three-star hotel has 13 double rooms and two suites. Downstairs, local seafood and lamb dishes are served in a loggia with an open fireplace overlooking the sea.

Island of Rab

Arbiana €€€
Obala Petra Krešimira 12, Rab Town, T051-775900, arbianahotel.com.
Standing on the harbour front, this building dates back to 1924. Now a lovely boutique hotel offering the best accommodation in town, it has 28 rooms with sumptuous furnishing and sweeping curtains. Known for its friendly staff and personal service, it also has a highly regarded restaurant.

Hotel Imperial €€
Palit bb, Rab Town, T051-724522, imperial.hr.
Rab Town's oldest hotel sits on the edge of the old town, amid the greenery of Komrčar Park. The 134 rooms are smart and modern and a decent buffet breakfast is served in the hotel restaurant. The town beach lies just a 10-minute walk away and the hotel operates taxi boats (free) to Frkanj nudist beach.

Pansion Tamaris €€
Palit 285, T051-724925, tamaris-rab.com.
Overlooking the sea in St Euphemius Bay in Palit, this friendly little hotel has just 14 rooms plus a restaurant serving excellent seafood on a pleasant terrace. You can walk through Komrčar Park to be in Rab Town in just a few minutes, and there are taxi boats from the jetty to the beaches on Frkanj peninsula.

Eating & drinking

Rijeka

Zlatna Školjka €€€
Kružna 12a, in a side street off the Korzo, T051-213782.
Mon-Sat lunch and dinner, closed Sun.
Serves creative seafood dishes in a sedate pastel-coloured dining room with a combination of modern furniture and antiques.

Trsatika €€
J Rakovca 33, Trsat, T051-217455.
Thu-Tue lunch and dinner, closed Wed.
High up on Trsat, below the pilgrimage church, this popular restaurant has a summer terrace offering fantastic views over Rijeka. Favourite dishes include *gulaš* (goulash) and *škampi na buzaru* (shrimps prepared with onion and tomato). Pizza makes a cheap option.

Pod Voltun €€-€
Pod voltun 15, T051-330806.
Daily lunch and dinner.
This informal *konoba* is popular with locals for *merenda* (early lunch) and serves hearty home cooking with favourites including *brudet* (fish stew) and *bakalar* (salted cod).

Bracera €
Kružna 12, T051-213782.
Daily lunch and dinner.
Rijeka's favourite pizzeria is opposite the more upmarket fish restaurant, Zlatna Školjka.

Around Rijeka

Opatija & around
Le Mandrać €€€
Obala F Supila 10, Volosko, 4 km from Opatija, T051-701357, lemandrac.com.
Daily lunch and dinner.
Opened in 2004 and now regarded as one of Croatia's best restaurants, Le Madrać is housed in a minimalist glass conservatory with ambient music, candles and a sea view. There's a special 'slow food' menu consisting of nine courses including delicacies such as foie gras, truffles and oysters.

Plavi Podrum €€€-€€
Supilova Obala 4, Volosko, 4 km from Opatija, T051-701223.
Daily lunch and dinner.
This classic seafood restaurant has a formal dining room and outdoor tables overlooking a pretty fishing harbour. It's noted for excellent fresh fish and an outstanding wine list.

Lovran & around
Najade €€€
Šetalište Maršala Tita 69, T051-291866.
Daily lunch and dinner.
This restaurant has long been popular with Croatians, who come here to eat fish on a terrace overlooking the sea. It's close to the harbour, and the owner reputedly gets first choice of the catch when the fishermen come in.

Dopolavoro €€
Učka 6, Ičići, T051-299641.
Daily lunch and dinner.
On the old road up Mount Učka, at an altitude of 1000 m, Dopolavoro's front terrace affords great views down onto Kvarner Bay. Come here for hearty local meat dishes such as venison, wild boar and lamb, as well as seasonal specialities including wild mushrooms, asparagus and truffles.

Island of Krk

Konoba Šime €€
Antuna Mahnića 1, Krk Town, T051-220042.
Daily lunch and dinner.
One block in from the Riva, on the left as you pass through Mala Vrata, this typical *konoba* is noted for tasty, reasonably priced pasta dishes.

Bracera €€-€
OK-Kvarnerska 1, Malinska, T051-858700, bracera.hr.
Daily lunch and dinner.
In Malinska, 13 km north of Krk Town, this friendly eatery is run by an owner-chef who also catches the seafood on offer. Food is prepared over an open fire in the old-fashioned dining room, which has a wooden-beamed ceiling hung with fishing nets and old fishing tools, plus heavy wooden tables and benches.

Listings

Punat & the Islet of Košljun
Marina €€
Puntica 9, T051-654380.
Daily lunch and dinner.
Based in the marina with a view over the bay and the Islet of Košljun, this highly regarded restaurant serves up local specialities.

Baška
Cicibela €€
Emila Geistlicha bb, T051-847747, cicibela.hr.
Daily lunch and dinner.
This cosy restaurant is known for its discreet waiters and romantic atmosphere. There's a good selection of fish and seafood dishes, with pizza providing a cheaper option.

Vrbnik
Nada €€€-€€
Ulica Glavača 22, T051-857065, nada-vrbnik.hr.
Daily lunch and dinner.
Close to the harbour, Nada doubles as a restaurant, where you can eat fresh fish and seafood on a terrace with views out to sea, and a *konoba* (wine cellar), where you can sample the Žlahtina Nada along with nibbles such as *ovči sir* (sheep's cheese) and *pršut* (smoked ham). Reservations recommended. By prior agreement you can also visit their main wine cellars (Zagrada 4, below the town walls) for a guided tour, a video presentation and wine tasting.

Island of Cres

Belona €€
Šetalište 20 Aprila 24, Cres Town, T051-571 203.
Daily lunch and dinner.
This old-fashioned eatery is known for oven-baked *arbun* (sea bream), pasta with lobster, and oven-baked lamb with potatoes. In warm weather eat outside on the terrace.

Konoba Bukaleta €€
Loznati, T051 571606.
Daily lunch and dinner.
In the mountains, 5 km from Cres Town, this modern white building has a large terrace affording fine views over the Kvarner Gulf. The speciality here is local Cres lamb, prepared in a variety of ways: roast lamb, lamb goulash with gnocchi, lamb's liver and so on. They also serve sheep's cheese and home-baked bread. Be sure to reserve a table in advance during high season.

Island of Lošinj

Mali Lošinj
Corrado €€€-€€
Sv Marije 1, T051-232487.
Daily lunch and dinner.
This is the best place to try traditional Lošinj fare such as *gulaš od junjetine* (lamb goulash). The owner is a cook and fisherman, so you can also expect top-class seafood dishes such as squid and scampi with pasta.

Artatore €€
Artatore 132, Uvala Artatore, T051-232932.
Daily lunch and dinner.
Located 7 km north of Mali Lošinj, this restaurant is especially popular with yachters, who moor up in front of the terrace overlooking the bay. The owner does the cooking himself and his top dishes are *škampi rižot* (shrimp risotto), *jastog s rezancima* (lobster with pasta) and *ribe na žaru* (barbecued fish).

Pizzeria Draga €€
Braće Vidulića 77, T051-231132.
Daily lunch and dinner.
This friendly, bustling restaurant offers a range of pasta dishes and salads at lunchtime, and in the evenings adds a vast choice of brick-oven baked pizzas to the menu. There's a covered terrace area so you can eat outside.

Veli Lošinj
Bora Bora €€
Rovenska 3, T051-867544, borabar.com.
Daily lunch and dinner.
In Rovenska Bay near Veli Lošinj, funky Bora Bar is run by an Italian-born owner-chef who is married to a Croatian. Expect modern Mediterranean cuisine using local produce, with an emphasis on seafood and truffles, plus fresh home-made pasta. Popular with sailing types, there are water and electricity connections for boats out front, as well as Wi-Fi.

Entertainment

Activities & tours

Astoria €€€
*Dinka Dokule 2, Rab Town,
T051-774844, astoria-rab.com.*
Daily lunch and dinner.
On the first floor of Residence
Astoria, this restaurant has a
terrace overlooking Rab's main
square and the harbour. The
menu features local meat and
fish dishes using organic
ingredients and fresh herbs.

Konoba Rab €€€-€€
*Kneza Branimira 3, Rab Town,
T051-725666.*
Daily lunch and dinner.
In a side street running between
Srednja Ulica and Gornja Ulica,
this *konoba* serves up meat and
fish prepared either on a
barbeque or under a *peka*.

Zlatni Zalaz €€€-€€
*Supertarska Draga 379, about
10 km northwest of Rab Town,
T051-775150.*
Daily lunch and dinner.
This restaurant serves some of
the best food on the island. The
speciality is *janjeai but s jabukama*
(lamb with apple) but there's also
a choice of fish dishes.

Restoran Paradiso €€
*Stjepana Radića 1, Rab Town,
T051-771109, makek-paradiso.hr.*
Daily lunch and dinner.
In the heart of the old town, this
romantic restaurant is hidden
away in a courtyard garden and
serves tasty Croatian cuisine.

Rijeka

Bars & clubs
Hemingway
*Korzo 28, T051-272887,
hemingway.hr.*
One of a chain of bars on Rijeka's
pedestrian shopping street.

Indigo
*Stara Vrata 3, T051-325300,
indigo.com.hr.*
In the old town, this lounge-
restaurant-bar has a pop feel.

Jazz Tunnel
*Školjić 12, 051-327116,
jazztunel.com.*
Live jazz, blues, soul and funk in
a tunnel-like space near Titov Trg.

Nina 2
*Adamićev Gat, T091-5317879,
nina2.com.*
In a boat on Rijeka's seafront,
DJs playing house and R&B.

Palach
Kružna 6, T051-215063.
In a street off the Korzo, Palach has
been hosting concerts for 25 years.

Festivals & events
Rijeka Karneval, see page 49.

Around Rijeka

Bars & clubs
Disco Seven
*Maršala Tita 125, Opatija,
T099-4777000, discoseven.hr.*
On the seafront in Opatija, this
summer disco plays house music.

Rijeka

Ad Natura
*S.V.Čiče 4, Rijeka, T091-5907065,
adnatura.com.*
Organizes mountain biking, free
climbing and kayaking in the
mountains of Risnjak and Učka.

Island of Krk

Squatina Diving Centre
*Zarok 88a, Baška, T051-856034,
squatinadiving.com.*

Island of Cres

Diving Club Beli
*Pansion Tramontana, T051-
840519, diving-beli.com.*

Island of Lošinj

Diving Center Sumartin
*Sv. Martin 41, T051-232835,
sumartin.com.*

Island of Rab

Aqua Sport
*Supetarska Draga 331,
T051-776145, aquasport.hr.*

Moby Dick
*Lopar 493, T051-775577,
mobydick-diving.com.*

Contents

161 Introduction
162 Zadar
166 Island of Pag
168 Paklenica National Park
170 Kornati National Park
172 **Listings:**
172 Sleeping
173 Eating & drinking
176 Entertainment
176 Shopping
177 Activities & tours

Greeting to the sun.

Introduction

North Dalmatia, south of Kvarner, is centred on the port of Zadar, its historic centre. Packed with Roman ruins, Byzantine churches and Venetian-style town houses, it was once the capital of all Dalmatia, an honour it has shared through the centuries with Split (Central Dalmatia).

The most interesting island in the region is Pag, renowned for its delicious salty sheep's cheese and a long tradition of lacemaking. Its chief settlement, Pag Town, is a perfect model of Renaissance urban planning, having been designed entirely by one architect. On the northern tip of Pag, Novalje has fine pebble beaches and one of the hottest clubbing scenes in Croatia.

North Dalmatia's main attraction, though, especially for yachters, has to be Kornati National Park, a unique seascape of almost 90 scattered islands and islets. Dry, rocky and practically devoid of vegetation, the islands are uninhabited. If you don't have your own boat, it's possible to visit them on an organized day trip.

If you prefer terra firma and the sweet smell of pinewoods, you can retreat to Paklenica National Park on the seaward slopes of the rugged Velebit mountain chain – an area criss-crossed by well-marked hiking paths and much loved by free climbers. And, nearby, you can try rafting down the River Zrmanja, marking the southern limits of Velebit.

Kornati islands

What to see in...

...a one day
Explore **Zadar's** old town with its Roman monuments, Romanesque churches, and a modern-day sea organ, all tightly packed on a medieval walled pedestrian-only peninsular. In the evening, party at **Garden Zadar** or **Arsenale** and if funds permit, take a room at **Hotel Bastion**.

...a weekend or more
Lovers of the big blue might opt for a one-day boat trip round the scattered islands of **Kornati National Park**, while keen hikers could pack a picnic and tackle the rocky slopes of **Paklenica National Park**. Adventure sports fanatics might try whitewater rafting down the River Zrmanja.

Zadar

Sitting compact on a rectangular peninsula, accessible only to pedestrians, the historic centre of Zadar is renowned throughout Croatia for its beautiful medieval churches, the most impressive being St Donat, which stands on the site of the ancient Roman forum. Close by, in the St Mary's Convent complex, the Gold and Silver of Zadar exhibition is a stunning collection of minutely detailed Byzantine reliquaries. The narrow cobbled streets are lined with fine Venetian-style town houses, many converted into shops and cafés at ground level, giving the old town the buzz of a modern-day urban centre. The surrounding modern suburbs are dispersed and more difficult to negotiate: most of the hotels, restaurants and sports facilities lie 5 km along the coast at Puntamika and Borik. All the sights listed here are in Zadar's old town and are within walking distance of one another.

St Mary's and the adjoining Benedictine convent.

Forum

Zeleni Trg.

The Romans founded Zadar as Jadera, and developed it into a port and fortified market town with a forum, theatre and public baths). Now known as Zeleni Trg, the ancient forum dates from between the first century BC and the third century AD. In Roman times it served as the main market place and public meeting space; still today the city's top monuments, floodlit at night, are found here. On the northwest corner stands an ancient Roman column used as a 'pole of shame' from the Middle Ages up until 1840, where criminals were chained and exposed to public scorn and ridicule.

Crkva Sv Donat

Zeleni Trg.
Jul-Aug daily 0900-2200, May-Jun and Sep-Oct daily 0900-1300, 1600-1900, closed Nov-Apr.

Following the fall of the Western Roman Empire in the fifth century, Zadar became the capital of the Byzantine *thema* (province) of Dalmatia. Standing in the centre of the Forum, the ninth-century Church of St Donat dates from that period. An imposing rotonda, it's Zadar's best-known monument and the largest Byzantine building in Croatia. Standing 27 m high, it's a robust cylindrical structure flanked by three circular apses. Fragments of Roman stones have been incorporated into the sturdy outer walls, and inside a matroneum (womens' gallery) is supported by six pilasters and two Roman columns, and capped by a central dome. St Donat ceased to function as a church during the early 19th century. Today it stands empty, but due to its excellent acoustics it hosts the annual summer festival of medieval, Renaissance and baroque music.

Essentials

⊖ **Bus station** The bus station is on Ante Starčevića 2, T023-211555, liburnija-zadar.hr. For regional bus travel, see page 272.

⊅ **Ferry** Jadrolinija, www.jadrolinija.hr, runs a ferry service from Zadar to Mali Lošinj (Kvarner), stopping at several smaller islands en route. It also operates daily local ferries to nearby islands.

⊙ **Train station** The train station is next to the bus station, T060-333444 (national train information) hznet.hr. For regional train travel, see page 272.

⑤ **ATM** Cash machines are plentiful in Zadar old town – you'll find two in Široka ulica.

⊕ **Hospital** Bože Peričića 5, between the old town and the bus station, T023-315677.

✚ **Pharmacy** Each pharmacy is marked by a glowing green cross. **Ljekarna Donat**, Braće Vranjanina 14, T023-251342, is usually open 24 hours. If closed, there will be a notice on the door saying which pharmacy to go to.

⌐ **Post office** The main post office is at Kralja S Državislava 1, Monday to Saturday 0700-2100.

❶ **Tourist information** Zadar city tourist office at Ilije Smiljanića bb, T023-212222, www.tzzadar.hr. The regional tourist office at is Leopolda Mandića 1, T023-315107, zadar.hr.

Church of St Donat.

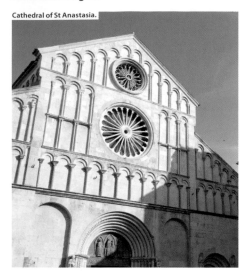

Cathedral of St Anastasia.

Katedrala Sv Stošije

Zeleni Trg.
Jul-Aug daily 0800-2000, Sep-Jun daily
0800-1200, 1700-2000.

Next to Sv Donat stands the 12th-century, late
Romanesque Cathedral of St Anastasia. Built on a
rectangular ground plan, it has a splendid façade
bearing three doors, a series of blind arches and
two central rose windows, the lower one
Romanesque and the upper one Gothic. Inside,
you'll find a stone altar and wooden choir stalls
from the 15th century. At the end of the left aisle, a
smaller altar displays a ninth-century stone casket
containing the remains of St Anastasia, to whom
the cathedral is dedicated. Work on the bell tower
began in the 15th century, though the upper three
floors weren't completed until 1892 to drawings by
the English architect TG Jackson.

Tip...

If you have a head for heights it's well worth
climbing to the top of the cathedral's bell
tower for spectacular views over the city.

Arheološki Muzej

Trg Opatice Čike 1, T023-250516, amzd.hr.
Apr-Sep 0900-1400, 1700-2100, Oct-Mar
0900-1400, 10Kn.

Housed in a modern concrete building close to
the Forum, the Archaeological Museum traces
local history from the Stone Age to the late Middle
Ages. The ground floor is devoted to finds from
between the seventh and 12th centuries, and
includes several fine examples of medieval stone
carving. The first floor examines North Dalmatia
under the Romans, while the second floor is given
over to the Palaeolithic, Neolithic, Copper, Bronze
and Iron Ages.

Riznica

Trg Opatice Čike, T023-250496.
May-Sep Mon-Sat 1000-1300, 1800-1930,
Sun 1000-1300, Oct-Apr Mon-Sat 1000-1230,
1800-1930, Sun 1000-1230, 30 Kn.

Standing next door to the early Romanesque
Church of St Mary, the treasury houses a stunning
collection known as *Zlato i Srebro Zadra* (Gold and
Silver of Zadar), curated by the Benedictine nuns
who live in the neighbouring Convent of St Mary.
   The first floor displays a hoard of sumptuous
reliquaries – arms and legs of various saints,
encased in minutely detailed gold plating – and
gold and silver processional crosses. On the
second floor you'll find an equally well-displayed
collection of religious paintings – look out for
three panels from a 15th-century polyptych by the
Venetian artist Vittore Carpaccio (1455-1526) and a
striking Assumption of the Virgin from 1520 by
Lorenzo Luzzo.

Morske Orgulje

Obala Kralja Petra Krešimira IV.

On the tip of the old town peninsula, the
extraordinary Sea Organ is made up of 35 pipes
forming whistles that are played by the sea. The
notes produced depend on the size of the waves,

Maraschino

While in Zadar, be sure to try Maraschino, a bittersweet syrupy liquor made from Marasca cherries and manufactured here since 1821. Its unique almond-flavour is obtained by crushing the cherry stones, and it can be drunk straight or mixed in cocktails. Through the decades it has been exported far and wide and is said to have won the hearts of world figures such as Napoleon and Queen Victoria.

with the sea's energy creating ever-changing sounds. It was designed by Nikola Bašić and installed in 2005.

Zadarski Pozdrav Suncu

Obala Kralja Petra Krešimira IV.

Set into the stone-paved waterfront, next to the Sea Organ, the Greeting to the Sun is a 22-m circle made up of 300 multi-layered glass plates. Below the glass, light-sensitive solar modules absorb the sun's energy during the day, then transform it into electrical energy. Just after sunset, the lighting elements create an impressive light show, in harmony with the sounds of the Sea Organ. The pavement lights up in shades of blue, green, red and yellow, and local children meet here and race around chasing the light patterns. The solar modules can produce 46.500 kW per year – this energy is used for the Greeting to the Sun installation and for lighting the rest of the waterfront. It was installed in 2008 and, like the Sea Organ, was created by local architect Nikola Bašić.

Narodni Trg

The People's Square took over the role of the Forum as the city's main square in the 16th century. On the west side stands the City Guardhouse, dating from 1562, with an imposing 18th-century clock tower. On the opposite side of the square, the 16th-century Renaissance loggia now houses an exhibition centre (Mon-Fri 0900-1200, 1700-2000, Sat 0900-1300).

Sea Organ.

Island of Pag

Long and skinny, rocky and barren, Pag's sparse pastures, scented with wild sage, support sheep farming, an important industry here, with twice as many sheep on the island as people. The island is known throughout the country for its *paški sir* (Pag cheese, made from sheep's milk) and *janjetina* (roast lamb). Several fertile valleys are given over to vineyards, producing two dry white wines, the golden-coloured Žutica and the light, crisp Gegić.

The chief settlement is the picturesque 15th-century Pag Town, with a long tradition of salt production and lacemaking, while the main tourist destination is Novalja, a seaside resort with some decent pebble beaches and several late-night dance clubs.

Note that while the southern half of Pag is considered North Dalmatia, the northern half officially belongs to the Kvarner region. However, to simplify the matter, the entire island is included in North Dalmatia here.

Island of Pag.

Pag Town.

Essentials

⊕ **Bus station** Pag Town bus station is 500 m from the old town, T023-600276. **Novalja** bus station lies 500 m from the centre of town, T053-661500. For regional bus travel, see page 272.

➔ **Ferry** The southern tip of the island of Pag is joined to the mainland by a bridge. However, **Jadrolinija**, www.jadrolinija.hr, runs daily ferries from Rijeka in the Kvarner region (see page 141) to Novalja (northern tip of Pag), stopping at Rab Town (island of Rab) en route.

⊖ **ATM** Cash machines are plentiful in both **Pag Town** and **Novalja**.

❶ **Tourist information** Trg Petra Krešimira IV, **Pag Town**, T023-611286, and **Novalja**, T053-661404, tz-novalja.hr.

Pag Town

Located at the end of Pag Bay, Pag Town has been the island's capital since the 15th century. Its wealth was based on salt production and the salt pans can still be seen here today. Although there are no notable beaches, and the surrounding landscape is somewhat dreary, the old town is a gem of Renaissance architecture.

In 1443, while under Venetian rule, plans were drawn up to build a new fortified town, to defend against the Turks. The renowned architect Juraj Dalmatinac (also responsible for Šibenik Cathedral, see page 195) masterminded the project, which took several decades to build. A grid of narrow streets, centring on a main square with a cathedral and Rector's Palace, were to be enclosed by sturdy walls and 10 towers.

Today, apart from the walls, the complex remains intact. On the main square, Trg Kralja Petra Krešimira IV, stands the 15th-century Church of St Mary. Although it was never awarded the status of cathedral, it remains a proud monument based on the form of a three-nave Romanesque basilica, with a fine façade featuring a Renaissance rose window above an elegant Gothic portal. Café life centres on the main square, while much of the post-1960s tourist development such as hotels, apartments and restaurants lie west of town, overlooking a family beach, with shallow water suitable for kids.

Novalja

21 km northwest of Pag Town.

Connected to Pag Town by daily buses, Novalja lies in a sheltered cove backed by pinewoods, and is Pag's largest and busiest resort. Pristine, clear, emerald seawater and a number of bays with fine pebble beaches make it the best place for sunbathing on the island, while sports and late-night dance clubs compensate in part for its lack of cultural attractions.

The most popular bathing areas are the pebble beaches of Zrče, 2 km northeast of Novalja (served by shuttle bus in July and August), and Straško, a short walk south of Novalja town centre. Both are equipped with watersports facilities, showers, sun beds and umbrellas for hire, lifeguards, bars and eateries.

Tip...

Since 2007, Zrče beach has had a special 24-hour licence, meaning that its bars and clubs can work non-stop, making it the only place of its kind in Croatia.

Paklenica National Park

Paklenica National Park office
*Tudjmana 14a, Starigrad Paklenica (42 km
north of Zadar), T023-369202, paklenica.hr.*
Apr-Oct 40Kn, Nov-Mar 30Kn.

The best starting point for exploring the park is the seaside town of Starigrad Paklenica, overlooking the narrow Velebitski Kanal (Velebit Channel). Here, in the national park office at the entrance to the park, you can pick up hiking maps and information about mountain refuges.

Lying on the southeast slopes of the Velebit mountain chain, Paklenica National Park runs for 20 km along the Riviera, combining coastal and mountain scenery, which makes it it a haven for hikers and free-climbers. The lower levels are covered with beech forests, which give way to pines, dramatic rocky outcrops, mountain meadows and scree slopes. A refuge for wildlife, bears and wild boars are sighted in the more remote areas of Velebit.

Peak to peak

The most popular walking route leads up the impressive limestone gorge of Velika Paklenica, which is 10 km long and up to 400 m deep, and runs from the highest peaks down to the sea. The path starts about 4 km inland from the park entrance at Starigrad Paklenica. Passing a couple of mountain refuges, a stiff climb will bring you to the 1757-m peak of Vaganski Vrh, the highest point on southern Velebit, offering stunning views over the sea and islands. This walk requires an entire day, and you should only set out armed with good hiking boots and a plentiful supply of water. Alternatively, a little way up the gorge, a secondary path branches off to the right, leading to Anića Kuk, a bizarre 721-m vertical rock form and a popular training ground for free-climbers. From here the path continues, passing through a dense forest, and eventually arrives at a height of 550 m, where you will find Manita Peč, a 500-m-long illuminated cave, filled with stalactites and stalagmites, which can be visited as part of a guided tour (ask at the national park office for details). A final stretch of path brings you to the 800 m peak of Vidakov Kuk.

Birdwatchers should note that rock partridges are often spotted on Paklenica's stony slopes, while birds of prey such as peregrine falcons and golden eagles may be sighted in Velika Paklenica gorge.

River Zrmanja

The River Zrmanja is a typical karst river – its source lies in the Velebit mountains and it flows down to the Adriatic Sea. Its emerald-blue waters run 64 km, passing through valleys and magnificent steep-sided canyons, and over waterfalls and rapids en route. Various agencies (see page 177) arrange rafting, kayaking and canoeing here. A popular stretch for these tours lies between the villages of Kaštel Zegarski (15 km from Starigrad Paklnecia) and Muškovci, between which the river passes through a dramatic canyon.

Kornati National Park

I f you visit the park as part of an organized group, the entrance fee will be included in the price of the trip. If you're travelling by private boat, you pay depending on the size of your vessel. This can be done at any one of a number of kiosks scattered through the park (in June-September), from the national park head office in Murter (all year), or from nearby marinas.

Although the Kornati are best explored by private sailing boat, they can also be visited as part of an organized day trip, arranged by private agencies operating from nearby coastal resorts including Zadar and Šibenik (see respective sections for details).

Parallel to the mainland coast midway between Zadar and Šibenik, Kornati National Park covers an area 35 km long and 13 km wide, containing 89 islands, islets and reefs. Declared a national park due to its wealth of underwater life and its unique natural beauty, the area is made up of crystal-clear blue sea and a scattering of eerie 'moonscape' islands supporting scanty vegetation.

Having no fresh water sources and little fertile land, the Kornati passed through the centuries with minimum human intervention. During the 17th century, noble families from Zadar, with the blessing of the Venetians, used the islands for sheep rearing, employing serfs from Murter as shepherds. Later, the Murterini bought rights to 90% of the Kornati, and continued to use them for seasonal farming: grazing sheep, cultivating olives, grapes and figs and keeping bees (there are few wild animals here other than lizards). They also built some 300 simple stone cottages, mainly in sheltered coves, which they used as temporary homes when fishing or tending the land. Today many of these cottages, still without running water and electricity, have been turned over to tourism, and are available for rent through the summer months, often with a small boat included, as 'Robinson Crusoe' retreats (see Sleeping, page 173).

Kornati National Park office
Butina 2, Murter,
T022-435740, www.kornati.hr.

Sleeping

Zadar

Hotel Bastion €€€€
Bedemi zadarskih pobuna 13,
T023-250724,
hotel-bastion.hr.
This stylish four-star boutique hotel is ideally located, right in the heart of the old town, near the sea. It has 23 rooms and five suites, all with wooden floors and modern 'baroque' furnishing, plus shiny marble-and-tile bathrooms. Breakfast includes a buffet and cooked-to-order sausages, omelettes and pancakes. The staff are exceptionally friendly, and there's a small wellness centre, a restaurant, free parking and free Wi-Fi. It is a little pricey, but worth it if you can afford it.

Hotel Niko €€€
Obala Kneza Domagoja 9,
Puntamika-Borik, T023-337880,
hotel-niko.hr.
What started out as the excellent Restaurant Niko (see Eating, page 173) with a romantic waterside terrace, now also has 12 guest rooms. Elegantly furnished with reproduction antiques, plush red carpets and sweeping curtains, each room has air conditioning, minibar and satellite TV.

Villa Hrešč €€
Obala kneza Trpimira 28,
T023-337570, villa-hresc.hr.
This modern pink villa has been renovated to form a luxurious establishment with six spacious apartments and two rooms. It's on the coast, offering a view of the old town across the water. Facilities include an upmarket restaurant and a garden with a pool.

Pansion Albin €
Put Dikla, T023-331137,
albin.hr.
In the Borik area, this B&B offers 16 comfortable rooms with hot showers and breakfast (buffet and cooked to order). The owners provide guests with a welcome drink upon arrival and are happy to offer local advice and help with plans. There's a restaurant (see Eating, page 174) and a pool in the garden.

Tamaris €
Zagrebačka 5, T023-318700,
tamaris-zadar.com.hr.
On the edge of town, this small modern hotel has nine doubles, two singles and one apartment, all with en suite bathroom and TV. The adjoining restaurant is popular with business people, and is reputed to serve excellent spit-roast lamb.

Island of Pag

Hotel Boškinac €€€
Novaljska Polje bb, Novalja,
T053-663500, boskinac.com.
Set amid vineyards, 3 km outside Novalja, this small, luxury hotel occupies a stone building with seven rooms and four apartments, plus a gourmet restaurant with an open fire and a leafy terrace. The interior features natural materials combined with modern design and vivid colours. They also have their own wine cellars and tasting is available on request.

Hotel Pagus €€€
Ante Starčevića 1, Pag Town,
T023-492050, coning-turizam.hr
This modern, three-storey hotel is close to the centre of Pag Town and looks out onto the beach. It has 117 comfortable rooms, a restaurant with a sunny terrace overlooking Pag Bay, plus a wellness centre offering massage, a sauna, beauty therapies, and an indoor and outdoor pool with jacuzzi.

Hotel Loža €€
Trg Loža 1, Novalja, T053-663380, turno.hr.
Bang in the centre of Novalja, this comfortable hotel has 35 rooms, each with satellite TV and a minibar – the best ones have a balcony and sea view. There's also a ground-floor restaurant and café with a summer terrace overlooking the seafront, plus an internet corner.

Paklenica National Park

Hotel Vicko €€
Joze Dokoze 20, Starigrad Paklenica, T023-369304, hotel-vicko.hr.
A comfortable, modern hotel with 23 rooms and a pleasant restaurant with a summer terrace shaded by pine trees. They also offer three- to seven-day adventure sports packages with hiking, climbing, cycling, rafting and kayaking.

Hotel Rajna €
Tudjmana 105, Starigrad Paklenica, T023-369130, hotel-rajna.com.
Popular with Croatian and foreign climbers and walkers thanks to its location close to the national park entrance, Rajna has 10 guest rooms (most with balconies) and a highly regarded restaurant serving tasty local seafood and meat dishes. The owner also runs photo-safari trips and can provide lots of information about the park.

Kornati National Park

Camping within the park is strictly forbidden. The following Murter-based agencies both have a selection of Robinson Crusoe-type accommodation: simply furnished cottages with gas lighting and water from a well, no cars, no shops and probably no neighbours.

Kornat Turist
Hrvatskih vladara 2, T022-435854, kornatturist.hr.

Lori
Zdrače 2, Betina, T022-435631, touristagency-lori.hr.

Eating & drinking

Zadar

Foša €€€
Foša 2, T023-314421.
Daily lunch and dinner.
Close to the Land Gate, just outside the city walls, this is probably the best centrally located fish restaurant. Pasta, risotto, seafood and steak are served on a lovely terrace looking out onto a small harbour.

Kornat €€€
Liburnska obala 6, T023-254501.
Daily lunch and dinner.
On the seafront promenade, close to the ferry port, Kornat is said by many to be the best restaurant in town. It has a stylish modern interior, and serves Croatian dishes spiced up with a dash of Italian flair: look out for tuna carpaccio with rocket, and gnocchi with gorgonzola and pine nuts.

Niko €€€
Obala Kneza Domagoja 9, Puntamika-Borik, T023-337888, hotel-niko.hr.
Daily lunch and dinner.
Regarded by many as one of the best restaurants in town, Niko has been serving Mediterranean cuisine, with an emphasis on seafood, since 1963. There's a lovely waterside terrace and the adjoining hotel has 12 guest rooms (see Sleeping, page 172).

Albin €€
Put Dikla 47, 2km from the old town, on the road to Puntamika and Borik, T023-331137, albin.hr.
Daily lunch and dinner.
This long-standing favourite has been serving up fresh fish for 30 years. What's on offer depends on the night's catch, but the *riblja juha* (fish soup) wins endless praise. They also have rooms to rent (see Sleeping, page 172).

Dva Ribara €€
Blaža Jurjeva 1, T023-213445.
Daily lunch and dinner.
Most people come here to eat pizza, but it's also possible to order pasta, risotto, fish and meat dishes. You'll find it in the old town, with a small terrace for outdoor dining in warm weather.

Konoba Martinac €€
A Paravije 7, T091-579 9883.
Daily lunch and dinner.
Home cooking with a creative twist, served in a courtyard garden on sunny days. Look out for veal in tuna and caper sauce. It is in the old town, in a side street close to the cathedral.

Na po Ure €€
Špire Brusine 8, T023-312004.
Daily lunch and dinner.
This small *konoba* has an exposed stone interior and serves dishes such as *morki pas* (shark) and *pašticada* (beef stewed in *prošek* and prunes). You'll find it in the old town, on the main street as you enter from Kopnena Vrata (Land Gate).

Pizzeria Pet Bunara €€
Trg Pet Bunara bb, T023-224010, petbunara.hr.
Daily lunch and dinner.
In the old town, close to Trg Pet Bunara, this restaurant takes pride in using fresh seasonal ingredients to create tasty pizzas, pasta dishes and salads, plus a limited selection of meat and fish dishes.

Roko €€
Put Dikla 54, Brodarica, on the road from the old town to Borik, T023-331000.
Daily lunch and dinner.
This restaurant is owned by a fisherman and serves up spaghetti with shrimps, and lobster, on a summer terrace.

Konoba Stomorica €
Ulica Stomorica 12, T023-315946.
Daily lunch and dinner.
In the heart of the old town, this tiny *konoba*, frequented by local fishermen, serves *girice* (small fried fish) and *pržene lignje* (fried squid), with house wine on tap.

Cafés & bars
Forum
Široka bb, T023-250537.
Pleasant café with a terrace overlooking the Roman Forum and the Church of Sveti Donat.

Kavana Sv Lovre
Narodni Trg bb, T023-212678.
Occupying a former church next to Gradska Straža (City Guardhouse), this is an ideal place to stop while sightseeing in the old town.

Riva
Zadarskog Mira 1358, T023-251462.
A great spot to have coffee on the seafront promenade in the old town, close to the Forum.

Island of Pag

Pag Town
Na Tale €€
S Radića 2, T023-611194, ljubica.hr.
Daily lunch and dinner.
Close to the harbour, with outdoor tables and sea views, this small restaurant specializes in barbecued fish and Pag lamb, which you might round off with *palačinke* (pancakes). Pizzas are also available.

Novalja

Boškinac €€€
Novaljska Polje bb, T053-663500, boskinac.com.
Daily, lunch and dinner.
For a true gourmet experience, splash out on dinner at this excellent hotel-restaurant (see Sleeping, page 172), popular with locals and non-residents. Expect a romantic candlelit stone terrace and innovative dishes prepared exclusively from fresh local ingredients – notably seafood, lamb and sheep's cheese. To try a bit of everything opt for one of the *degustacija* (degustation) menus, featuring small portions of either three, five or seven of the chef's signature dishes. The wines served here come from the Boškinac vineyards. Reservations are recommended.

Starac i Mora €€€-€€
Brače Radić bb; T053-662423.
Daily lunch and dinner.
Excellent seafood and fresh fish. Just off the seafront, a wooden door takes you into a courtyard garden with outdoor seating. The main dining room has exposed stone walls and a rustic interior, and the kitchen turns out excellent local seafood specialities.

Antonio €€
Obala Petra Krešimira 4, T053-661280.
Open all year for lunch and dinner.
On a waterside terrace looking out over Novalja bay, close to the main square, this family-run eatery serves up tasty pizza and pasta dishes, as well as local specialities such as Novaljski *brodet sa palentom* (Novalja fish stew with polenta). Open all year.

Moby Dick €€
Obala Petra Krešimira IV bb, T053-662488.
Daily lunch and dinner.
Located on the seafront promenade, in the centre of town, Moby Dick serves Dalmatian seafood dishes, barbecued fish and meat, plus pizzas, on an open-air terrace.

Steffani €€-€
Skopljanska 20, T053-661697.
Daily lunch and dinner.
In the centre of Novalja, Steffani is popular with both locals and visitors who come here to savour barbecued meat and fish, along with local specialities such as snails and dried octopus. Pizza and pasta dishes make a cheap option.

Kornati National Park

The restaurants listed here are all on the west coast of the largest island, Kornat.

Restoran Beban €€
Uvala Gujka (Gujak Cove), T099-475739 (mob).
Mid-Apr to early Oct, daily lunch and dinner.
One of the few restaurants in the area to offer *janjetina* (roast lamb), as well as *brodet* (fish stew), seafood and barbecued fish.

Restoran Darko-Strižnja €€
Uvala Strižnja (Strižnja Cove), T098-435988 (mob).
Early May to early Oct, daily lunch and dinner.
Fisherman-owner Darko serves up seafood risotto and pasta dishes, *brodet* (fish stew), seafood and barbecued fish, plus fantastic lobster.

Restoran Opat €€
Uvala Opata (Opat Cove), T091-473 2550.
Daily lunch and dinner.
This highly regarded eatery serves delicious seafood specialities such as fish pâté, salted anchovies and tuna carpaccio, plus locally grown olives preserved in sea water, and cake made from carob.

Entertainment

Shopping

Zadar & around

Bars & clubs
Arsenal
Trg Tri Bunar 1, T023-253820,
arsenalzadar.com.
Mon-Thu 0800-2400,
Fri-Sat 0800-0200.
In the vast 18th-century
Venetian arsenal, this arts and
entertainment centre includes
a bar, a gallery for exhibitions,
a wine shop and a tourist
information area.

The Garden Petrčane
Petrčane, thegardenzadar.com.
In the grounds of Hotel Pinija in
Petrčane, 12 km northwest of
Zadar, this club is run by the
same people who run the
Garden Zadar (see below).
Set on a peninsula, backed by
pinewoods and giving onto the
sea, it combines an open-air
dance floor and a waterside bar.
Through summer, it hosts several
music festivals attracting
international performers.

The Garden Zadar
Bedemi zadarskih pobuna,
Zadar, watchthegardengrow.eu.
In a garden above the city walls,
on the edge of the old town,
Zadar's coolest club closed some
years ago. It has now been
revived by two members of the
British band UB40, and is a
romantic hideaway for cocktails
and cool music.

Island of Pag

Bars & clubs
Aquarius Club
Zrče Beach, Novalja, aquarius.hr.
Through summer, Zagreb's
hottest club moves from the
capital to the island of Pag for
open-air drinking and dancing
by the sea, with regular live
concerts given by popular
Croatian musicians.

Kalypso
Zrče Beach, Novalja, zrce.hr.
Palm trees, straw umbrellas,
bathing, badminton and beach
volleyball by day; music, dancing
and cocktails by night.

Papaya
Zrče Beach, Novalja,
papaya.com.hr.
A beach complex with water
slides, a bar and a restaurant.
Resident and international guest
DJs generate a party mood, daily
after 2000. It also hosts
occasional music festivals.

Zadar

Books
Algoritam
Murvićka 1, T023-493050.
Algoritam is the best bookshop
for foreign-language
publications, including novels,
travel guides and maps.

Clothing
Boutique Croata
Široka ulica 24, T023-250597;
croata.hr.
Croata sells original Croatian ties
in presentation boxes with a
history of the tie (a Croatian
invention) included.

Cro à Porter
Široka ulica 18, T023-204902,
callegro.com.
In the Callegro shopping
centre, this is the place to shop
for fashion items created by
young Croatian designers.

Food & drink
Bibich
Kraljskog Dalmatina, T023-
250246.
The Bibić family produce their
own high-quality wines and
herb-flavoured *rakija*, which
you can taste and buy here.

Activities & tours

Tržnica
Old town.
Daily 0700-1400.
Open-air fruit and vegetable market in the old town.

Vinoteka Arsenal
Trg Tri Bunar 1,
arsenalzadar.com.
Mon-Sat 0900-2200.
Inside the arsenal complex, this wine shop stocks wines from Croatia, Australia, Spain, France, Portugal, Chile and Argentina, as well as virgin olive oil from South Dalmatia.

Zadar & around

Tour operators
Generalturist
Branimirova obala 1, Zadar,
T023-318997, generalturist.com.
One-day rafting, kayaking and canoeing trips on the River Zrmanaja.

Surfmania
Kraljičina plaža, Nin,
22km from Zadar,
T098-9129818, surfmania.hr.
A windsurfing, kitesurfing and kayaking centre.

Terra Travel Agency
Matije Gupca 2a, Zadar,
T023-337294, terratravel.hr.
Excursions from Zadar to Kornati and Paklencia national parks.

Zadar Sub
Dubrovačka 20a, Zadar,
T023-214848, zadarsub.hr.
A diving centre at Sali on the island of Dugi Otok.

Zara Adventure
Danijela Farlattija 7, Zadar,
T023-342368, zara-adventure.hr.
Caving, trekking, rafting and climbing and rafting in Paklenica National Park and the surrounding area.

Island of Pag

Diving
Blue Bay Diving
Stara Novalja, T091-8871810,
bluebaydiving.com.
Instruction and diving trips for all levels, with nearby sites including several wrecks, a cave and abundant underwater life.

Contents

181 Introduction
182 Split & around
184 *Map: Split*
192 Northwest of Split
196 Southeast of Split
200 Island of Brač
202 Island of Hvar
204 *Map: Hvar Town*
208 Island of Vis
210 Listings:
210 Sleeping
214 Eating & drinking
219 Entertainment
222 Shopping
222 Activities & tours

Detail from Roman ruins at Split.

Central Dalmatia

Introduction

More wild and mountainous than the northern regions, Central Dalmatia is home to several of Croatia's most beautiful coastal towns and loveliest islands. Its main city, Split, dates back to Roman times. With a busy ferry port, it's a perfect point of arrival if you're coming from Italy and a good launching pad if you intend to explore the surrounding islands.

The nearest island is Brač. Its top resort, Bol, owes its wealth to the stunning Zlatni Rat beach, which lies in the shadow of Vidove Gora, the highest peak on all the Adriatic islands.

For many people, the most beautiful island is Hvar. Its capital, Hvar Town, is Croatia's hippest island resort – a huddle of proud stone houses built around a harbour and backed by a hilltop fortress. The rest of the island falls away into a wilderness of lavender fields and vineyards.

Further out to sea, Vis is Croatia's most distant inhabited island and a place that, for now at least, has been spared commercial tourism. Its two main settlements, Vis Town and Komiža, are popular with yachters and offer authentic fish restaurants and wine cellars.

Back on the mainland, north of Split, is the little medieval town of Trogir and, further north still, Dalmatia's second largest city, Šibenik, with its magnificent cathedral. Nearby, Krka National Park conceals a series of dramatic waterfalls and steep wooded slopes. South of Split, the Makarska Rivijera offers a string of decent pebble beaches and is a good starting point for hiking up Mount Biokovo in spring and autumn.

What to see in...

...one day
Explore **Split's** magnificent Roman-era Diocletian's Palace and browse the open-air market. Walk along the coast to check out the **Meštrović Gallery**, then hike up on **Marjan** to watch the sunset over town. Stay overnight in a small hotel in the old town or Varoš and feast on a seafood dinner with local wine.

...a weekend or more
Board a ferry to either **Brač** or **Hvar**, where you should divide your time between the beaches (try scuba-diving, windsurfing or sea kayaking) and the cultural sights – the old stone buildings that make up these proud Venetian-era harbour towns.

Split city view.

Split & around

Split is Croatia's second largest city, after Zagreb, and the main point of arrival for visitors to Dalmatia. The old town lies within the walls of Diocletian's Palace – a vast structure commissioned by Roman Emperor Diocletian in AD 295. When the palace was completed in AD 305, Diocletian resigned and retired to his beloved homeland until his death in AD 313.

The palace then lay semi-abandoned until 615, when refugees from Salona – which had been sacked by tribes of Avars and Slavs – found shelter within its sturdy walls, and divided up the imperial apartments into modest living quarters. It thus began to develop into a city in its own right. By the 11th century the settlement had spread beyond the ancient walls, and during the 14th century, an urban conglomeration west of the palace was fortified, thus doubling the city area.

Today it's an extraordinary mix of the old and the new: magnificent ancient buildings, proud baroque palaces, romantic cobbled back streets, a palm-lined seafront promenade with a string of open-air cafés, and a vibrant nightlife. With several well-equipped marinas, it's also Croatia's top base for yacht charter companies, should you wish to explore the region in the best way possible, aboard a sailing boat.

Dioklecijanova Palača

Map: Split, p184.

The heart of the city lies within the massive walls of Diocletian's Palace, a splendid third-century structure combining the qualities of an imperial villa and a Roman garrison. Rectangular in plan, this monumental edifice measures approximately 215 m by 180 m, with walls 2 m thick and 25 m high. Each of the four outer walls bears a gate: Zlatna Vrata (Golden Gate), Željezna Vrata (Iron Gate), Srebrena Vrata (Silver Gate) and Mjedna Vrata (Bronze Gate). Originally, there were two main streets: the Decumanus, a transversal street running east-west from Srebrena Vrata to Vrata, and the Cardo, a longitudinal street running from the main entrance, Zlatna Vrata. Both streets were colonnaded, and intersected at the central public meeting space, Peristil. On the east side of Peristil lay the mausoleum, and on the west, Jupiter's Temple. Diocletian's imperial apartments were located on the south side of the palace, overlooking the sea, while the servants' and soldiers' quarters overlooked the main land entrance. The stone used to build the palace came from the nearby quarries of Brač and Trogir. From the early Middle Ages onwards, new buildings were erected within the palace, so that the original Roman layout has been largely obscured.

Essentials

Bus station At Obala Kneza Domagoja 12, T060-327777, ak-split.hr. For regional bus travel, see page 272.

Ferry The ferry port is immediately in front of the bus and train stations. **Jadrolinija**, jadrolinija.hr, and **Blue Line**, blueline-ferries.com, both operate overnight ferries from Split to Ancona in Italy. Through summer, the Italian company **SNAV**, snav.it, runs a high-speed catamaran to Ancona. Jadrolinija also runs frequent local ferries and catamarans to the surrounding Dalmatian islands.

Train station At Obala Kneza Domagoja 9, T021-338525, national train information, T060-333444, hznet.hr. For regional train travel, see page 272.

ATM Cash machines are plentiful in Split – there are several on the Riva (seafront promenade) just outside the walls of Diocletian's Palace.

Hospital Hospital Firule, Spinčićeva 1, a 15-minute walk east of the centre, T021-556111 (24-hour casualty).

Post office The main post office is at Obala kneza Domogoja, near the bus station and ferry port, and is open daily 0700-2000.

Tourist information There's a tourist information office in the old town at Peristil bb, T021-345606, visitsplit.com. The **Turistički Biro** on the seafront at Obala Hrvatskog narodnog preporoda 12, T021-347100, turistbiro-split.hr, deals with private accommodation in and around Split.

The Peristil, inside Diocletian's Palace.

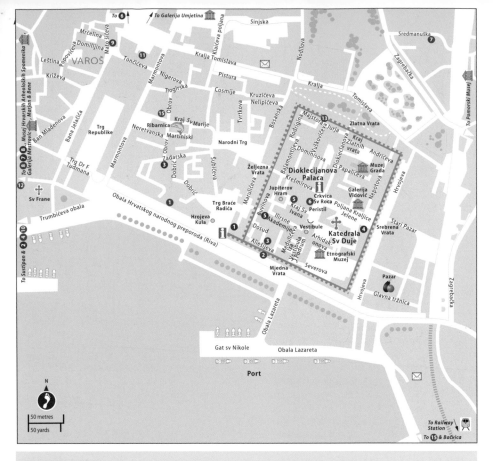

Split listings

❶ Sleeping

1 Hotel B&B Kaštel *1700 Mihovilova Sirina 5*
2 Hotel Jadran *Sustipanjska Put 23*
3 Hotel Marmont *Zadarska 13*
4 Hotel Peristil *Poljana Kraljice Jelena 5*
5 Hotel Slavija *Buvinova 2*
6 Villa Marjela *Jobova 5*
7 Villa Matejuška *Tomića stine 3*
8 Villa Varoš *Miljenko Smoje 1*

❶ Eating & drinking

1 Adriana *Obala Hrvatskog narodnog preporoda 6*
2 Bobis *Obala Hrvatskog narodnog preporoda 20*
3 Dioklecijan (Tri Volta) *Dosud 9*

4 Fife *Trumbićeva obala 11*
5 Kibela *Kraj Sv Ivana 5*
6 Luxor *Peristil bb*
7 Kod Jose *Sredmanuška 4*
8 Konoba Varoš *Ban Mladenova 7*
9 Pizzeria Galija *Tončićeva 12*
10 Restoran Jugo *Between the gardens of Sveti Stipan and the ACI Marina*
11 Rizzo *Tončićeva 6*
12 Šperun *Šperun 3*
13 Teak Caffe *Majstora Jurja 11*
14 Žbirac *Bačvice Bay*
15 Zlatna Ribica *Kraj Sv Marije 8*

Riva (Seafront promenade)

Obala hrvatskog narodnog preporoda.
Map: Split, p184.

In Roman times, the south façade of the palace rose directly from the sea, and ships would have docked immediately in front of the palace walls. Today it gives onto Obala Hrvatskog narodnog preporoda (better known to locals as the Riva, from the Italian, *riva*, meaning 'shore'), a pedestrian-only promenade, lined with palm trees and open-air cafés. In 2007, the Riva was given a €1.3 million facelift, with the installation of controversial new concrete paving and modern, white, retractable awnings for the café terraces. The project was proposed by 3LHD architects from Zagreb.

Podrum

Between Obala Hrvatskog narodnog preporoda and Peristil.
Daily 0600-2300.
Map: Split, p184.

From the Riva, the Mjedna Vrata (Bronze Gate) leads into the underground chambers, which would originally have used as storerooms and maybe a prison. Today, through daylight hours the main passageway, lined with stalls selling handmade souvenirs, is kept open and leads onto Peristil.

Robert Adam

The first detailed plans and drawings of how Diocletian's Palace must have once looked were published in 1764, by the Scottish neoclassical architect, Robert Adam, in *The Ruins of the Palace of the Emperor Diocletian at Spalato in Dalmatia*. Adam, who is generally regarded as the greatest British architect of the 18th century, was fascinated by the scale and quality of Diocletian's building projects, and stayed in Split for five weeks in 1757 to investigate the palace. By asking permission to enter people's houses and inspecting their walls, he managed to trace the original Roman structure through the medieval buildings. This was no easy task – the Venetian governor of the time suspected the Scot of spying and nearly had him deported. Fortunately, Adam completed his research, and the space and symmetry of Diocletian's Palace is said to have inspired some of his greatest buildings, which in turn became models for neoclassical architects throughout Europe.

Peristil

Map: Split, p184.

Ever since Roman times, this spacious central courtyard has been the main public meeting place within the palace walls. It is here that Diocletian would have made his public appearances – probably flanked by a guard, and dressed in a silk toga – and his subjects would have kneeled or even prostrated themselves before him.

The two longer sides of the square are lined with marble columns, topped by Corinthian capitals and richly ornamented cornices linked by arches. On the east side, Diocletian's mausoleum (now the cathedral), is guarded by a black granite Egyptian sphinx dating back to 1500 BC. On the west side, the Roman arches have been incorporated into the 15th-century Grisogono-Cipci Palace, now housing Luxor Café (see box, above).

At the south end of the square, immediately above the podrum exit, four columns mark the monumental arched gateway to the Vestibule, a domed space that served as the main entrance into Diocletian's private living quarters.

Split cathedral.

Katedrala Sveti Duje

Peristil.
Jul-Aug daily 0800-2000, Sep-Jun daily
0800-1200 and 1630-1900. Bell tower: daily
May-Sep 0900-1900, Oct-Apr 0900-1200, 5Kn.
Map: Split, p184.

Diocletian's mausoleum, an octagonal structure
surrounded by 24 columns, now forms the main
body of the Cathedral of St Domnius. Before the
third century, to prevent the spread of disease,
dead bodies (no matter how illustrious) were
disposed of outside the city walls. However,
Diocletian had raised the Emperor's status to that
of divine, so as an 'immortal' he was to be an
exception. Upon his death, he was laid to rest here,
though his body later mysteriously disappeared.

During the seventh century, refugees from
Salona converted the mausoleum into an early
Christian church, ironically dedicating it to Sv
Duje, after Bishop Domnius of Salona, who
Diocletian had had beheaded in AD 304 for
sowing the seeds of Christianity.

In 1214, local sculptor Andrije Buvina carved
the wooden cathedral doors (now kept behind
glass screens in the main entrance). They are quite
magnificent, ornamented with reliefs portraying
28 scenes from the life of Christ.

The interior space is round in plan: eight
columns with Corinthian capitals support a central
dome (symbolizing the Emperor's divine nature),
which would originally have been decorated with
golden mosaics.

In front of the main entrance, the elegant 60-m
Romanesque-Gothic bell tower was constructed
in stages between the 12th and 16th centuries,
but it then collapsed at the end of the 19th century
and had to be rebuilt in 1908. If you have a good
head for heights, climb to the top for a bird's-eye
view of the palace layout.

Galerija Vidović

Poljana Kraljice Jelene bb, T021-360155,
galerija-vidovic.com.
Jun-Sep Tue-Fri 0900-2100, Sat-Sun 1000-1300;
Oct-May Tue-Fri 0900-1600, Sat-Sun 1000-1300,
10Kn.
Map: Split, p184.

Opened in spring 2007, the long-awaited Vidović
Gallery displays bold oil paintings of local sights
by Split's best-known painter, Emanuel Vidović
(1870-1953). He donated these works to the city
when he died.

Pazar

Just outside the eastern wall of Diocletian's Palace.
Mon-Sat 0700-1300, Sun 0700-1100.
Map: Split, p184.

Split's open-air fruit and vegetable market is held
daily just outside the palace walls. It's well worth a
look to size up the season's fresh produce: spinach,
wild asparagus and strawberries in spring;
tomatoes, peaches and melons in summer; grapes,
pomegranates and walnuts in autumn; and
cabbages, potatoes and oranges in winter.
Dalmatians prefer local seasonal produce – while
choice may be limited, quality is assured.

Zlatna Vrata

Map: Split, p184.

The largest and most monumental of the four
palace gates, the Golden Gate originally opened
onto the road to the nearby Roman settlement of
Salona (see page 190). It was walled up during the
14th century, and only uncovered again during the
19th century. Just outside the gate stands a
colossal bronze statue of Grgur Ninski (Bishop
Gregory of Nin) by Ivan Meštrović. The ninth-
century bishop infuriated Rome by campaigning
for the use of the Slav language in the Croatian
Church, as opposed to Latin. The statue of him was
created in 1929 and placed on Peristil (where its
proportions must have been daunting) to mark the

Narodni Trg.

1000th anniversary of the Split Synod. Under Italian occupation in 1941, the statue was seen as a symbol of Croatian nationalism and promptly removed. It was re-erected here in 1957. Touch the big toe on the left foot of the bronze statue of Grgur Ninski; it is considered good luck, and has been worn gold by hopeful passers-by.

Narodni Trg

Map: Split, p184.

Immediately west of Diocletian's Palace lies Split's medieval old town. Here life centres on the Narodni Trg (People's Square), better known to locals as Pjaca, from the Italian, 'piazza'. Paved with gleaming white marble, this is contemporary Split's main square, and you'll find a number of open-air cafés, where you can happily sit and watch the world go by. In the middle of the square stands the former Town Hall, constructed under Venice in 1443, and easily recognized by its three pointed Gothic arches. Nowadays it is used to host temporary art exhibitions.

Ribarnica

Kraj Sv Marije
Mon-Sat 0700-1300, Sun 0700-1100.
Map: Split, p184.

West of Narodni Trg, at the covered fish market you'll find a daily selection of fresh fish and seafood. Locals also call it *peškarija*, from the Italian *pescaria*.

Varoš

Map: Split, p184.

West of the centre, built into the hill leading up to Marjan, Varoš is a labyrinth of winding cobbled streets and traditional Dalmatian stone cottages, dating back to the 17th century. The oldest church in Varoš is the tiny 12th-century Romanesque Sv Nikola (St Nicholas), hidden away in the side street of Stagnja.

Galerija Umjetina

Kralja Tomislava 15, T021-480151, galum.hr.
Tue-Sat 1100-1900, Sun 1000-1300, 20Kn.
Map: Split, p184.

Behind the palace, near the Golden Gate, the Gallery of Fine Arts reopened in May 2009 following renovation. Centring on an internal courtyard garden, it extends over two floors.

The permanent exhibition features icons, old masters, and modern and contemporary art. Croatian works predominate, notably 19th-century portraits of European aristocrats by Vlaho Bukovac, hazy Dalmatian seascapes by Emanuel Vidović, and bronze sculptures by Ivan Meštrović. There are also several pieces by important European artists, including Paolo Veneziano and Egon Schiele.

Pomorski Muzej

Glagoljaška 18, T021-347346, hpms.hr.
Mon-Wed and Fri 0900-1400, Thu 1700-2030,
Sat 0900-1300, 15Kn.
Map: Split, p184.

A 10-minute walk east of the palace walls, past the old stone cottages of Radunica, brings you to the 17th-century Gripe Fortress, built by the Venetians.

Inside is the Maritime Museum. There are two distinct sections, one dedicated to naval war and the other to naval trading. You'll see scale models of ships, sailing equipment and a fine collection of early 20th-century naval paintings by Alexander Kircher. Of particular note are the world's first torpedoes, made in Rijeka in 1866, designed by a Croat, Ivan Blaž Lupis, and manufactured by an Englishman, Robert Whitehead.

Marjan

Map: Split, p184.

West of the historic centre, a 15-minute uphill hike through Varoš brings you to Vidilica Café, where an ample terrace offers panoramic views over the city. From here you can begin to explore Marjan, a nature reserve planted with Aleppo pines, holm oak, cypresses and Mediterranean shrubs such as rosemary and broom, located on a compact peninsula, 3.5 km long. From Vidilica, a path along the southside of Marjan leads to the 13th-century Romanesque church of Sv Nikola (St Nicholas) and, further on, to the 15th-century church of Sv Jere (St Jerome), built on the remains of an ancient temple. At the western tip of Marjan, Bene is a recreation area with a family beach and sports facilities.

Top of Marjan hill.

Sustipan

Map: Split, p184.

The gardens of Sustipan, planted with elegant cypress trees and dotted with benches, offer views out to sea, and over the ACI Marina back to town. A Benedictine monastery was established here in the 11th century, only to be abandoned 300 years later – some ruins from that time can still be seen. The centrepiece to the gardens is a neoclassical pavilion, erected by the French when Split spent a brief period under Napoleon's Illyrian Provinces.

Muzej Hrvatskih Arheoloških Spomenika

Šetalište Ivana Meštrovića bb, 2 km west of town, T021-323901, mhas-split.hr.
Mon-Fri 0900-1600, Sat 1000-1300, 10Kn.
Map: Split, p184.

Overlooking the sea and sheltered to the north by Marjan Hill, you'll find the Museum of Croatian Archaeological Monuments. It displays early Croatian religious art from between the seventh and 12th centuries. Unfortunately only one floor is now in use, many exhibits having been lent to other museums abroad. However, worth seeing are the stone carvings decorated with plaitwork design. In the garden are *stečci*, stone tombs dating back to the cult of the Bogomils, an anti- imperial sect that developed in the Balkans during the 10th century.

Galerija Meštrović

Šetalište Ivana Meštrovića 46, T021-340800, mestrovic.hr.
May-Sep Tue-Sun 0900-1900; Oct-Apr Tue-Sat 0900-1600, Sun 0900-1500, 30Kn.
Map: Split, p184.

Close to the Museum of Croatian Archaeological Monuments lies one of Split's most delightful cultural institutions: the Meštrović Gallery. Croatian sculptor Ivan Meštrović designed this monumental villa in the early 1930s, and used it as his summer residence and studio until fleeing the country during the Second World War. On display in the villa and the garden are 200 sculptures and reliefs, in wood, marble, stone and bronze, created between the beginning of the century and 1946. The entrance ticket is also valid for the Holy Cross Chapel within Kaštelet, a 17th-century complex bought by Meštrović in 1932, which is situated 100 m down the road at Šetalište Ivana Meštrovića 39. Here you can see a cycle of New Testament wood carvings, that are considered to be Meštrović's finest work.

Beaches

Locals generally prefer to go to the islands. However, the main city beach at **Bačvica** is clean and functional; it is possible to rent a sunlounger and umbrella, and there are showers and bars. **Bene**, on the tip of Marjan Peninsula, offers a number of small, secluded, rocky coves backed by pine trees; there are also showers and a bar.

Around Split

Salona

6 km north of Split.

Just outside the modern town of Solin, Salona is Croatia's most important archaeological site. As the largest Roman settlement on the Dalmatian coast, during the third century it is said to have had a population approaching 60,000, who were catered for by a forum, temples, an amphitheatre and *therme* (baths).

Following the legalization of Christianity in AD 313, a Christian community rapidly developed here, and in the early fifth century Salona's bishop became the Metropolitan of the province of Dalmatia. Many churches were built on the Salona site, and the centre moved from the Forum to what is now Manastirine, where a basilica was built over the site of Domnius' grave.

Salona was devastated by the Avars and Slavs in the seventh century, and has lain in ruins ever since. It was the surviving Salonites who founded Split, when they fled to Diocletian's Palace for shelter following the destruction of their homes.

Arheološki Kompleks Salone (Put Starina bb, Solin, T021-212900. Jun-Sep Mon-Fri 0700-1900, Sat 0900-1900, Sun 0900-1300, Oct-May Mon-Sat 0900-1500, 20Kn). At first glance, the Salona Archaeological Site is an overgrown landscape of crumbling stones and fallen columns, but with a site plan (available at the entrance) and a little imagination, you can begin to visualize how it looked as a prosperous Roman settlement.

Manastirine, immediately south of the entrance, is the place where the early Christians buried their martyrs, notably Bishop Domnius. It subsequently became a place of worship, and countless sarcophagi were placed around the bishop's tomb. In the early fifth century a triple-nave basilica was built over the site. The foundations, sections of the crumbling walls and several sarcophagi can still be seen today. Nearby, you can see the second-century *therme* (Roman baths), which opened onto a central courtyard with a large pool.

Built into a hillside in the northwest corner of the site stands Salona's most impressive building, an amphitheatre from the late second century. It was designed to seat 18,000 spectators, and gladiators and wild animals, and later Christians, would have fought here. In the sixth century, Byzantine Emperor Justinian banned gladiator fights, and it was probably used instead for religious and defensive purposes.

Northwest of Split

If you're based in Split, Trogir, a short distance up the coast, with its magnificent UNESCO-listed medieval cathedral, makes a perfect half-day trip out of town. Following the coast further north, you arrive at Šibenik, home to another splendid cathedral, this time Gothic-Renaissance, and an old town built into a hillside overlooking the sea. Inland from Šibenik, Krka National Park comprises a wooded gorge with a series of spectacular thundering waterfalls.

St Lawrence cathedral.

Trogir.

Tip...

Just across the narrow Trogir Channel, on the island of Čiovo, a well-equipped marina makes a base for several companies chartering yachts.

Trogir

Tiny Trogir, 27 km west of Split, sits compact on a small island, connected to the mainland by one bridge and tied to the outlying island of Čiovo by a second. Founded by Greeks from Issa (on the island of Vis) in the third century BC, today Trogir is a romantic huddle of narrow cobbled streets and medieval stone buildings. Once protected by 15th-century city walls, a labyrinth of narrow cobbled streets twists its way between the medieval houses bringing you out on to a splendid main square, overlooked by a monumental 13th-century Romanesque cathedral. In 1997, Trogir was listed a UNESCO World Heritage Site and it is well worth a visit.

The south-facing seafront promenade is lined with cafés and restaurants, and there are also a couple of good, reasonably priced hotels.

Katedrala Sveti Lovrijenac

Trg Ivana Pavla II.
Daily 0900-1200 and 1600-1900.

On Trogir's main square, the Romanesque Cathedral of St Lawrence is a splendid example of medieval architecture. Constructed between 1213 and 1250, its most impressive feature is the main portal, which is sheltered within a spacious vestibule edged by a marble banquette, and adorned with elaborately detailed Romanesque sculpture by Master Radovan. The great door is flanked by a pair of burly lions that form pedestals for the figures of Adam and Eve. Around the portal, scenes from the Bible are mixed with references to everyday peasant life, in an extraordinary orgy of saints, apostles, animals and grotesques.

St Lawrence cathedral interior.

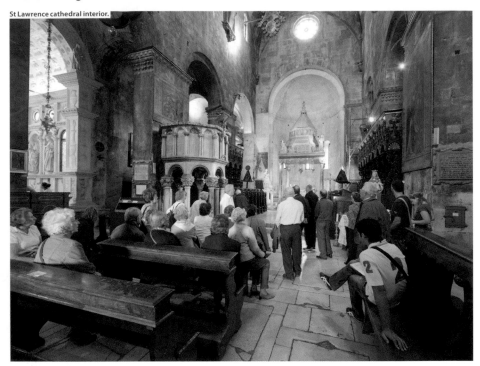

Inside, the cathedral is dimly lit. Look out for the 15th-century chapel to the left of the main aisle, featuring St John of Trogir lying upon a stone sarcophagus, watched over by statues of Mary, Christ, the saints and the apostles.

The cathedral also boasts an elegant 47-m bell tower. Building began in the early 15th century, and took place in successive stages – the first two storeys are Gothic, while the third and final level, in Renaissance style, was completed in 1610. You can climb to the top for stunning views across the ancient rooftops.

Šibenik & around

Some 75 km northwest of Split, Šibenik lies in a protected sea channel, at the mouth of the River Krka. The medieval old town is a warren of steep, winding alleyways and terracotta-roofed houses, built into a hillside below the remains of a Venetian fortress. Close to the seafront, the city's main sight is the monumental Renaissance Cathedral of St Jacob, which is included on the UNESCO list of World Heritage Sites.

Tip...

Šibenik is not geared towards tourists, but you can devote half a day to the historic centre, and it makes a good starting point for a visit to Krka National Park.

Essentials

⊖ **Bus station** Šibenik bus station lies at Draga 14, T060-368368, on the seafront, a five-minute walk from the city centre. For regional bus travel, see page 272.

⊙ **Train station** Šibenik train station, T022-333699, is at Milete bb, south of the bus station, a 10-minute walk from the city centre. For regional train travel, see page 272.

⊖ **ATM** Cash machines are plentiful in both Trogir and Šibenik.

⊕ **Hospital** Šibenik hospital, Stjepana Radića, a 15-minute walk southeast of the centre, T022-246246.

❶ **Tourist information** Trogir tourist office at Trg Ivana Pavla II 1, T021-881412, tztrogir.hr. Šibenik tourist office is at Obala Dr F Tudjmana 5, T022-214411, sibenik-tourism.hr.

On the edge of town, disused factories and sprawling modern suburbs reveal a period of 20th-century industrial development followed by economic collapse caused by the war.

Katedrala Sv Jakova

Trg Republike Hrvatske.
Daily 0900-1900.

Built between 1431 and 1536, the splendid Cathedral of St Jacob was constructed in several stages. The result, a mix of late Gothic and Renaissance styles, is a three-aisle basilica based on the plan of a Latin cross, with a trefoil façade and cupola. The project was initiated by Venetian architects, who worked here for 10 years. They were responsible for the ornate Gothic portals – the main door portrays The Last Judgement, surrounded by the Apostles and crowned by a portrait of Christ, and the side door, the Entrance to Paradise, guarded on either side by a lion, one carrying Adam and the other Eve. In 1441, Juraj Dalmatinac, a Dalmatian from Zadar, who had trained as an architect in Venice, took over. He proposed a far grander edifice, a three-aisle basilica topped by an octagonal cupola, introducing the newly emerging Renaissance style. He also created one of the building's best-loved features – a frieze running around the outer walls, made up of

74 faces, some moustachioed, some turbanned, said to be those citizens too stingy to contribute to the cost of the building. Sadly, Dalmatinac died in 1473, before his masterpiece was completed. The final works were conducted by one of his pupils, Nikola Fiorentinac, who oversaw the mounting of the cupola and the construction of the vaulted roof, employing a unique system of interlocking monolithic stone slabs cut to shape.

The baptistery was designed by Dalmatinac but completed by another of his pupils, Andrija Aleši, an Albanian from Durres. It is to the right of the main altar, and is accessed by a short flight of stone steps. It is an enchanting space, with decorative stonework. The final stone of the building was laid in 1536, and in 1555 it was dedicated to St Jacob.

Krka National Park

16 km north of Šibenik. The National Park office is in Šibenik at Trg Ivana Pavla II 5, T021-201777, npkrka.hr.
Jun-Sep daily 0800-2000, 80Kn, Mar-May and Oct daily 0900-1700, 65Kn, Nov-Feb daily 0900-1500, 25Kn. National park boats leave from Skradin for Skradinski Buk on the hour, departing for the return journey on the half hour. The cost of the ride is included in the entrance ticket.

Krka National Park encompasses a steep-sided, wooded canyon and a series of seven waterfalls. The main entrance is close to Skradinski Buk, the park's most spectacular falls, made up of a series of 17 cascades plunging over 40 m into a wide emerald-green basin, ideal for bathing. Next to the falls, a meadow, bordered by woods, offers an idyllic spot for picnicking. Above Skradinski Buk, a series of wooden bridges and well-marked footpaths lead to the next falls, Roški slap, 10 km to the north. If you don't fancy the hike, it's possible to catch a second national park boat, which runs several times a day, shuttling visitors between the two falls and calling en route at the 15th-century Visovac Samostan (Visovac Monastery) perched on a small island in the middle of Visovačko Jezero (Visovac Lake).

Southeast of Split

South of Split the coastal highway (Magistrala) twists and turns to follow the water's edge, affording fine views over the sea and islands to your right, and the rugged silhouette of the Dinaric Mountains to your left. A succession of coastal villages offers modest pebble beaches and rooms to rent in 1970s concrete-block houses mellowed by draping vines and balconies lined with potted geraniums. The most interesting destinations are Omiš, at the mouth of the Cetina Valley, and Makarska, at the foot of Biokovo mountain, on the so-called Makarska Rivijera.

Coast southeast of Split.

Omiš

28 km southeast of Split.

Omiš lies where the River Cetina emerges from a dramatic gorge to meet the sea. Many people pass straight through, but closer inspection reveals old stone houses and cobbled alleys, a colourful roadside fruit and vegetable market and a small harbour. The scene is presided over by a hilltop fortress backed by the spectacular Omiška Dinara Mountains.

Centuries ago, the people of Omiš were fearsome medieval pirates, who would raid Byzantine and Venetian ships, then sail away up the gorge, out of sight. Today, the town makes an ideal base for exploring the Cetina Gorge, where various agencies organize adventure sports.

There's a town beach just south of the centre, though it's somewhat spoilt by the nearby traffic. better still, head for Ruskamen (6 km southeast), where you'll find a lovely small pebble beach backed by pines with a stretch reserved for nudists.

Omiš.

Rijeka Cetina

With its source in the Dinara Mountains, the River Cetina runs through a gentle valley of green meadows, which in turn becomes a dramatic landscape of spectacular karst formations, the Cetina Gorge. Cutting a high-sided canyon between the mountains of Mosor and Biokovo, it then meets the sea at Omiš. A series of rapids makes the river ideal for rafting, canoeing and kayaking, while the sheer-faced cliffs attract free-climbing enthusiasts (see Activities & tours, page 222). Riverside restaurants serve up freshwater specialities such as trout, eels and frogs, making a welcome change from the omnipresent seafood of the coast.

Makarska

67 km southeast of Split.

Makarska combines the qualities of an old-fashioned Dalmatian port and a modern-day tourist resort. The setting is impressive: a palm-lined seafront promenade is built around a large cove, protected from the open sea by a wooded peninsula to the southwest, and sheltered from the cold bura wind by the craggy limestone heights of Mount Biokovo to the northeast. There's also a pleasant main square, Kačićeva Trg, rimmed with 18th-century baroque buildings. Through

Essentials

⊖ **Bus station** Makarska bus station, T021-612333, is on the main road above town. For regional bus travel, see page 272.

⊇ **Ferry Jadrolinija**, jadrolinija.hr, runs daily ferries from Makarska to Sumartin on the eastern tip of the island of Brač.

⊕ **ATM** Cash machines are plentiful in both Omiš and Makarska.

⊕ **Hospital** The nearest hospital is in Split.

❶ **Tourist information** Omiš tourist office is at Trg Kneza Miroslava bb, T021-861350, tz-omis.hr. **Makarska** tourist office is at Obala Kralja Tomislava 16, T021-612002.

Five of the best

Nudist beaches in Central Dalmatia

❶ **Nugal** Makarska. This lovely pebble beach sits in a small cove backed by steep cliffs, a 2-km walk east of Makarska.
❷ **Paklina** Island of Brač. A pebble beach and series of rocky coves, at the west end of the more commercial beach of Zlatni Rat, in Bol.
❸ **Jerolim** Island of Hvar. One of the scattered Pakleni islands, Jerolim is devoted to naturism and served by regular taxi boats from the harbour in Hvar Town.
❹ **Galerija Plavac** Zečevo, Island of Hvar. Popular with nudists since the 1960s, this islet has pebble beaches backed by pinewoods, and is served by taxi boats from Jelsa.
❺ **Žbirac** Srebrena, Island of Vis. Made up of smooth white pebbles (*srebrena* means silver), plus a series of rocky 'shelves', Srebrena is near Rukavac, on Vis's southeast coast.

summer it makes a perfect base for exploring the so-called Makarska Rivijera, a 60-km stretch of coast offering some of the best mainland beaches, while keen walkers are drawn to the rugged landscapes and rural villages of Biokovo Nature Park during spring and autumn.

Tourism here dates back to 1914, when the first hotel opened. In the 1970s, a string of modern hotels and houses with rooms to let were built along the coast. Today, come summer it's overrun with young visitors and families from all over Europe, who are drawn by its beaches, vibrant nightlife and reasonably priced accommodation.

Beaches Makarska's town beach, **Donja Luka**, is a 10-minute walk west of the centre and has umbrellas and sun loungers for hire, water-sports facilities and beach bars. East of the centre, a lovely 2-km footpath leads through pinewoods, following the coast, to arrive at **Nugal**, a pebble beach in a small cove backed by steep cliffs, which is popular with nudists (see box, above).

You might also check out some of the small low-key resorts of the **Makarska Rivijera**, which stretches from Brela in the north to Gradac in the south. Of these, Brela, Baška Voda and Tučepi all have fine pebble beaches and are served by local buses running along the coast from Makarska.

Makarska village.

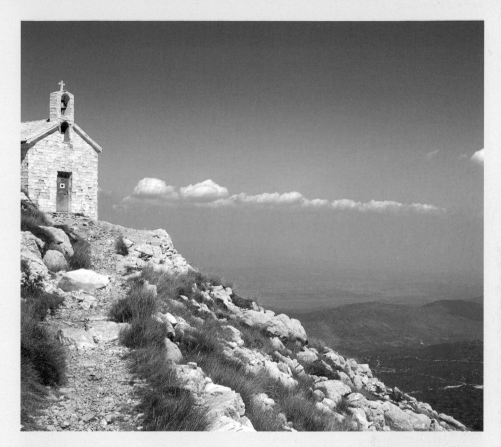

Mount Biokovo

Behind Makarska, a network of clearly marked footpaths lead up Mount Biokovo, a barren rocky karst landscape with scanty pastures and bare limestone rocks supporting only the hardiest indigenous species, such as chamois goats and mouflon sheep. From Makar, a semi-abandoned cluster of old stone cottages, a well-marked trail leads to the peak of **Vošac** (1440 m), which can be walked in four hours, while another trail departs from Kotišina to reach the same peak in five hours. From Vošac, the terrain becomes increasingly rocky, though hardened hikers can attempt a final 1½-hour pull to the highest peak, **Sveti Jure** (1760 m). The summit is capped by a slightly disheartening radio and TV transmitter, while its namesake, the tiny stone chapel of Sv Jure, is close by, but remains closed for most of the year. On a clear day you can see across the Adriatic Sea to Italy and inland to Bosnia Herzegovina. See Activities & tours, page 223, for agencies organizing hiking tours.

If the hike up looks too stiff, hire a jeep and drive from Makarska up to Sveti Jure (31 km). Take the road for Vrgorac, then swing sharp left for the park and follow a series of hairpin bends to the summit.

Island of Brač

As the closest island to Split and the only island in Dalmatia with an airport, Brač has the advantage of being easily accessible. The disadvantage of this, however, is that it has lost a degree of its island identity.

Its largest town and chief ferry port is Supetar. While the bulk of foreigners pass straight through, on their way to the more prestigious resort of Bol, many families from the mainland have summer homes in Supetar itself. It's a pleasant enough place, with the old town focusing on a crescent-shaped harbour, and a decent bathing area, backed by several large hotels, west of the centre. There is little of cultural interest here, though the town cemetery is noted for its beautifully carved tombstones.

The island's top destination is Bol, home to the lovely beach of Zlatni Rat, presided over by Vidova Gora, the highest peak on any of the Adriatic islands. Bol is crawling with tourists during July and August, but if you manage to visit outside peak season it's well worth it for the fantastic beach.

Bol.

Bol

On the south coast of Brač, Bol is home to Croatia's most-photographed beach, the spectacular Zlatni Rat. This once-idyllic little fishing village has somewhat lost its charm due to the rampant success brought upon it by its beach – it's one of Croatia's top package destinations, with several big hotels and a miniature train running from the village to the beach – but if you can visit outside peak season, it's more than worth the trip. The village itself is made of old stone cottages clustered round a pretty harbour filled with coloured wooden fishing boats. A short walk east of the harbour, the 15th-century Dominican Monastery is set in gardens overlooking the sea.

Zlatni Rat

2 km from Bol.

A pleasant tree-lined promenade leads 2 km from the village of Bol to the renowned beach of Zlatni Rat (Golden Cape). The promenade, overlooked by the big package hotels (discreetly hidden by the trees), makes a pleasurable walk (there are no buses). An extraordinary geographical feature, it's composed of fine shingle and runs 500 m perpendicular to the coast, moving and changing its shape slightly from season to season, depending on local winds and currents. It's a perfect beach for children as the water is shallow and the seabed easy on their feet. It's also Croatia's number one site for windsurfing (see Activities & tours, page 223. A cluster of pines at the top end of the cape offer respite from the sun, and there's a bar selling cold drinks and snacks. As well as Zlatni Rat there's a stretch reserved for nudists, known as **Paklina**, just 200 m west of the cape (see box, page 198).

Vidova Gora

The highest peak (778 m) on all the Croatian islands, offers a bird's-eye view of Zlatna Rat and Bol, plus distant views of Hvar, Vis, Pelješac Peninsula and Korčula. There's also a small *konoba*

(see Eating & drinking, page 217) serving local specialities. It's possible to walk or bike up, though the less athletic might opt for a tour by minibus. Enquire at Bol tourist office for details.

Pustinja Blaca

13 km west of Bol.

The impressive monastery complex of Blaca Hermitage is built into the cliffside high above the coast. It's possible to reach Blaca Bay by boat from the harbour in Bol – just as the monks used to do – and then walk up. The hermitage was founded by monks from Poljica, on the mainland, who fled here to escape the Turks in 1550. Originally they took shelter in a cave, subsequently building the church and hermitage, and later opening a printing press and a school for children from nearby hamlets. The last monk to live here, Father Niko Miličević Mladi, was a keen astrologer. He set up an observatory in 1926 and, besides his astronomical tools, left behind a collection of old clocks. Visitors can see these, along with the old-fashioned kitchen, an armoury and a display of period furniture. Blaca is on the UNESCO World Heritage 'Tentative List'.

Island of Hvar

A long, thin island, trendy Hvar is a land of vineyards, lavender fields and old Venetian coastal villages with an altogether slower, more pleasurable way of life than the mainland. The most popular and by far and away the most charming resort is Hvar Town. Close by, on the western end of the island, is Stari Grad, the main ferry port, and Jelsa, a pleasant fishing village and low-key seaside resort. The eastern end of Hvar is sparsely populated and offers little of cultural interest.

Hvar.

Hvar Town is probably Croatia's most fashionable resort after Dubrovnik. Old stone houses are built into the slopes of three hills surrounding a bay, with the highest peak crowned by a Venetian fortress, which is floodlit by night. Café life centres on the magnificent main square, giving directly onto the harbour and backed by a 16th-century cathedral. The bay is protected from the open sea to the south by the scattered Pakleni Otoci (Pakleni islets), which are covered with dense pine forests and rimmed by rocky shores, offering secluded coves for bathing.

Hvar Town is a favourite overnight port of call for sailing boats and many people come here exclusively for the nightlife – it's been billed the Croatian Ibiza. Expect hip design hotels, upmarket seafood eateries, chi-chi cocktail bars and occasional celebrities – recent illustrious visitors include George Clooney, Sharon Stone and Roman Abramovich.

Trg Sv Stjepan

St Stephen's Square.
Map: Split, p204.

This, the largest piazza in Dalmatia, dates back to the 13th century. The east end is backed by the cathedral, while the west end opens out onto the Mandrac, an enclosed harbour for small boats, which in turn gives onto the bay. The paving dates from 1780 and in the centre stands a well from 1520. Today many of the old buildings lining the square house popular cafés, restaurants and galleries at street level.

Essentials

➜ **Ferry** The main ferry port is Stari Grad, served by regular Jadrolinija ferries from Split. **Jadrolinija**, jadrolinija.hr, also runs a daily catamaran from Split to the island of Lastovo (South Dalmatia), stopping at Hvar Town and Vela Luka (island of Korčula) en route. In addition, the same company runs a high-speed catamaran from Split to Jelsa, calling at Bol (island of Brač) en route.

○ ATM There are cash machines in Hvar Town (on the seafront), Stari Grad and Jelsa.

⊕ **Hospital** The nearest hospital is in Split on the mainland.

✛ **Pharmacy** You will find pharmacies in Hvar Town (T021-741002), Stari Grad (T021-765061) and Jelsa (T021-761108).

➔ **Post office** There are post offices in Hvar Town, Stari Grad and Jelsa.

ℹ **Tourist information** Hvar Town tourist office is at Trg Sv Stjepana bb, T021-741059, tzhvar.hr. **Stari Grad tourist office** is at Nova Riva 2, T021-765763, stari-grad-faros.hr. **Jelsa tourist office** is at Riva bb, T021-761017, tzjelsa.hr.

Trg Sv Stjepan.

Hvar Town listings

❶ **Sleeping**
1 Aparthotel Pharia *Majerovića bb*
2 Hotel Podstine *Pod Stine*
3 Hotel Riva *Riva bb*
4 Palmižana *Sveti Klement*
5 Villa Town Gate *Hektorovićeva 1*

❶ **Eating & drinking**
1 Alviž *Dolac bb*
2 Konoba Menego *Groda bb*
3 Luna *Grod bb*
4 Macondo *Groda bb*
5 Yakša *Petra Hektorovića bb*

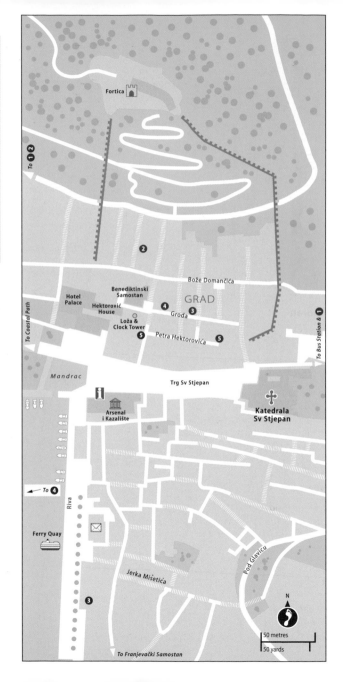

Trg Sv Stjepan and the cathedral.

Katedrala Sv Stjepan

Trg Sv Stjepana bb, Hvar Town, T021-741152.
Daily 0700-1200 and 1700-1900 (in summer it
sometimes stays open all day).
Map: Hvar Town, p204.

Providing a majestic backdrop to the main square,
St Stephen's Cathedral was built in stages between
the 16th and 17th centuries on the foundations of
an earlier monastery, to produce a trefoil façade
standing in perfect harmony with a four-storey bell
tower. There is also a treasury.

Arsenal i Kazalište

Trg Sv Stjepana bb, Hvar Town, T021-741009.
Under restoration at the time of writing but
should be open in for summer 2010.
Map: Hvar Town, p204.

On the south corner of the main square, looking
onto the harbour, the 16th-century Arsenal is easily
identified by its huge front arch, which allowed
Venetian galleys to dock inside for repair work.
    The upper floor houses the Arsenal Gallery,
displaying a collection of paintings by local artists.

Passing through the gallery you arrive at the
theatre, which opened in 1612 and welcomed all
citizens regardless of their social standing, making
it one of the first institutions of its kind in Europe.
The interior was refurbished in 1803, and is still
used for performances today.

Franjevački Samostan

Križa bb, Hvar Town, T021-741193.
Summer daily 1000-1200, 1700-1900,
winter daily 1000-1200, 20Kn.
Map: Hvar Town, p204.

South of the centre, a pleasant seafront path leads
to the 15th-century Franciscan Monastery. The
entrance is through a charming cloister – used for
classical music concerts during the summer festival
– into the former refectory, now a museum. The
most impressive piece on show is undoubtedly *The
Last Supper*, a vast 17th-century canvas by an
unknown Venetian artist, measuring 2.5 m by 8 m.
The refectory opens onto a beautiful garden, with
a magnificent 300-year-old cypress tree,
overlooking the sea.

Around the region

Fortica

Hvar Town, T021-742620.
Summer daily 0800-2400, winter by
appointment, 20Kn.
Map: Hvar Town, p204.

Above town, a winding footpath leads through a
garden of dense Mediterranean planting, to arrive
at the fortress. A medieval castle once stood here,
though the present structure was erected by the
Venetians in 1557, and the ochre-coloured barracks
were added by the Austrian military authorities
during the 19th century. From the ramparts, you
have fantastic views down onto the town and
harbour, and out across the sea to the Pakleni islets.

Beaches

The nearest beach to the centre of Hvar Town is
Bonj Les Bains, a concrete bathing area rimmed by
a 1930s stone colonnade and overlooked by the
vast Hotel Amfora. It's a 10-minute walk west of
town, though you need to pay for the sunloungers
and private cabanas (reservations recommended).

For a more back-to-nature experience, take a
taxi-boat (0800-2000) from Hvar Town's harbour to
the Pakleni islets. Covered with dense pine forests
and surrounded by rocky shores, they offer
secluded pebble coves for bathing. The nearest
islet, **Jerolim**, is predominantly nudist, while the
largest, **Sveti Klement**, is home to an ACI sailing
marina and the lovely boho-chic retreat of
Palmižana (see Sleeping, page 213).

To join the see-and-be seen crowd, head for
Stipanksa (also one of the Pakleni islets), where
Carpe Diem Stipanska (carpe-diem-beach.com,
Jun-Sep 1000-1900) is a smart beach club with a
pool, restaurant, bar, two beach areas lined with
palm umbrellas and teak lounge chairs, a beach
volleyball court and a diving centre.

Stari Grad

Stari Grad is Hvar's oldest settlement and chief ferry
port. It's a more relaxed, slightly less swish resort
than Hvar Town, with an easygoing village
atmosphere. Founded by Greeks from the Aegean
island of Paros in 385 BC, it was originally known as
Pharos. Little of the original Greek settlement
remains today, other than the 11-m-long **Cyclop's
Wall**, now a UNESCO World Heritage Site, which is
made up of massive stone blocks and can be
traced through some of the buildings on the
south side of the bay.

Today, most of the buildings in the old part of
town date from the 16th and 17th centuries – the
best examples can be seen on Škor, a picturesque
square enclosed by baroque houses. However,
there aren't many great beaches or decent hotels,
and little of cultural interest other than the
16th-century Hektorović House.

Tvrdalj (Trg Tvrdalj, Stari Grad, T021-765068;
Jul-Aug daily 1000-1300, 1700-2000, May-Jun and
Sep-Oct daily 1000-1300, Nov-Apr by request,
15Kn) Stari Grad's best-loved building is the
fortified Hektorović House, on the south side of the
bay, in the old town. It was built by Petar
Hektorović (1487-1572) in 1520, as a home for him
and his friends, and also as a place of refuge for the
entire town, in the event of a Turkish invasion.
Hektorović was a local aristocratic landowner, who
had been educated in Italy and became one of
Dalmatia's most prominent Renaissance poets.
Tvrdalj's centrepiece is a long rectangular fishpond,
surrounded by a fine cloister, around which the
living quarters, domestic area and servant quarters
are arranged. The walls of the interior bear many
plaques, with witty and philosophical inscriptions
in both Croatian and Latin, and there's a walled
garden where Hektorović cultivated both
indigenous Mediterranean and exotic plants.

Stari Grad.

Jelsa

10 km east of Stari Grad.

Jelsa is a lively fishing town and seaside resort, built around a natural harbour. Everyday life focuses on the 19th-century seafront promenade, lined with cheerful cafés and pizzerias, while to each side of the bay, dense pinewoods have been used to conceal a number of large hotel complexes, built during the 1970s.

Jelsa in connected to Bol on the island of Brač by a daily catamaran service – something to bear in mind if you want to visit both islands without returning to Split first.

Humac

8 km east of Jelsa.

A poorly maintained local road leads all the way to Sućuraj, on the eastern tip of the island. If you follow this road for 8 km, you'll see a sign to the right for Humac. Walk the final 400 m along a rough track, to arrive at a romantic cluster of abandoned stone cottages, founded as a temporary dwelling for shepherds in the 16th century. No one lives here anymore, but during summer it's possible to eat at the unforgettable **Konoba Humac** (see Eating & drinking, page 219).

A 30-minute walk from Humac, **Grapčeva Špilja** is a vast chamber of underground stalactites and stalagmites, with traces of human civilization from the third millennium BC. Through summer (June-September) you can visit the cave with a guide. Contact Jelsa tourist office for details.

Island of Vis

Closed to foreigners until 1989 due to the presence of a Yugoslav naval base, Croatia's most distant inhabited island was spared the commercial brand of tourism that flourished along much of the Adriatic during the 1970s. It's now rapidly developing into a discreet but rather upmarket destination, thanks to its wild, rugged landscapes and the insight it offers into the way people once lived throughout Dalmatia. The two main settlements, Vis Town and Komiža, both lie on the coast, while there are also about a dozen semi-abandoned inland villages. There is limited holiday accommodation, but the restaurants are truly wonderful, the wines, notably the white Vugava and the red Viški Plavac, are organically produced, and there are several peaceful beaches where you can soak up the sun and swim in crystal-clear waters, said to be among the cleanest in the Adriatic.

Vis island.

Essentials

⛴ **Ferry** The main ferry port is in Vis Town, served by daily **Jadrolinija**, jadrolinija.hr, ferries from Split.
⑤ **ATM** Cash machines are plentiful in Vis and Komiža, but not in smaller settlements.
⊕ **Hospital** The nearest hospital is in Split, on the mainland.
✚ **Pharmacy** There are pharmacies in Vis Town and Komiža.
⤷ **Post office** There are post offices in Vis Town and Komiža.
❶ **Tourist information** Vis Town tourist office is at Šetalište Stare Isse 5, T021-717017, tz-vis.hr. **Komiža tourist office** is at Riva Sv Mikule 2, T021-713455, tz-komiza.hr.

Vis Town

On the north coast of Vis, this is the island's largest town and chief port. The ancient Greeks founded Issa, their first colony in Dalmatia, on the slopes above the northwest part of the bay, in 389 BC. Unfortunately there's not much left of it today, but excavations have unearthed finds now on display in the archaeological museums in both Split and Vis itself. The Vis Town you see today grew out of two separate settlements, Kut and Luka, which have joined together to form a 3-km string of buildings, ranging from humble fishermen's cottages to noble baroque villas, hugging the large sheltered bay. Jutting out into the bay, Prirov Peninsula is capped by a proud 16th-century Franciscan monastery. The entire scene is backed by craggy hills, promising the wild, unspoilt landscapes of the interior. Through summer, yachts moor up along the seafront, their crews drawn by Vis's authentic fish restaurants and fine wines.

Komiža

18 km southwest of Vis Town.

On the west coast of Vis, this friendly fishing village is built around a small harbour. Old stone buildings with wooden shutters and terracotta-tiled roofs line a series of narrow alleys, each of which runs down to the seafront. Here, locals of all generations meet for morning coffee, conduct their evening promenade and put the world to rights. Above the village, from the weather-beaten slopes of Hum Hill, a 13th-century monastery surveys the open waters of the Adriatic and the outlying islet of Biševo, home to the Blue Cave. Through winter 20 or so fishing boats animate the harbour but, come summer, elegant yachts from all parts of Europe call here. It's probably one of the most unspoilt places on all the islands in a fantastic setting and with excellent restaurants.

Modra Spilja

On the east coast of the islet of Biševo, 5 km southwest of Komiža.

Biševo's Blue Cave is often compared to the Blue Cave on Capri, Italy. Some 24 m long, 12 m wide and with water 10-20 m deep, sunlight enters the cave through a submerged side entrance, passes through the water and reflects off the seabed, casting the interior in a magnificent shade of blue. Small boats ferry visitors in and out to see this natural wonder. You can visit the cave as part of an organized day trip from Komiža. Excursions are planned so you enter the cave around midday when the light is at its best, then continue to the west side of Biševo for a few hours in Porat Uvala (Porat Bay), where there's a pleasant sand beach and a couple of simple restaurants. Boats depart at 0900 from the harbour and return at 1700. Enquire at Komiža tourist office for further details.

Beaches

In Komiža, the main town beach, **Gospa Guzarica**, lies west of the centre in front of Hotel Komiža and has a diving club. Southeast of Komiža town centre, **Kamenica** beach is home to the Aquarius open-air club. Some of the best beaches are on the southeast coast of Vis. If you have a car, head for Rukavac, where you'll find **Uvala Srebrena** (Silver Bay), a popular bathing spot backed by pinewoods with a series of white rocky ledges stepping down to the water, or Milna, where the small beach in **Uvala Zaglav** (Zaglav Bay) offers shallow water suitable for kids.

Listings
Sleeping

Split

Diocletian's Palace & the historic centre

Hotel Marmont €€€€
Zadarska 13, T021-308060,
marmonthotel.com.
Map: Split, p184.
Opened in summer 2008, this chic hotel occupies a restored 15th-century building near Narodni Trg, the main square. It has 21 smart rooms with minimalist furniture and oak floors, flat-screen TV and Wi-Fi. There's also a first-floor terrace café with potted olive trees.

Hotel Peristil €€€
Poljana Kraljice Jelena 5,
T021-329070, hotelperistil.com.
Map: Split, p184.
Within the palace walls, next to Srebrena Vrata, this small hotel has 12 rooms – the best ones have views onto the Roman Peristil and the cathedral. Restaurant, great location, helpful staff, plus a lovely terrace out front where breakfast is served through the summer months.

Hotel Slavija €€€
Buvinova 2, T021-323840,
hotelslavija.com.
Map: Split, p184.
Within the walls of Diocletian's Palace, this building dates from the 17th century and has been a hotel since 1900, making it the oldest in town. It was fully renovated in 2004 and now has

25 basic but comfortable rooms. The location is fantastic, if you don't mind the noise from surrounding bars. The best rooms are on the top floor and have private terraces.

Hotel B&B Kaštel 1700 €€
Mihovilova Sirina 5, T021-343912,
kastelsplit.com.
Map: Split, p184.
Brilliantly located, overlooking the palm-lined seafront promenade, but entered from around the back, off Vočni Trg. There are 10 rooms, all with wooden floors and simple furniture, plus air conditioning, satellite TV, minibar and hairdryer. The staff are friendly and helpful, there's an internet corner next to reception, plus a breakfast room with exposed Roman stone walls.

Outside the historic centre

Hotel Jadran €€
Sustipanjska Put 23, T021-398622, hoteljadran.hr.
Map: Split, p184.
Overlooking Uvala Zvončac, close to the gardens of Sveti Stipan, this pleasant but basic 1970s hotel has 30 rather dated rooms and two suites, most with a sea view and balcony. In summer, guests have the use of an outdoor swimming pool, gym and sauna.

Villa Marjela €€
Jobova 5, T021-384623,
villamarjela.hr.
Map: Split, p184.
A 15-minute walk northwest of the old town, near Poljud Stadium, this friendly family-run hotel has eight comfortable rooms, all with wooden floors, air conditioning and TV, plus decent bathrooms. It's a peaceful place and reasonably priced.

Villa Matejuška €€
Tomića stine 3, T021-321086,
villamatejuska.hr.
Map: Split, p184.
In a narrow cobbled alley in Varoš, one block back from the seafront, this old stone building has been renovated to make a small family-run hotel. There are six apartments, each with air conditioning, satellite TV, Wi-Fi and a fully equipped kitchenette. Breakfast is served in the ground-floor Konoba Matejuška.

Villa Varoš €
Miljenko Smoje 1, T021-483469,
villavaros.hr.
Map: Split, p184.
In Varoš, this small family-run hotel occupies a traditional Dalmatian stone building with green wooden window shutters. There are eight basic but comfortable rooms, plus one apartment with a terrace and jacuzzi. Breakfast is served at the nearby Konoba Pizzeria Leut, looking out over the fishing boats of Matejuška.

Trogir

Hotel Pašike €€
Sinjska bb, T021-885185,
hotelpasike.com.
This small hotel in the old town
has 14 rooms with antique
furniture and modern en suite
bathrooms, plus one apartment
with a hydro-massage tub. On
the ground floor, Konoba Pašike
serves barbecued Dalmatian
meat and fish dishes at outdoor
tables, with live music. A double
in August costs 800Kn.

Hotel Tragos €€
Budislavićeva 3, T021-884729,
tragos.hr.
In an 18th-century baroque
palace in the old town, Tragos
has 12 simply furnished, modern
rooms, decorated in warm
creams and yellows. In the
courtyard garden, Restaurant
Tragos serves Dalmatian
favourites such as *pasticada*
(beef stewed in sweet wine) and
brudet (fish stewed in a tomato
and onion). They also offer free
parking and transfers to and
from the airport.

Villa Sikaa Hotel €€
Obala kralja Zvonimira 13,
T021-881223, vila-sikaa-r.com.
This small family-run hotel
occupies an 18th-century villa
looking out over Trogir Channel
with a view back to the old town.
The eight rooms and two suites
have wooden floors and newly
tiled bathrooms.

Šibenik & around

Hotel Skradinski Buk €€
Burinovac bb, Skradin,
T022-771771, skradinskibuk.hr.
On the edge of Krka National
Park, this small family-run hotel
occupies a carefully renovated
old stone building in the centre
of Skradin. There are 28 rooms,
and a third-floor terrace offering
views down onto the River Krka.

Jadran Hotel €€
Obala Franje Tudjmana 52,
T022-242000, rivijera.hr.
In the centre of Šibenik, on the
seafront promenade, just a
five-minute walk from the bus
station and the cathedral, this
hotel provides 57 smart,
comfortable rooms. There's
also a restaurant and café
with outdoor tables overlooking
the water.

The Konoba €€
Andrije Kačića 8, T022-214397,
bbdalmatia.com.
In Šibenik's old town, this B&B
occupies two traditional stone
buildings. The five rooms all
have wooden floors and antique
furniture, and three have en suite
bathrooms. The Dutch owner
prepares an excellent breakfast,
and there's a roof terrace with
views out to sea.

Omiš

Hotel Villa Dvor €€
Mosorska cesta 13, T021-863444,
hotel-villadvor.hr.
Built into a cliff overlooking
the River Cetina, this hotel has 23
comfortable rooms and a terrace
restaurant affording impressive
views onto the canyon. It's
approached up a steep flight of
106 stone steps. The hotel boat
shuttles guests down the river to
nearby beaches.

Makarska

Hotel Biokovo €€€
Obala Kralja Tomislava bb,
T021-615401, hotelbiokovo.hr.
Comprising 55 rooms and one
apartment, this pleasant,
old-fashioned hotel in the centre
of town was fully refurbished in
2004, and has a ground floor café
and restaurant giving onto the
seaside promenade, and a small
wellness centre.

Hotel Osejava €€€
Šetalište Dr Fra Jure Radića,
T021-604300, osejava.com.
Opened in summer 2009, this
hotel has a cool minimalist pop
interior and stands on the
seafront, a 10-minute walk from
the main town beach. There are
40 rooms and five suites, each
with an oversized photo of a
landscape, seascape or cityscape
covering an entire wall, and a
slick bathroom with a glass door,
making it visible from the

Eating & drinking

Komiža

Villa Kamenica €€
*Mihovila Pavlinovića 15,
T021-713883, villa-kamenica.hr.*
Just a five-minute walk from the
harbour, this villa is set in a lush
garden with lemon trees and
lavender, a barbecue and a big
outdoor table. There are three
apartments, each with air
conditioning, satellite TV, a fully
equipped kitchenette and a
furnished balcony. The owners
are kind and helpful and full of
local advice.

Villa Nonna €€
*Ribarska 50, T021-713500,
villa-nonna.com.*
This old stone townhouse,
overlooking the harbour, was
renovated in 2005 to provide
seven bright and airy
apartments, each named after
a local plant and painted in
appropriate shades. Expect
wooden floors and some
exposed stonework, air
conditioning, satellite TV and
a fully equipped kitchenette.

Split

Diocletian's Palace & the historic centre

Dioklecijan (Tri Volta) €
Dosud 9, no phone.
Daily lunch and dinner.
Map: Split, p184.
Known affectionately as Tri Volta,
after the three arches on the
terrace that form part of the
palace walls, this bar is popular
with local fishermen. You can get
merenda here the year through:
early morning helpings of hearty
dishes such as *gulaš* (goulash)
and *tripice* (tripe). During summer
the menu is refined and
extended to cater for tourists.

Kibela €
*Kraj Sv Ivana 5, in front of
Jupiter's Temple, T021-346205.*
Daily lunch and dinner.
Map: Split, p184.
Hidden away in a passageway off
Peristil, this small family-run bar
serves up simple *merenda* at
lunchtime. During winter, the
house speciality is *fažol sa
kobasicom* (beans and sausage).

Cafés & bars

Luxor
Peristil bb, T021-341082.
Map: Split, p184.
Ideal stopping place while
sightseeing, on Peristil opposite
the cathedral. They do light
snacks as well as drinks, and even
put cushions out so you can sit
on the Roman steps if all the
tables are full. There's a rather

formal restaurant on the first
floor, under the same
management as Hotel Marmont.

Teak Caffe
*Majstora Jurja 11, close to
Zlatna Vrata.*
Map: Split, p184.
Still 'in' with locals, probably
because of the free newspapers,
Teak's smart interior comprises
rough stone walls and polished
woodwork. There are several
tables outside in summer.

Outside the historic centre

Kod Jose €€€-€€
*Sredmanuška 4, just outside the
palace walls, close to Zlatna
Vrata, T021-347397.*
Daily lunch and dinner.
Map: Split, p184.
This typical Dalmatian *konoba*
combines rough stone walls,
heavy wooden tables and
candlelight. Top dishes are the
risottos and fresh fish – the
choice changes daily so you'll
need to ask to see what's on
offer. The discreet waiters
deserve a special mention.

Konoba Varoš €€€-€€
*Ban Mladenova 7, between the
centre and Marjan, T021-396138.*
Daily lunch and dinner.
Map: Split, p184.
Less atmospheric than Kod Jose,
though some believe the food to
be better here. The walls are
decorated with seascapes and
paintings of ships, and the ceiling
hung with fishing nets.

Restoran Jugo €€€-€€
Close to Hotel Jadran, between
the gardens of Sveti Stipan and
the ACI Marina, T021-398900.
Daily lunch and dinner.
Map: Split, p184.
Worth the 15-minute walk from
the centre for its summer terrace
with views of the marina, and a
fantastic view of the city behind.
Serves up passable Dalmatian
dishes and pizza.

Adriana €€
Obala Hrvatskog narodnog
preporoda 6, T021-344079.
Daily lunch and dinner.
Map: Split, p184.
A large and boisterous restaurant
in the centre, with an ample
terrace overlooking the seafront.
Popular dishes include *rižot fruta*
di mare (seafood risotto), *pohani*
sir (cheese fried in breadcrumbs),
frigane lignje (fried squid) and
ražnjići (kebabs). It gets very
crowded in summer, and the
music is often rather loud.

Šperun €€
Šperun 3, T021-346999.
Daily lunch and dinner.
Map: Split, p184.
In a side street between the
Riva and Varoš, this cosy but
sophisticated restaurant offers
typical Dalmatian dishes such
as *brodet* (fish stew), *bakalar*
(dried cod) and *crni rižot* (risotto
prepared in cuttlefish ink).

Fife €
Trumbićeva obala 11,
T021-345223.
Daily lunch and dinner.
Map: Split, p184.
Overlooking Matejuška, where
fishermen from Varoš keep
their boats, this eatery is truly
local and down-to-earth. The
menu changes daily: look out
for *juha* (soup), *crni rižot* (risotto
prepared with cuttlefish ink)
and *palačinke* (pancakes).

Pizzeria Galija €
Tončićeva 12, T021-347932.
Daily lunch and dinner.
Map: Split, p184.
Close to the fish market, Galija
reputedly does the best pizzas in
town, plus pasta dishes and
salads. The informal atmosphere
and set up – wooden tables and
benches, draught beer and wine
by the glass – make it popular
with locals. The owner, Željko
Jerkov, is an Olympic gold
medal-winning basketball player.

Rizzo €
Tončićeva 6, T021-348349.
Daily lunch and dinner.
Map: Split, p184.
Excellent sandwich bar, hidden
away between the fish market
and Pizzeria Galija. Oven-warm
bread rolls are filled with
cheese, salami, tuna and salad
of your choice.

Zlatna Ribica €
Kraj Sv Marije 8, T021-348710.
Mon-Fri until 2000 and Sat
until 1400.
Map: Split, p184.
This stand-up seafood eatery
is five minutes from to the fish
market, so everything on offer is
guaranteed to be fresh. Try *girice*
(small fried fish) or *frigane ligne*
(fried squid), accompanied by a
glass of *bevanda* (half white wine,
half water).

Cafés & bars
Bobis
Obala Hrvatskog narodnog
preporoda 20, T021-347962.
Daily lunch and dinner.
Map: Split, p184.
With tables outside lining the
seafront promenade, Bobis is
known for its *krafne* (doughnuts)
and *pita sa sirom* (cheese pie) as
well as coffee and drinks.

Žbirac
Bačvice Bay, zbirac.hr.
Daily lunch and dinner.
Map: Split, p184.
Overlooking the beach and
much loved by locals, this
low-key café has outdoor tables
on a wooden deck shaded by
tamarisk trees.

Trogir

Restaurant Fontana €€€
Obrov 1, T021-884811.
Daily lunch and dinner.
This highly esteemed
restaurant has tables outside
on a waterfront terrace through
summer. The fish and seafood
dishes can be pricey; pizza
is a cheaper option.

Čelica €€
Čiovo bridge, T021-882344.
Daily lunch and dinner.
This old wooden car ferry,
anchored by Čiovo bridge,
has been converted to form
an unusual restaurant. The
owner catches and cooks the
seafood, his speciality is *riblja
juha* (fish soup).

Škrapa €€-€
*Augustina Kazotića,
T021-885313.*
Daily lunch and dinner.
Popular with both locals and
visitors, Škrapa serves up large
platters of delicious *frigne ligne*
(fried squid) and *ribice* (small
fried fish). It's informal and fun,
with heavy wooden tables and
benches both indoors and out.

Šibenik & around

Gradska Vijećnica €€€
*Trg Republike Hrvatske 1, Šibenik,
T022-213605.*
Daily lunch and dinner.
Commanding a prime site, with
tables on Šibenik's main square
opposite the cathedral, this
restaurant is based in the
16th-century Venetian Town Hall.
The house speciality is *paprika
punjena sirom* (peppers stuffed
with cheese).

Konoba Toni €€€-€€
*Trgovačka 46, Skradin,
T022-771177.*
Daily lunch and dinner.
On the edge of Krka National
Park, this rustic *konoba* specializes
in traditional Dalmatian dishes
such as *brudet sa purom* (fish stew
with polenta) prepared over an
open fire, and lamb and veal
cooked under a *peka*.

Zlatne Školjke €€€-€€
*Grgura Ninskog 9, Skradin,
T022-771022.*
Daily lunch and dinner.
On the edge of Krka National
Park, in an old stone house with a
summer terrace overlooking
Skradin's ACI Marina, this
restaurant is best known for *crni
rižot* (black risotto), *špageti
plodovima mora* (spaghetti with
seafood) and *riba na žaru*
(barbecued fish).

Konoba Dalmatino €€
*Fra Nikole Ružiča 2, Šibenik,
T091-542 4808.*
Daily lunch and dinner.
In Šibenik's the old town, this
tiny old-fashioned eatery is a
great spot for fresh fish and
Dalmatian specialities such
as *pršut* (prosciutto) and *sir*
(cheese). It doubles as an
upmarket wine shop.

Omiš

Radmanove Mlinice €€
*Cetina Valley, T021-862073,
radmanove-mlinice.hr.*
Apr-Oct for lunch and dinner.
On the banks of the River Cetina,
6 km upstream from Omiš, this
old watermill was once the
home of the Radman family.
Today it's a pleasant garden
restaurant serving local *pastrva*
(trout) and *janjetina* (roast lamb)
at tables under the trees.

Restoran Kaštil Slanica €€
*Cetina Valley, 4 km upstream
from Omiš, T021-861783,
radmanove-mlinice.hr.*
Daily lunch and dinner.
This riverside restaurant
specializes in *žabji kraci* (frog's
legs), *jegulje* (eels) and *janjetina*
(roast lamb), while the bread
comes freshly baked from a *peka*.

Stari Mlin €€€-€€
Prvosvibanjska 43, T021-611503.
Mon-Sat for lunch and dinner,
closed Sun.
Housed in an 18th-century
baroque building, a few blocks
back from the seafront, Stari Mlin
specializes in fish and seafood,
plus a small selection of Thai
dishes. The cavernous interior is
warm and cosy through winter,
while a large vine-covered
terrace comes into use through
summer.

Hrpina €€
Trg Hrpina 2, T021-611619.
Apr-Oct lunch and dinner;
through winter it works just
as a bar.
This long-standing, family-run
restaurant has a terrace lined
with potted geraniums
overlooking a small piazza just
off the main square. They serve
traditional Dalmatian dishes.

Island of Brač

Supetar
Vinotoka €€€-€€
Jobova 6, T021-631341.
Daily lunch and dinner.
Said by locals to be one of the
best restaurants on the island,
Vinotoka is a couple of blocks
back from the bay. Fresh fish and
shellfish top the menu, with
most dishes prepared outside
on a *roštilj* (barbecue).

Kopačina €€
*Donji Humac, 8 km from Supetar,
T021-647707.*
Daily lunch and dinner.
In the hill village of Donji Humac,
this old-fashioned *konoba* is
much loved by locals and
manages to stay open all year.
Most people come here
especially to eat *janjetina* (roast
lamb) at wooden tables and
benches on a raised front terrace.

Bol
Gušt €€€-€€
Frane Radić 14, T021-635911.
Daily lunch and dinner.
In an old stone building in the
centre of Bol, this small
restaurant offers a good range
of fish and lobster dishes, as well
as *janjetina* (roast lamb) and
pašticada (beef stew). There are
a few tables outside on the
terrace, but you may have to
queue for a seat.

Ribarska Kučica €€€-€€
Ante Starčevića bb, T021-635033.
Jun-Sep for lunch and dinner.
On the coastal path, a 10-minute
walk east of the crowds in the
centre of Bol, this informal eatery
serves fresh fish, pasta and pizza
at romantic, candlelit tables
overlooking the open sea.

Konoba Vidova Gora €€
Vidova Gora, T098-225999.
Open Feb-Dec for lunch
and dinner.
On highest point of Vidova Gora,
this informal *konoba* specializes
in local roast lamb, served with
seasonal salad, bread and wine.
The front terrace affords a
fantastic view down onto the
sea and nearby islands, but as
it's often very windy you may
prefer to sit inside.

Island of Hvar

Hvar Town
Yakša €€€
*Petra Hektorovića bb,
T021-717202.*
Lunch and dinner.
Map: Hvar Town, p204.
In the old town, this
sophisticated candlelit restaurant
opens onto a romantic stone
courtyard with funky modern
furnishing. The menu features
creative salads, pasta dishes
combining delights such as
rocket, pesto and shrimps, local
seafood, and delicious deserts.
They do brunch too.

Luna €€€-€€
Grod bb, T021-741400.
Lunch and dinner.
Map: Hvar Town, p204.
On the first floor of a stone
building in the old town, Luna's
dining room has a large open
space in the roof so you can see
the sky and stars at night. Try the
excellent fresh fish (they'll bring

specialities such as *kožji sir* (goat's cheese), *pršut* (prosciutto) and *salata od hobotnice* (octopus salad), plus carafes of home-made wine. Typical of a *konoba*, it has exposed stone walls, a wooden-beamed ceiling and candlelit tables.

Stari Grad
Stari Mlin €€€-€€
Iza škole, T021-765804.
Lunch and dinner.
Opened in 2008 by owner-chef Damir Cavić, who used to run the very popular Jurin Podrum, this small family-run eatery occupies a traditional stone building in the old town. The menu features fresh local fish and seafood. It's popular with locals and stays open all year.

Jelsa
Napoleon €€€-€€
Mala Banda, T099-526 9990, napoleon-hvar.com.
Lunch and dinner.
Looking out over the harbour, this friendly eatery serves up delicious Dalmatian seafood specialities – choose the *jastog* (lobster) if you want to splash out. The stone-walled dining room is decorated in naval style, with blue and white table linens, and outdoor tables line the water's edge.

you a platter of uncooked fish so you can choose which one you want before it's cooked), while meat eaters might opt for chicken with truffles, or a steak.

Macondo €€€-€€
Groda bb, T021-742850.
Lunch and dinner.
Map: Hvar Town, p204.
This excellent fish restaurant is in a narrow alleyway between the main square and the fortress. In summer there are several tables outside, while the indoor space has a large open fire and is hung with discreet modern art. Start with scampi pâté, followed by a platter of mixed fried fish, and round it off with a glass of home-made *orahovica* (*rakija* made from walnuts). The food and service are practically faultless, but you may have to queue for a table.

Alviž €
Dolac bb, T021-742797, hvar-alviz.com.
Lunch and dinner.
Map: Hvar Town, p204.
This friendly, family-run pizzeria occupies an old stone building behind the cathedral, opposite the bus station. The shabby-chic interior with whitewashed stone walls opens onto a lovely peaceful courtyard garden with grape vines. Besides pizzas they also do excellent *palažinke* (crêpes).

Konoba Menego €
Groda bb, T021-742036, menego.hr.
Lunch and dinner.
Map: Hvar Town, p204.
On the steps leading up to the castle, this informal eatery and wine bar serves small platters of locally produced Dalmatian

Konoba Humac €€
Humac, 8 km east of Jelsa,
T021-761405.
Daily Jun-Sep for lunch
and dinner.
There's no electricity so
everything is cooked as it would
have been over a century ago:
under a *peka* or on a *roštilj*. The
bread is home-made and the
cheese, salad and wine locally
produced. You can't get much
more authentic than this.

Island of Vis

Vis Town
Villa Kaliopa €€€
V Nazora 32, Kut, T021-711755.
Lunch and dinner.
Close to the Town Museum, this
enchanting restaurant is set in
the walled garden of a
Renaissance villa. The menu
changes daily, depending on
what fresh products are
available. Dinner here is an
event in itself, and worth
dressing up for.

Konoba Vatrica €€€-€€
Kralja Krešimira IV 15,
T091-594 9047, vatrica.hr.
Jun-Sep daily lunch and dinner,
Oct-May dinner only.
With an ample vine-covered
terrace on the seafront, this
restaurant gets incredibly busy in
summer. Guests sit at heavy
wooden tables and feast on
barbecued fish and meat dishes.

Pojoda €€€-€€
Don Cvjetka Marasovic 8,
T021-711575.
Lunch and dinner.
Hidden away in a courtyard
garden, this is a fine spot to taste
local seafood specialities such as
salata od hobotnice (octopus
salad) and *brodet* (fish stew)
along with a carafe of house
wine. Round it all off with *rožata*,
a Dubrovnik speciality similar to
crème caramel.

Komiža
Konoba Bako €€€-€€
Gundulićeva 1, T021-713742,
konobabako.hr.
Dinner only.
This informal and friendly
seafood restaurant is in a tiny
bay with tables right up to the
water's edge. The indoor dining
area has rough stone walls and a
pool stocked with fresh fish and
lobster. The former Croatian
president, Stjepan Mesić, has
eaten here.

Konoba Jastožera €€€-€€
Gundulićeva 6, T021-713859,
jastozera.com.
May-Sep.
Opened in 2002, this restaurant
is based in the former town
lobster-pot house. The interior
has been beautifully refurbished
with tables set on wooden
platforms above the water, and
small boats can still enter the
central space. Needless to say,
the house speciality is lobster.

Entertainment

Split

Bars & clubs
Fluid
Dosud 1.
A tiny, cosy, stone-walled late-
night drinking den, popular
with both locals and visitors.

Galerija Plavac
Trg braće Radiča (off Vočni Trg).
Bar staging temporary
exhibitions by local artists and
occasional live music, tables
indoors and outside in a small
internal courtyard.

Ghetto Club
Dosud 10.
The alternative crowd meet
here for drinks, occasional
exhibitions and performances.
Throughout the summer, tables
spill outside onto a delightful
candlelit courtyard.

Hemingway
VIII Mediteranskih igara 5,
T099-211 9993, hemingway.hr.
Open daily; Fri and Sat until
0500.
Opened in summer 2008, Split's
Hemingway is part of a chain
of pricey clubs, which started
out in North Croatia. Attracting
the see-and-be-seen crowd, it
has a big summer terrace
overlooking Poljud Marina.
Expect guest DJs from abroad
and a good mix of dance, disco,
1970s and house music.

Jungla
Šetalište Ivana Meštrovića bb.
Open daily; until 0300 in
summer.
Sometimes referred to as Hula
Hula (the name has changed
several times), grungy Jungla
serves drinks and loud music
on a terrace overlooking
Zvončac Bay.

Ovčice
*Put Firule 4, T021-489759,
ovcice.hr.*
A five-minute walk along the
coast from Bačvice Bay, this
pleasant sea-view terrace café
stays open until 0100. In summer
you can hire an umbrella and
sunlounger on the pebble beach
during the day.

Puls 2
Buvinina 1, opposite Hotel Slavija.
Probably still the most 'in' bar for
the mainstream 16-25 age group.
Industrial interior with thumping
techno music and a crowded
summer terrace outside with
cushions so you can sit on the
stone steps.

Festivals & events
Sudamje
7 May.
The Feast of St Domnius
celebrates the patron saint of
Split, whose bones go on
display for a week in the
cathedral. It's a local public
holiday. Stands sell handmade
wooden objects and basketry.

Split Sumer Festival
splitsko-ljeto.hr.
Jul-Aug.
Hosts opera, theatre and dance
at open-air venues within the
walls of Diocletian's Roman
Palace. The highlight is Aida
on Peristil.

Around Split
Festivals & events
Ethnoambient Salona
Salona, ethnoambient.net.
Late Jul.
A three-day open-air event
attracting musicians from as
far afield as Scotland, Portugal
and Greece.

Northwest of Split
Bars & clubs
Aurora Club
*Kamenar bb, Primošten (20 km
southeast of Šibenik),
auroraclub.hr.*
Mid-Jun to early Sep.
One of the largest discos
in Dalmatia.

Hacienda
*Magistrala bb, on the road
between Šibenik and Vodice,
hacienda.hr.*
Jun-Sep.
The biggest nightclub for miles,
in a walled garden out of town.

Southeast of Split
Bars & clubs
Beach Bar Buba
Donja Luka beach, Makarska.
Open May-Oct.
On the main town beach, a
10-minute walk west of the
centre, during the day Buba hires
out sunloungers and umbrellas,
then plays electronic and dance
music come sunset.

Deep
Osejava Peninsula, Makarska.
Open Jun-Sep.
A small summer bar and disco, in
a natural cave overlooking the
sea, playing electronic music
with laser shows. It is a 10-minute
walk east of the centre, just after
Hotel Osejava.

Grotta
Šetalište Sv Petra bb, Makarska.
Open Jun-Sep.
A long-standing small bar and nightclub, playing rock and dance music, in a natural cave overlooking the sea on St Peter's peninsula.

Petar Pan
Fra Jure Radića bb, Makarska, petarpan-makarska.com.
Open Jun-Sep.
At the south end of the seafront promenade, this open-air disco has a sophisticated sound and light system and space for 1500 guests. It opened in summer 2008 and attracts visiting house DJs such as StoneBridge from Sweden.

Island of Brač

Bars & clubs
Luna
Supetar, summerclubluna.com.
An open-air summer club hosting occasional visiting international DJs (Terry Francis and Tom Baker have played here), on the hillside above Supetar.

Varadero
Frane Radić 1, Bol.
On the ground floor of Hotel Kaštil, close to the harbour, this cocktail bar pulls the crowds through summer and hosts occasional guest DJs.

Island of Hvar

Bars & clubs
Carpe Diem
Riva bb, Hvar Town, T021-717234, carpe-diem-hvar.com.
Open until 0300 in the peak season.
Trendy cocktail bar with oriental furniture and a plant-filled summer terrace looking out to sea. Through peak season it's so popular they have two bouncers outside, controlling the people waiting to get in. A great venue for celebrity spotting, if that's your thing.

Hula Hula
Hvar Town, on the seaside path between Hotel Amfora and Hotel Podstine.
Daily Jun-Sep.
This wooden beach bar makes the perfect spot to watch the sunset with chill-out music and a drink, in a small pebble cove looking out to sea.

Kiva
Hvar Town, in a narrow side street off the harbour.
Apr-Oct 2100-0300.
This tiny, informal wine bar plays classic rock and alternative music. Popular with young Croatians and hard-drinking sailing types; once it's full inside customers spill out onto the street. Many visitors cite it as their favourite bar on Hvar.

The Top
Fabrika bb, Hvar Town.
On the top floor of Hotel Adriana, this stunning rooftop lounge-bar affords views over the old town and out to sea. Tables and lounge sofas are arranged on a series of multi-level garden terraces. Chic but informal, it serves cocktails, wine and light snacks through the day and into the early hours.

Veneranda
Gornja cesta bb, Hvar Town, T098-855151, veneranda.hr.
Open Jun-Sep.
Above the coastal path west of town, in the grounds of a former 16th-century Greek Orthodox Monastery, this complex includes a cocktail bar (in the former church), a pool and a dance floor playing techno and electronic music.

Island of Vis

Aquarius
Kamenica Beach (a 10-min walk east of the harbour), Komiža.
Open Jun-Sep.
This tiny beach bar offers sunloungers, umbrellas and chill-out music by day, followed by house, dance and electronic music with drinks at night.

Shopping

Activities & tours

Lambik
Kralja Krešimira 2, Vis Town,
T021-711575.
Popular with the yachting
crowd for a pre-dinner aperitif,
this bar serves coffee, local
wines and slightly pricey
cocktails the day through.

Peronospora Blues
Obala Sv Jurja bb, Vis Town.
A *vinerija* and gallery. Try the
excellent Plavac Mali, a red wine
produced by the owner, served
with platters of ham and cheese.
It's also possible to buy bottles
to take home.

.

Split

Books
Algoritum
Bajamontijeva 2, between Peristil
and Narodni Trg, T021-348030.
The best bookshop for
foreign-language publications,
including novels, travel guides
and maps.

Food & drink
Pazar
Colourful open-air market just
outside the palace walls, with
stalls selling fruit and vegetables,
plus clothes and leather goods.

Vinoteka Bouquet
Obala hrvatskog narodnog
preporoda 3, on the seafront,
T021-348031.
A tiny shop well-stocked with
the best Croatian wines, truffle
and olive oil products.

Souvenirs
Aromatica
Šubićeva 2, T021-344061,
aromatica.hr.
Delicious-smelling soaps,
shampoos and massage oils
made from local aromatic herbs.

Croata
Krešmirova 11, T021-314055,
croata.hr.
Sells original Croatian ties in
presentation boxes, with a
history of the tie.

Split & around

Adventure sports
Adventure Dalmatia
Matije Gupca 26, Split, T021-
540642, adventuredalmatia.
com.
Arranges rafting, canoeing,
canyoning and free climbing in
the Cetina Valley near Omiš, and
sea kayaking in Trogir and Brela.

Sailing
Ultra Sailing
Uvala baluni bb, T021-314589,
ultra-sailing.hr.
Arranges one-day private
charters aboard a yacht – the
best way to explore the islands.

Northwest of Split

Adventure sports
Nik
A Šupuka 5, T022-338550,
Šibenik, nik.hr.
Arranges excursions to the
nearby national parks of Krka
and Kornati.

Southeast of Split

Adventure sports
Active Holidays
Knezova Kačića bb, Omiš,
T021-863015, activeholidays-
croatia.com.
Organizes rafting, canoeing,
free-climbing, paragliding,
windsurfing and scuba-diving in
Omiš and the surrounding area.

Biokovo Active Holidays
Kralja P Krešimira IV 7B,
Makarska, T021-679655,
biokovo.net.
Organizes one-day and
several-day adventure sports
programmes including hiking
and mountain biking on Biokovo
and the island of Brač, and sea
kayaking at Brela.

Diving
More-Sub
Kralja P Krešimira 43,
Makarska, T021-611727,
more-sub-makarska.hr.

Island of Brač

Adventure sports
Big Blue
Podan Glavice 2, Bol,
T021-635614, big-blue-sport.hr.
Arranges scuba-diving, wind-
surfing and sea kayaking at Zlatni
Rat, and rents out mountain bikes.

Diving
Amber Dive Center
Supetar, T098-922 7512,
amber-divecenter.com.

Island of Hvar

Adventure sports
Hvar Adventure
Obala bb, Hvar Town, T021-
717813, hvaradventure.com.
Sea-kayaking tours, sailing
expeditions, hiking and
rock climbing.

Diving
Diving Center Viking
Podstine bb, T021-742529,
viking-diving.com.

Spas & retreats
Sensori Spa
Hotel Adriana, T021-750250,
suncanihvar.com.
A luxurious wellness centre
comprising an indoor rooftop
pool filled with heated seawater,
plus a selection of massage
treatments, facials and
aromatherapy.

Suncokret
Dol, 6 km from Jelsa,
T091-739 2526,
suncokretdream.net.
Suncokret (Sunflower) offers
holistic wellness retreats
combining yoga, nature walks
and reiki. Guests are
accommodated in cottages
in the village and typical
Dalmatian meals are provided.
Most courses last one-week,
but visitors are also welcome
to drop in for a session.

Island of Vis

Adventure sports
Alternatura
Hrvatskih Mučenika 2, Komiža,
T021-717239, alternatura.hr.
Activities and tours such as boat
trips to the Blue Cave on Biševo
and the distant island of
Palagruža, as well as free
climbing and wine tasting.

Diving
Dodoro Diving Tours
Trg Klapavica 1, Vis Town,
T091-251 2263,
dodoro-diving.com.

Issa Diving Centre
Ribarska 91, Komiža, T021-
713651, scubadiving.hr.

Contents

227 Introduction
229 Dubrovnik & around
230 *Map: Dubrovnik*
240 Great days out:
    Elafiti islands
242 Pelješac Peninsula
246 Island of Korčula
252 Island of Mljet
254 Island of Lastovo
256 Listings:
256 Sleeping
259 Eating & drinking
263 Entertainment
265 Shopping
265 Activities & tours

South Dalmatia

Dubrovnik old town.

Introduction

The southernmost region of Croatia, South Dalmatia is a long, thin, coastal strip backed by the dramatic Dinaric Alps, which form the natural border with Bosnia and Herzegovina. Urban life centres on the former city-republic of Dubrovnik, an architect's dream contained within medieval defensive walls, facing out to sea and packed with baroque churches and elegant 17th-century town houses.

A two-hour ferry ride west of Dubrovnik lies the island of Mljet, one third of which is a national park. Most visitors arrive as part of an organized day trip, so if you decide to stay the night you'll have the place (almost) to yourself. Be sure to try the lobster – Mljet's culinary speciality.

Further west still, Lastovo is one of Croatia's most remote and least visited islands, where you can escape the crowds and wallow in unspoilt nature.

The region's most visited island is Korčula, with Korčula Town renowned for its fine cathedral and re-enactments of the medieval Moreška sword dance. The easiest way to reach Korčula from Dubrovnik is to drive along the mountainous Pelješac Peninsula then take a short ferry ride. Pelješac is renowned for its vineyards, which produce the sophisticated red Dingač – several cellars here offer wine tasting.

What to see in...

...one day
If time is limited, devote your energy to exploring **Dubrovnik's** magnificent old town, beginning with a circuit of the city walls, checking out the museums and indulging in a seafood lunch.

...a weekend or more
With more time to spare, get a taste of island life with an overnight stay on tiny car-free **Lopud**, or an excursion to **Mljet** with its dense pinewoods and two interconnected saltwater lakes. If wine is your thing, head for **Pelješac Peninsula** and the island of **Korčula**, which produce some of Croatia's top vintages.

Mljet.

Dubrovnik & around

Lying 216 km southeast of Split, backed by rugged limestone mountains and jutting out into the Adriatic Sea, Dubrovnik, for centuries the independent Republic of Ragusa, is one of the world's finest and best-preserved fortified cities. Its gargantuan walls and medieval fortress towers enclose the historic centre, which is filled with terracotta-roof town houses and monuments such as the 15th-century Rector's Palace, two monasteries with cloistered gardens and several fine baroque churches with copper domes. The old town is traversed by the main pedestrian promenade, Stradun (Placa), which is paved with glistening white limestone and lined with open-air cafés. In 1979, the city became a UNESCO World Heritage Site.

Tourism has a long history here and the museums, churches, hotels and restaurants are all well geared to foreign visitors – beware that in Dubrovnik you can expect to pay almost double what you would anywhere else in Croatia. Dubrovnik is considered one of Europe's most exclusive destinations, heaving with visitors through high season and attracting more than its share of international celebrities. Cruise ships en route from Venice to the Greek islands stop here, several of the country's plushest and most expensive hotels can be found here, and it's the main base for charter companies hiring out yachts in South Dalmatia.

Dubrovnik fortress.

Gradske Zidine

citywallsdubrovnik.hr.
May-Sep daily 0800-1900, Oct-Apr daily
1000-1500, 70Kn.
To reach the city walls, climb the steps
immediately to your left after passing through
Pile Gate.
Map: Dubrovnik, p230.

The walls, as they stand today, follow a ground plan
laid down in the 13th century. However, the fall of
Constantinople to the Turks in 1453 sent panic
waves throughout the Balkans, and Ragusa hastily
appointed the renowned Renaissance architect,
Michelozzo di Bartolomeo (1396-1472) from
Florence, to further reinforce the city fortifications
with towers and bastions. On average the walls are
24 m high and up to 3 m thick on the seaward side,
6 m on the inland side.

Essentials

⊗ **Airport** For airport information, see page 268.

⊖ **Bus station** At Obala pape Ivana Pavla II 44, T060-
305070, libertasdubrovnik.com. For regional bus travel,
see page 272.

➜ **Ferry** Dubrovnik's port is at Gruž, 3 km west of the
old town. **Jadrolinija**, jadrolinija.hr, operates daily local
ferries from Dubrovnik to the nearby Elafiti islands.
Jadrolinija also runs a ferry to Sobra on Mljet, while **G&V
Line**, gv-line.hr, cover the same route by catamaran,
stopping at the Elafiti islands en route. Lastovo is not
connected to Dubrovnik by boat, instead it is served
by ferry and catamaran from Split (Central Dalmatia).
Jadrolonija also runs a coastal ferry several times weekly
from Dubrovnik to Rijeka (Kvarner), stopping at the
islands of Korčula and Hvar, and at Split, en route. The
same ferry sometimes also does an overnight trip from
Dubrovnik to Bari (Italy).

◉ **Train station** Note that there is no train service to
Dubrovnik.

⊖ **ATM** There are ATMs in the old town, notably on
Stradun, and close to the ferry port.

⊕ **Hospital** Roka Mišetića bb, T020-431777.

✛ **Pharmacy** Gruž at Gruška obala (T020-418990)
and Kod Zvonika on Stradun (T020-321133) alternate as
24-hour pharmacies.

➋ **Post office** The most central post office is at
Široka 8, in the old town, Monday-Friday 0800-1500.

❶ **Tourist information** The new walk-in tourist
information centre is at Široka bb (T020-323587)
within the city walls, while there is a second tourist
information centre at Branitelja Dubrovnika 7 (T020-
427591), just outside Pile Gate. In addition, there is
a tourist information centre at Obala S Radića 32
(T020-417983) close to the ferry landing station in
Gruž harbour. The following websites are also useful:
Dubrovnik City Tourist Board, tzdubrovnik.hr, and
Dubrovnik County Tourist Board, visitdubrovnik.hr.

Tip...

The highlight of any visit to Dubrovnik has to be a
walk around the city walls. To walk the full circuit,
2 km, you should allow at least an hour.

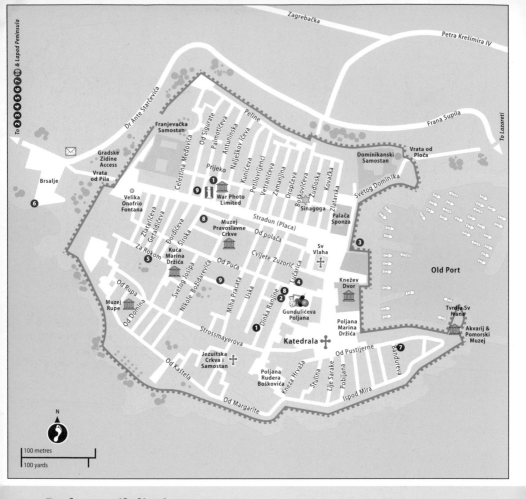

Dubrovnik listings

❶ Sleeping

1 Amoret Apartments *Dinka Ranjine ulica*
2 Berkeley Hotel *Andrije Hebranga 116A*
3 Hotel Aquarius *Mata Vodopića 8, Lapad Peninsula*
4 Hotel Bellevue *Pera Cingrije 7*
5 Hotel Lapad *Lapadska obala 37*
6 Hotel More *Kardinala Stepinca 33, Lapad Peninsula*
7 Karmen Apartments *Bandureva 1*
8 Pučić Palace *Ulica od Puca 1*
9 Stari Grad Hotel *Od Sigurate 4*

❶ Eating & drinking

1 Buffet Škola *Antuninska ulica bb*
2 Kamenica *Gundulićeva Poljana 8*
3 Lokanda Peškarija *Na Ponti bb*
4 Marco Polo *Lučarica 6*
5 Mea Culpa *Za Rokom 3*
6 Orhan *Od Tabakarije 1*
7 Orsan *Ivana Zajca 2, Lapad Peninsula*
8 Proto *Široka 1*
9 Taj Mahal *Gučetića 2*
10 Tovjerna Sesame *Dante Alighieria bb*

Vrata od Pila

Map: Dubrovnik, p230.

There are two gates into the city walls – Pile Gate is to the west. The name Pile comes from the Greek *pili* meaning 'gate'. During the time of the republic, they were closed each evening at 1800 and reopened at 0600 the next morning; the keys were kept under the custody of the rector. Pile Gate, as it stands today, combines a stone bridge, a wooden drawbridge on chains, and an outer Renaissance portal from 1537 followed by a Gothic inner gate from 1460. From May to October, guards in period costume stand vigilant by both gates, just as they would have done when the city was an independent republic.

Velika Onofrio Fontana

Poljana Paska Miličevića.
Map: Dubrovnik, p230.

Located in the square just inside Pile Gate, Onofrio's Greater Fountain was part of the city's water supply system, designed by the Neapolitan builder Onofrio de la Cava to bring water from the River Dubrovačka 20 km away. It was completed in 1444. Topped with a dome, water runs from 16 spouting masks around the sides of the fountain. Originally it would have been decorated with ornate sculptures, which were unfortunately destroyed during the earthquake of 1667.

Stradun

Map: Dubrovnik, p230.

Up until the 12th century, Stradun (also known as Placa) was a shallow sea channel, separating the island of Laus from the mainland. After it was filled in, it continued to divide the city socially for several centuries, with the nobility living in the area south of Stradun, while the commoners lived on the hillside to the north. It forms the main thoroughfare through the old town, running 300 m from Pile Gate to Ploče Gate. The glistening white limestone paving dates from 1468, though

Dubrovnik under siege

In the early 1990s, when the war of independence broke out, Yugoslav forces placed the city under siege. From November 1991 to May 1992, the ancient fortifications stood up to bombardments; fortunately none of the main monuments were seriously damaged, though many of the terracotta rooftops were blasted to fragments. The international media pounced on the story, and it was the plight of Dubrovnik that turned world opinion against Belgrade, even though less glamorous cities, such as Vukovar in Eastern Slavonia (see page 35) were suffering far worse devastation and bloodshed. During the second half of the 1990s, money poured in from all over world and today, thanks to careful restoration work (costing an estimated US$10 million), few traces of war damage remain and Dubrovnik is once again a fashionable, high-class holiday resort.

the stone buildings to each side were constructed after the earthquake of 1667. While the upper levels were residential, the ground floors were used as shops. Still today Stradun serves as the city's main public gathering place, where locals conduct their morning and evening promenades and meet at rather pricey open-air cafés.

Franjevačka Samostan

Placa 2, T020-321410, malabraca.hr.
Summer daily 0900-1800, winter daily 0900-1700, 25Kn.
Map: Dubrovnik, p230.

The Franciscan Monastery complex centres on a delightful cloister from 1360 – late Romanesque arcades are supported by double columns, each crowned with a set of grotesque figures, beside an internal garden filled with palms and Mediterranean shrubs. There's a small museum displaying early laboratory equipment, ceramic bowls and old medical books from the pharmacy, founded by the monks in 1318 and said to be the oldest institution of its kind in Europe.

Palača Sponza

Luža, T020-321032.
Daily 0900-1500, free (ground floor only).
Map: Dubrovnik, p230.

At the east end of Placa, the Sponza Palace was designed by Paskoje Miličević in 1522 and displays a blend of Renaissance arches on the lower level and Venetian-Gothic windows on the first floor. Through the centuries it has been used as a customs office and the city mint (Ragusa minted its own money, a convertible currency known as the *perpera*) though it now houses the state archives. The ground floor is open for temporary exhibitions, and during the Summer Festival concerts take place in the internal courtyard. This is one of the few buildings to survive the 1667 earthquake.

Dominikanski Samostan

Sv Dominika 4, T020-321423.
Summer daily 0900-1800,
winter 0900-1700, 20Kn.
Map: Dubrovnik, p230.

Behind the Sponza Palace, in a passageway leading to Ploče Gate, the Dominican Monastery centres on a 15th-century late-Gothic cloister, designed by the Florentine architect Michelozzo di Bartolomeo (1396-1472) and planted with orange trees. The east wing of the complex houses a museum exhibiting 15th- and 16th-century religious paintings by members of the Dubrovnik School – notably a triptych featuring the *Virgin and Child* by Nikola Božidarević and a polyptych centring on the *Baptism of Christ* by Lovro Dobričević – as well as works by the city's goldsmiths and reliquaries collected by the monks through the centuries. The rather plain interior of the monastery church is worthwhile for the *Miracle of St Dominic* by Vlaho Bukovac (1855-1922), a local painter from Cavtat.

Sponza Palace.

St Blaise church.

Vrata od Ploča

Map: Dubrovnik, p230.

The main entrance into the old town from the east, Ploče Gate, like Pile Gate, combines a 15th-century stone bridge with a wooden drawbridge and a stone arch bearing a statue of St Blaise.

Crkva Svetog Vlaha

Luža.
Daily 0800-1200 and 1630-1900.
Map: Dubrovnik, p230.

Opposite the Sponza Palace, the baroque Church of St Blaise, built between 1705 and 1717, replaced an earlier 14th-century structure destroyed by fire following the earthquake of 1667. It is dedicated to the city's patron saint, St Blaise, and on the high altar stands a silver statue of him, holding a model of the city from the 16th century, which is paraded around town each year on 3 February, the Day of St Blaise. The stained-glass windows, a feature rarely seen in churches in southern Europe, were added in the 1970s.

Knežev Dvor

Pred Dvorom 3, T020-321497.
Summer daily 0900-1800, winter
Mon-Sat 0900-1600, 35Kn.
Map: Dubrovnik, p230.

Behind the Church of St Blaise, the Rector's Palace is the building where the citizen holding the one-month term as rector was obliged to reside during his time in office; he could only leave for official business and his family remained in their own home.

The building dates from the 15th-century, though the arcaded loggia and internal courtyard, combining late-Gothic and early-Renaissance styles, were largely built after the 1667 earthquake.

In the courtyard (where classical music concerts are held during the Summer Festival) stands a bust of Miho Pracat (1528-1607), a powerful merchant and ship owner from the nearby island of Lopud, who left his wealth to the republic for charitable purposes when he died. When the bust was erected in 1638, he became the only man to be honoured in such a way – the production of

Around the region

Gundulićeva Poljan.

Gundulićeva Poljana

Map: Dubrovnik, p230.

Each morning, from Monday to Saturday, an open-air fruit and vegetable market sets up on Gundulićeva Poljana, west of the Rector's Palace. Come sunset, the market stalls are packed away and several restaurants put out tables in their place. In the middle of the square is a bronze statue of the Ragusan writer Ivan Gundulić (1589-1638), completed by Ivan Rendić in 1892. Gundulić is best known for his epic poem *Osman* (1626), describing the Poles' victory over the Turks, and the four sides of the stone pedestal upon which the statue is mounted are decorated with reliefs of scenes from the poem.

Katedrala

Poljana Marina Držića, T020-323459 (Treasury). Daily 0800-1200 and 1500-1730, 10Kn (Treasury). Map: Dubrovnik, p230.

The original 12th-century cathedral, said to have been sponsored in part by Richard the Lionheart of England out of gratitude for having been saved from a shipwreck on the nearby island of Lokrum on his return from the Crusades in 1192, was destroyed in the 1667 earthquake. What you see today is a splendid baroque structure with three aisles and a cupola, designed by Andrea Buffalini of Rome in 1671. The light but rather bare interior contains a number of paintings, notably a large polyptych above the main alter depicting *The Assumption of Our Lady*, attributed to the Venetian master, Titian (1485-1576). Adjoining the cathedral, the rich Treasury displays 138 gold and silver reliquaries, originating primarily from the East and brought to the city by the local seafarers. Pride of place is held by the skull of St Blaise in the form of a bejewelled Byzantine crown; an arm and a leg of the saint are also on show, likewise encased in elaborately decorated golden plating.

statues of local personalities was generally forbidden to prevent the cult of hero worship. Next to the courtyard are a series of large rooms where the Great Council and Senate held their meetings; over the entrance to the meeting halls a plaque reads *Obliti privatorum publica curate* (Forget private affairs, and get on with public matters).

Upstairs, the rector's living quarters now accommodate the *Gradski Muzej* (City Museum), offering an idea of how people once lived in the Republic of Ragusa. Exhibits include paintings by Venetian and Dalmatian artists, period furniture, costumes and a curious collection of clocks, each one stopped at 1745, the hour Napoleon's men took the city on 31 January 1806, symbolizing the fall of the republic.

Akvarij

Damjana Jude 2, Tvrdja Sv Ivana (St John's Fortress), T020-323978.
Summer daily 0900-2000, winter Tue-Sun 1000-1300, 30Kn.
Map: Dubrovnik, p230.

The St John's Fortress complex, behind the cathedral, guards the entrance to the old city port. At night, the port used to be closed by stretching a chain from the fortress to Kaše, a breakwater built in the 15th century. The ground floor of the fortress now houses the Aquarium, where several saltwater pools and 27 well-lit tanks display an impressive variety of Adriatic fish including ray and small sharks, and other underwater life such as octopuses, sponges and urchins.

Pomorski Muzej

Tvrdja Sv Ivana (St John's Fortress), Damjana Jude 2, T020-323904.
Summer daily 0900-1800, winter Tue-Sun 0900-1600, 35Kn.
Map: Dubrovnik, p230.

Above the Aquarium, on the first floor of St John's Fortress, the Maritime Museum traces Dubrovnik's development into one of the world's most important seafaring nations, with exhibits including intricately detailed model ships, as well as engine room equipment, sailors' uniforms, paintings and maps. There are also sections dedicated to the age of steam, the Second World War, and sailing and navigation techniques.

Jezuitska Crkva i Samostan

Poljana R Boškovića.
Daily 0900-1200 and 1500-1900.
Map: Dubrovnik, p230.

Completed in 1725, the Jesuit Church is Dubrovnik's largest and was modelled on the baroque Il Gesu in Rome, which was designed by Giacomo da Vignola in the mid-16th century. To

Aquarium at the St John's Fortress complex.

reach it, follow Uz Jezuite and climb an imposing staircase dating from 1738, often compared to Rome's Spanish Steps. Next to the church stands the Jesuit College, where many illustrious local citizens were educated.

Muzej Pravoslavne Crkve

Od Puča 8, T020-323283.
Summer daily 0900-1400, winter Mon-Fri 0900-1400, 10Kn.
Map: Dubrovnik, p230.

Next door to the Orthodox Church, built in 1877, stands the Orthodox Church Museum, with a collection of // religious icons, originating largely from the island of Crete and the Bay of Kotor (a short distance down the coast in Montenegro) and painted between the 15th and 19th centuries.

Benedictine monastery on Lokrum.

War Photo Limited

Antuninska 6, between Placa and Prijeko,
T020-322166, warphotoltd.com.
Jun-Sep daily 0900-2100; May and Oct Tue-Sat
0900-1500, Sun 1000-1400; Nov-Apr closed,
30Kn.
Map: Dubrovnik, p230.

This is a beautifully designed two-floor gallery
dedicated to photo-journalism from war zones
around the world. It has staged exhibitions from
Afghanistan, Iraq, former Yugoslavia, Israel and
Palestine and is emotionally gruelling but well
worth visiting.

Islet of Lokrum

During the summer, regular taxi boats shuttle
visitors back and forth from the old port.

East of the city walls, just 700 m from the old port,
you'll find the lush island of Lokrum. A Benedictine
Monastery was founded here in 1023, and legend
has it that when French authorities began closing
down religious institutions in the early 19th

century, local Benedictines placed a curse upon
anyone who should try to possess Lokrum. A
succession of subsequent owners died mysterious
and horrific deaths, one being the unfortunate
Archduke Maximilian von Hapsburg, who bought
the island in 1859, only to be taken prisoner and
shot in Mexico in 1867. Before departing,
Maximilian built a summer home here, set amid a
Botanical Garden filled with exotic plants and
peacocks, which can still be seen today. Even now,
locals remain superstitious about Lokrum, and
while it is a popular bathing area during daylight
hours, no one stays on the island after sunset.

There are some decent beaches on the
southwest side of the island, plus a small saltwater
lake, and beyond it an area reserved for nudists.

Beaches

The main bathing area close to the old town is
Eastwest Beach Club between the city walls and
Lazareti, while the best bathing spot on Lapad
Peninsula is Lapad Cove, where there's a pebble
beach in a deep bay.

Trsteno Arboretum

24 km northwest of Dubrovnik, T020-751019.
Summer daily 0700-1900, winter daily 0800-
1500, 25Kn.

All buses heading north up the coast from
Dubrovnik stop in Trsteno (45 mins), though you
should tell the driver in advance otherwise he
may drive straight on.

The small village of Trsteno is on the main coastal
road. Its 16th-century Renaissance arboretum, one
of the oldest and most beautiful landscaped parks
in Croatia, makes a pleasant outing at any time of
the year, though the trees and planting are at their
most attractive in spring and autumn.

The park, laid out in the grounds of a
Renaissance villa belonging to the Gucetić family,
was designed to emphasize the magnificence of
its clifftop setting: a series of terraces tumble
down to the sea, offering stunning views over
Trsteno's harbour and out across the water to
the Elafiti Islands.

Traditionally the men of Trsteno were sailors,
and wherever they went in the world they would
collect seeds and saplings for the Gucetić gardens.
Today, the arboretum contains pines from Japan,
palms from Mexico and cypress trees from various
parts of the Mediterranean, as well as
pomegranate, almond and lemon trees, and exotic
climbing plants such as sweet jasmine and passion
flower. Pride of place is taken by a 500-year-old
plane tree, with a 12-m circumference and boughs
so massive that one of them has to be supported
by a concrete pillar.

Behind the villa stands an ornate water garden
from 1736, featuring a grotto presided over by
baroque statues of Neptune and two nymphs, and
a pool fed with water from a trickling stream.

On October 1991, during the war of
independence, the arboretum was shelled from
the sea and part of the pinewoods was consumed
by fire. However, careful restoration work has
covered up the worst of the damage, and today
Trsteno still evokes the sophisticated lifestyle of
Renaissance Dubrovnik.

Trsteno arboretum.

Cavtat.

Cavtat

17 km southeast of Dubrovnik.

The pretty fishing town of Cavtat is Croatia's southernmost seaside resort. It was originally founded by ancient Greeks from Issa (Island of Vis, Central Dalmatia) and was called Epidauros. During the 15th century, it was incorporated into the Republic of Dubrovnik. Town walls were erected, and a rector installed to govern the rural hinterland region known as Konavle. Tourism began in the early 1900s under Austro-Hungary; during the 1980s several large hotel complexes were built and Cavtat turned into a popular package resort. For a year from October 1991, it was occupied by the JNA (Yugoslav Peoples' Army). The town suffered minimal material damage, though many houses in Konavle were looted and burnt during this period.

Today café life centres on the palm-lined seafront promenade giving onto a deep curving bay protected by a peninsula. Most of the hotels are located north of town, set amid lush Mediterranean vegetation and overlooking a second bay.

Baltazar Bogišić Collection

Obala Ante Starčevića 18, T020-478556.
Mon-Sat 0900-1300, 15Kn.

Housed within the 16th-century Renaissance Rector's Palace, this collection includes drawings by Croatian and foreign artists, and an impressive canvas, *Carnival in Cavtat*, by Vlaho Bukovac. There is also a lapidarium with Roman stone pieces from the first century AD and a display of old coins, some from the Republic of Ragusa (Dubrovnik).

Vlaho Bukovac Gallery

Bukovčeva 2, T020-478646, kuca-bukovac.hr.
May-Oct Tue-Sat 0900-1300, 1600-2000,
Sun 1600-2000; Nov-Apr Tue-Sat 0900-1300,
1400-1700, Sun 1400-1700, 20Kn.

The birthplace of the realist painter Vlaho Bukovac (1855-1922) has been turned into a gallery dedicated to him. Bukovac spent most of his years abroad: studying in Paris, visiting England and painting portraits of various aristocrats, and later becoming a professor at the Academy of Art in

Prague. However, from time to time he returned to Cavtat, and used this late 18th-century stone building as an atelier. In 1964 it was converted into a gallery displaying a collection of his paintings, drawings, furniture and mementoes.

Račić Mausoleum

Rat Peninsula, T020-478646.
By appointment only, enquire at the Vlaho Bukovac Gallery.

This impressive white stone mausoleum, designed by sculptor Ivan Meštrović in 1921, stands on the highest point of the town cemetery, on Rat Peninsula. An octagonal structure with a cupola, it is made of white stone from the island of Brač. The entrance features a pair of art nouveau-style caryatids (statues of female figures, used as columns to support the porch) and impressive bronze doors. The interior is decorated with reliefs of angels and birds in scenes symbolizing the three stages of life: birth, fate and death. Meštrović built the mausoleum to keep his promise to Marija Račić (a member of a family of wealthy ship owners), who was rumoured to have been his lover. The bronze bell, hanging from the cupola, is inscribed with a touching epitaph, "Know the mystery of love and thou shalt solve the mystery of death and believe that life is eternal."

Račić Mausoleum.

Elafiti islands

The tiny Elafiti islands – Koločep, Lopud and Šipan – offer unspoilt nature just a short ferry ride away from Dubrovnik. Pinewoods and scented shrubs cover the islands – the natural vegetation has been largely untouched, apart from on the inland area of Šipan, where there are cultivated fields of grape vines and olive trees. Being car free, the pace of life here is relaxed. Through summer, all three islands offer a number of small hotels and a modest choice of no-frills fish restaurants.

Koločep

Seven kilometres northwest of Gruž harbour, Koločep, with a population of around 150, is the smallest of the inhabited Elafiti islands. There are two settlements: the port of Donje Čelo on the northwest coast and Gornje Čelo on the southeast side; they are linked by a pleasant footpath, shaded by pine trees. The best beach, overlooked by a modern hotel in Donje Čelo, is sandy; there are also secluded pebble beaches, some given over to nudism. Historically the islanders lived from diving for coral, exploiting the nearby reef of Sv Andrija.

Lopud

The island of Lopud is 12 km northwest of Gruž and is 4.5 km long and 2 km wide. The sole village, also called Lopud, is made up of old stone houses built around the edge of a wide northwest-facing bay, with a view of Sudjuradj on Šipun across the water.

Guarding the entrance to the harbour, on the north side of the bay, stands a semi-derelict 15th-century Franciscan monastery, which was fortified to provide a place of refuge for the entire population in the case of a Turkish attack, and is now under restoration. Close by, the abandoned and roofless Rector's Palace is easily recognized by its fine triple Gothic windows. In stark contrast, on the south side of the bay stands the colossal Lafodia Hotel complex, erected in the 1980s. From Lopud a footpath (15-minute walking time) leads across the island, passing through lush vegetation scented with sage and rosemary to Šunj, a south-facing cove with a generous stretch of sand beach and a couple of summer restaurants.

Šipan

Šipan, the largest of the Elafiti islands, is 9 km long with a width of just over 2.5 km. The main settlements, Šipanska Luka (on the northwest coast) and Sudjuradj (on the southeast coast), are both built at the end of deep narrow inlets and account for a total population of around 500. Šipanska Luka has a palm-lined seafront overlooked by old stone buildings and a hotel – there is a decent beach a short distance from the centre. Sudjuradj is a sleepy fishing village with several small Renaissance villas and a pair of 16th-century watchtowers set back from the harbour, plus the island's second hotel. The two villages lie at opposite ends of Šipansko Polje, a fertile valley planted with olive trees and grape vines, and are connected by a 5-km asphalt road and a network of hiking paths.

Pelješac Peninsula

Beginning 46 km northwest of Dubrovnik, this long, skinny mountainous peninsula stretches almost 90 km from end to end. High above the coast, a single road runs its entire length, linking a succession of pretty hamlets and offering fine views out over the sea and nearby islands. In the past, fear of pirates meant that most settlements developed on the south-facing slopes, and it was only from the 18th century onwards that any sizeable villages grew up along the coast. Today, its relative lack of development and isolation from the mainland give Pelješac something of an island identity, and most Croatians know it purely for its red wines – Postup and Dingač. Both are truly excellent and can be tasted at several vineyards, which open their cellars to the public throughout the summer. Pelješac's main settlements are Ston and Orebić, both by the sea.

Pelješac Peninsula.

Ston

Eight kilometres along Pelješac Peninsula.

This fortified settlement is made up of two towns, Veli Ston and Mali Ston. It was founded when Dubrovnik took control of Pelješac in 1333, and soon became the Republic's second most important centre. Lying on opposite sides of the peninsula, each with its own bay, the two towns were originally fortified and connected by 5.5 km of defensive walls and 40 towers, effectively controlling land access onto Pelješac. Today the complex is on the UNESCO World Heritage 'Tentative List'.

Veli Ston, on the south side of the peninsula, is made up of Gothic and Renaissance buildings from the 14th and 15th centuries. Below town lies an expanse of saltpans, which once covered more than 400 sq km and provided the Republic of Dubrovnik with one-third of its annual revenue.

The smaller town of Mali Ston, 1 km northeast of Veli Ston, on the north side of the peninsula, can be reached in 15 minutes on foot, following the walls. It's known throughout Croatia for oysters (February-May) and mussels (May-September), which are farmed in the channel of Malostonski Zaljev, between the mainland and the peninsula. The mix of freshwater (from the River Neretva) and saltwater is ideal for cultivating shellfish.

Orebić

Close to the western tip of Pelješac Peninsula and 67 km northwest of Ston.

Orebić is now Pelješac's top resort, thanks to its fine south-facing beaches and attractive seafront. In the past, it produced many able sea captains, and when they retired they built villas here, which you can still see today. The town is protected from the bura wind by the heights of Sv Ilija Hill (961 m), whose south-facing slopes are dotted with pinewoods, cypresses and agaves. From here it's just 2 km across the Pelješac Channel to the island of Korčula: the two coasts are linked by a ferry service, making it possible for the people of Orebić to pop to Korčula for an evening out.

Essentials

⚓ **Ferry** A regular ferry plies the narrow sea channel between Orebić on Pelješac Peninsula to Dominče on the island of Korčula.

🏧 **ATM** There are cash machines in Veli Ston and Orebić.

ℹ **Tourist information** Ston tourist office is at Pelješki put 1, Veli Ston, T020-754452, ston.hr (summer only). **Orebić** tourist office is at Trg Mimbeli bb, T020-713718, tz-orebic.com.

Tip...

Most visitors come to Ston especially to eat at one of several excellent (but expensive) seafood restaurants.

Veli Ston with the saltpans and the walls clearly visible.

Franciscan monastery.

Franjevački Samostan

2 km west of Orebić, T020-713075.
Summer Mon-Sat 0900-1200 and 1600-1900,
Sun 1600-1900, 25 Kn.

A pleasant walk up a winding road lined with cypress trees brings you to the charming Gothic-Renaissance Franciscan Monastery, perched on a craggy cliff 152 m above the sea. It was built in the late 15th century by Franciscan monks, who chose this site for its vista onto the sea channel and surrounding islands. At that time nearby Korčula was under Dubrovnik's arch-rival, Venice. The monks constructed a loggia and terrace, which they used as a vantage point to spy on Venetian galleys; at the first sign of trouble they would send a warning to Dubrovnik by mounted messenger. 'Friendly' ships would let out three blasts of the siren as they passed below the monastery, to which the Franciscans would reply with a peal of the church bells. Inside the monastery you can see a fine collection of religious paintings, notably the *Our Lady of the Angels*, a Byzantine icon apparently washed up by the sea and said to protect sailors from shipwreck. There are also 20 or so votive paintings dedicated to the icon, commissioned by local seamen who survived danger on the ocean.

Beaches

A 15-minute walk east of Orebič, **Trstenica** is a 1500-m stretch of pebble and sand beach, equipped with sunloungers, parasols, showers and a café through summer. There is also a nearby nudist beach called **Ostupa**.

Pelješac's top vineyards & wine cellars

Podrum Bartulovića Prizdrina, T020-742346. On the road between Ston and Orebić, the Bartulovič family cellar offers wine tasting accompanied by platters of *pršut* (ham), *sir* (cheese) and *slane srdele* (salt sardines), in a beautifully restored traditional *konoba*.

Matuško Vina Potomje, T020-742393. Approached through a tunnel, the village of Potomje is the true home to the Dingač vineyards. Here, the Matuško family offer wine tasting and also have a shop selling reds from Pelješac and whites from Korčula.

Grgić Trstenik, T020-714244. On a promontory, at the mouth of the tiny port of Trstenik, stands the Grgić winery. Miljenko Grgić, who made his name with the exclusive Grgich Hills Estate, grgich.com, vineyards in California, returned to his Croatian roots in the 1990s to open this winery. Call first to taste white Pošip and red Plavac Mali.

Island of Korčula

This long, thin island is green and hilly, with a rocky, indented coastline. It was once covered with dense pine forest, leading the ancient Greeks to call it *Kerkyra Melaina* (Black Corfu). It seems the early Greek settlers lived in relative peace with the local Illyrian tribes, neither attempting to conquer nor assimilate them, but sharing land rights with them, as recorded by a stone inscription from the fourth century BC found in Lumbarda.

Between the 10th and 18th centuries the island came under Venice several times, and with arch-rivals the Republic of Dubrovnik and the Ottoman Empire in close proximity, La Serenissima did all it could to fortify and defend its main base here, the tiny yet culturally advanced Korčula Town. Legendary Venetian explorer, Marco Polo, is believed to have been born in Korčula Town, and an old stone building open to the public is said to have been his family home. Other attractions include the Moreška (a medieval sword dance) and excellent local white wines (Grk from Lumbarda and Pošip from the inland villages of Smokvica and Čara).

Korčula.

On the island's northeast coast, medieval Korčula Town is a compact cluster of terracotta-roofed houses perched graciously above the sea on a tiny peninsula fortified with walls and round towers. It is on the UNESCO World Heritage 'Tentative List'. The town is backed by hills covered with pinewoods, and faces onto a narrow sea channel offering views of the tall mountainous peaks of Pelješac in the distance. Large, modern hotels have been built a short distance from the centre, leaving the historic core as an open-air museum and making Korčula one of the most popular resorts on the islands, second only to Hvar.

Kopnena Vrata

The Land Gate is the principal entrance to the old town. A sweeping flight of steps leads up to the 15th-century Revelin Tower, a crenellated quadrangular structure forming an arched gateway into the historic centre. The tower houses a small museum to the Moreška sword dance (see page 248) with unpredictable opening hours.

From here, Korčulanskog Statuta runs the length of the tiny peninsula, with narrow streets branching off at odd angles to form a herring-bone pattern, ingeniously preventing local winds from blowing through the heart of town. Through summer, the Moreška sword dance is performed in a walled garden to the left of the Land Gate.

Katedrala Sv Marka

Strossmayerov Trg.
Summer daily 0900-1400, 1700-2000, winter by appointment.

Built of warm yellow-grey stone, Korčula's much-admired Gothic-Renaissance Cathedral of St Mark opens onto Strossmayerov Trg, the main square, in the heart of the old town. The magnificent Romanesque portal is flanked by finely carved figures of Adam and Eve and topped with a statue of St Mark.

Essentials

➲ **Ferry** A regular ferry plies the narrow sea channel between Orebić on Pelješac Peninsula and Dominče on Korčula. The catamaran Krilo makes daily runs from Split (Central Dalmatia) to Korčula Town. In addition, **Jadrolonija**, jadrolinija.hr) runs a coastal ferry several times weekly from Dubrovnik to Rijeka (Kvarner), stopping at the island of Korčula en route. Jadrolinija also runs a daily catamaran from Lastovo to Split (Central Dalmatia), stopping at Vela Luka (on Korčula's west coast) en route.

➒ **ATM** There are plenty of cash machines in Korčula Town.

➕ **Pharmacy** Ljekarna Korčula, Trg Kralja Tomislava bb, Korčula Town (T020-711057).

⊕ **Hospital** The nearest hospital is in Dubrovnik on the mainland.

➊ **Tourist information** Korčula Town tourist office is at Obala Dr Franje Tudjmana bb, T020-715701, korcula.net.

Cathedral.

Moreška

The Moreška (from *morisco*, meaning 'Moorish' in Spanish) came to Korčula via Italy in the 16th century. It originated in Spain in the 12th century, where it was inspired by the struggle of Spanish Christians against the Moors; on the East Adriatic, it was simply adapted to represent the ongoing fight of local Christians against the Turks.

Over the centuries the text, music and pattern of the dance have been altered and shortened, but the central story remains: Bula, a beautiful Muslim maiden, has been kidnapped by the Black Knight, and her sweetheart, the White Knight, comes to her rescue. The performance begins with the Black Knight (dressed in black) dragging Bula in chains, and the maiden crying out against his amorous proposals. The White Knight (confusingly, dressed in red) and his army then arrive, as do the Black Knight's army, ready to defend their leader. The two Knights hurl insults at one another, then cross their swords, and the dance begins. Their armies are pulled into the confrontation, with soldiers clashing swords in pairs within a circle, to the accompaniment of a brass band. The pace of the music gradually accelerates (in the past, performers were often wounded and had to replaced by reserves during the dance), with the black soldiers facing outwards and the circle contracting as they retreat inwards from the white army. Finally, all the black soldiers fall to the ground, the Black Knight surrenders, and the White Knight frees Bula from her chains and kisses her.

In the past, various versions of the dance were found throughout the Mediterranean, where they were probably used as much as an exercise for swordsmen as for entertainment. It also reached Northern Europe, and could well be the forerunner to English Morris dancing, where wooden poles are used instead of swords.

A traditional Moreška sword dance.

Inside, above the main altar stands a 15th-century ciborium (a canopy supported by four columns), carved by the local stonemason Marko Andrijic, who introduced the Renaissance style to the city. Beneath the ciborium, on the main altar, a 19th-century gilt sarcophagus holds the relics of St Theodore (the city's protector) brought to Korčula in 1736. Above it, the painting *St Mark with St Bartholomew and St Jerome* is an early work by the Venetian Mannerist, Tintoretto (1518-1594).

In the southern nave you'll find a curious collection of cannon balls and gruesome-looking weapons used against the Ottoman Turks. Above them, set in a gold frame, hangs a 13th-century icon, *Our Lady with the Child*, formerly kept in the Franciscan church on the island of Badija. When a Turkish fleet, commanded by the Algerian viceroy Uluz-Ali, attacked the town on 15 August 1571, children and the elderly prayed to the icon for divine intervention. Miraculously, a ferocious storm broke, destroying several galleys and causing others to retreat. Also in the southern nave is an *Annunciation* attributed to Tintoretto, while in the apse, a painting above the altar depicting the *Holy Trinity* is the work of another Venetian artist, Leandro Bassano (1557-1622).

Opatska Riznica

Strossmayerov Trg.
Summer daily 0900-1500 and 1700-2000, winter by appointment, 15Kn.

Next door to the cathedral, on the first floor of the 17th-century Renaissance-baroque Bishop's Palace, is the Abbey Treasury. Besides an impressive collection of icons and religious paintings, you'll see gold and silver chalices, mass vestments (garments worn by the clergy), ancient coins and a necklace donated to Korčula by Mother Theresa, which had been given to her by the town of Calcutta when she won the Nobel Peace prize in 1979.

Marco Polo

At the age of 17, Marco Polo (1254-1324), accompanied by his father and uncle, both of whom were Venetian merchants, travelled overland to China along the Silk Route, passing through the mountains and deserts of Persia, and then across the Gobi desert, to arrive, three years later, at the court of the great Mongol Emperor Kublai Khan.

Polo entered the Emperor's diplomatic service, acting as his agent on missions to many parts of the Mongolian Empire for the next 17 years, visiting, or at least gaining extensive knowledge about, Siam (present-day Thailand), Japan, Java, Cochin China (now part of Vietnam), Ceylon (present-day Sri Lanka), Tibet, India and Burma (present-day Myanmar). Some 24 years after their journey began, the Polos returned to Venice, laden with jewels, gold and silk, and eager to recount the extraordinary tales of what they had seen.

In 1298, as a captain in the Venetian fleet, Marco was taken prisoner during a sea battle against the Genoese close to Lumbarda, off the island of Korčula. During a year in prison in Genoa, he dictated the memoirs of his magnificent journeys to a fellow prisoner and romantic novelist, Rusticello of Pisa. Thus his tales of the exotic landscapes and highly refined lifestyles of the Orient first arrived in medieval Europe through *The Travels of Marco Polo*, a best-selling travelogue of its time, which later inspired Christopher Columbus and Vasco da Gama in their voyages of discovery.

Gradski Muzej

Strossmayerov Trg, T020-711420.
Jul-Sep daily 1030-2100, Apr-Jun, Mon-Sat 1030-1400 and 1900-2100, Oct Mon-Sat 1030-1400, 1900-2100, Nov-Mar Mon-Fri 1000-1300, 10Kn.

Opposite the cathedral, the 16th-century Renaissance Gabrielis Palace now houses the Town Museum. Exhibits include a copy of the fourth-century BC Greek *Lumbardska Psefizma* (see page 251), Roman ceramics and a section devoted to local shipbuilding. The building's interior gives some idea of how aristocrats lived between the 16th and 17th centuries, and on the top floor the kitchen is replete with pots and cookery utensils.

What the locals say

My perfect day starts with breakfast along the ancient city walls. I sit in the shade of the trees with a powerful macchiato, watching the fishing boats returning with their catch and enjoying the beautiful view of the Korčula archipelago, where I plan to spend the day swimming and relaxing.

I stroll through the history-rich and beautifully preserved old town on my way to the marina where I meet up with friends. We hop onto our sailing boat and head out to one of the many islands scattered off Korčula's coastline. The day is spent swimming, diving and relaxing. When we're peckish we dive down for sea urchins, which provide the perfect starter before heading to **Ante's** on the island of Stupa for the best waterside grill.

As the post-lunch slumber subsides and the refreshing maestral wind picks up we take to the sea again for an exhilarating sail up the channel. As the sun begins to set we turn back for the shore and a sunset cocktail at one of the bars that flank the western part of the old town.

A late dinner at **Marinero**, of whatever was freshly caught that day along with a glass or two of cold Pošip, with impromptu singing as we enjoy the moonlit seascape is the perfect end to a perfect day.

Tania Unsworth, hotel owner.

Marco Polo House.

Kuća Marca Pola

Marca Pola bb.
Jul-Aug daily 0900-2100, May-Jun, Sep-Oct daily 0900-1900, winter by appointment, 25Kn.

Northeast of the main square, behind the cathedral, stands the modest home and watchtower of the Depolo family, now known as the Marco Polo House. Local myth has it that Marco Polo, the legendary 13th-century traveller, was born here, though the present building was constructed several hundred years after his death. It's an amusing enough oddity, however.

Galerija Ikona

Trg Svih Svetih.
Summer daily 1000-1300, 1800-2000, winter closed, 10Kn.

Tucked away in a side street in the southeast part of the old town, the Icon Museum contains a display of Cretan School icons painted between the 14th and 17th centuries. They arrived in Korčula during the Candian Wars (1645-1669), when the town sent a galley to aid the Venetian fleet in its unsuccessful battle against the Turks for the possession of the Greek island of Crete.

Beaches

The main town beach is east of the centre, in front of Hotel Marco Polo. However, it gets very busy, so you're better off catching a taxi boat from the harbour to one of the nearby islets, or heading for the neighbouring village of Lumbarda (see right).

Lumbardska Psefizma

The Lumbardska Psefizma, a fourth-century BC inscription carved in stone, was found in Lumbarda. Proof of early Greek settlement on this site, it records a decree regarding land distribution, and includes the names of Greek and Illyrian families living here at the time. Today the original is in the Archaeological Museum in Zagreb, but you can see a copy at the Town Museum in Korčula Town.

Lumbarda

Six kilometres southeast of Korčula Town, at the eastern tip of the island, the tiny village of Lumbarda is best known for its sandy beach and surrounding vineyards, which produce a dry white wine, Grk. Today, a narrow road lined with mulberry trees leads from the village through vineyards planted with Grk vines, which some experts consider indigenous to Dalmatia, while others, due to its name, conclude that it must have arrived here during ancient times from Greece. Whatever its origin, it grows particularly well in the area's fine reddish sandy soil.

There's little of cultural interest in Lumbarda, though the village itself is a pleasant enough place, strung around a north-facing bay, lined with fish restaurants, cafés and rooms to let. Roads through the vineyards lead to several small beaches. The island's most popular bathing spot is the south-facing sand beach of **Pržina**, backed by a fast-food kiosk and bar, 2 km south of Lumbarda. A short distance east of Lumbarda, the north-facing beach of **Bili Žal** is made up of white stones beaten smooth by the water. A short distance east of Bili Žal is a rocky stretch reserved for nudists.

Island of Mljet

Mljet, the southernmost of the Croatian islands, is made up of steep rocky slopes and dense pine forests. The western third is a national park and within it is one of the country's most photographed sights: a proud but lonely 12th-century monastery perched on a small island in the middle of an emerald saltwater lake. Through the passing of the centuries, Mljet has remained something of a backwater. No great towns ever grew up here, and today it is home to half a dozen small villages, linked by a single road running the length of the island. Depopulation is a serious problem; the number of people living here has halved over the last 50 years. However, each summer Mljet is rediscovered by a steady flow of nature lovers, discerning travellers and escapists – in recent years visitors include Prince Charles and Steven Spielberg. The island isn't geared towards tourism – most arrive on organized day trips from Dubrovnik, and few remain overnight – but its natural beauty and lack of commercial development make it a wonderful escape for those in search of peace and tranquillity.

Looking from Montokuc onto Veliko Jezero.

Mljet National Park

Pristanište, T020-744041, np-mljet.hr.
The 90Kn entry fee is payable at one of a number of wooden kiosks within the park; if you stay overnight the fee is included in the price of your accommodation.

In 1960, the western third of the island was declared a national park to protect the indigenous forest of Aleppo pines and holm oaks, and the two magnificent interconnected saltwater lakes, **Malo Jezero** (Little Lake) and **Veliko Jezero** (Big Lake).

The park is ideal for those who enjoy walking or mountain biking: a network of paths criss-cross their way through the forests, and a 9-km trail runs around the perimeter of the two lakes. Southeast of Veliko Jezero, a steep, winding path leads to the highest point within the park, **Montokuc** (253 m), offering stunning views. For swimming, the best bathing areas are on **Solominji Rat**, just south of Mali Most, the bridge over the channel that connects the two lakes. The lakes offer an extended bathing season, the temperature of the water being 4°C warmer than that of the open sea.

It's possible to stay overnight within the park. The island's only hotel, the modern Hotel Odisej (see Sleeping, page 258) overlooks Pomena Bay, just a 15-minute walk from Malo Jezero. Alternatively, enquire at the tourist office for private accommodation and rooms to rent.

Saplunara

On Mljet's southeast tip, Saplunara (from the Latin *sabalum* meaning 'sand') is a protected cove with South Dalmatia's most spectacular sand beach. Close by, in a small, scattered settlement of the same name, several families let rooms and apartments throughout the summer (see Sleeping, page 259). There is also a handful of down-to-earth seasonal fish restaurants. A 20-minute walk from Saplunara, **Blace**, a 1-km long stretch of sand, faces south onto the open sea and backed by pines, is popular with nudists.

Essentials

➔ **Ferry** Jadrolinija, jadrolinija.hr, runs a ferry from Dubrovnik to Sobra port on Mljet. **G&V Line**, gv-line.hr, covers the same route by catamaran, stopping at the Elafiti islands en route.

🏧 **ATM** There is a cash machine in the port of Sobra.

ℹ **Tourist information** The tourist office is in Polače, T020-744086.

Pointing the way on Mljet.

Island of Lastovo

Lastovo is Croatia's second most isolated inhabited island (after Vis). Because of its remoteness it was chosen, like Vis, as a Yugoslav military base, and therefore closed to foreigners from 1976 to 1989. Fortunately this blocked all commercial tourist development and today it is undoubtedly one of the most unspoilt islands on the Adriatic, with dense pinewoods punctuated by meticulously cultivated farmland, an indented coastline with several sheltered bays, and only one true settlement, the charming semi-abandoned Lastovo Town, made up of old stone houses built prior to the turn of the 20th century.

Today, despite a serious problem of depopulation, life goes on. If you visit in spring you'll see a veritable troop of elderly women (plus the occasional donkey) hard at work in the fields. Lastovo is self-sufficient in fruit and vegetables even though only 35% of potential farmland is currently under cultivation. A network of footpaths criss-cross the island, passing through fields, woods and lush vegetation scented with sage, rosemary and mint, making walking a pleasurable pursuit. The islanders will assure you that there are no poisonous snakes – according to local myth, several centuries ago a priest saw an adder here and cursed it, after which all the island's snakes threw themselves into the sea.

Lastovo Town

10 km northeast of Ubli (the port).

One kilometre inland from the north coast, Lastovo Town stands 86 m above sea level. This once-wealthy community is made up of closely packed old stone houses, built into a south-facing slope, forming an amphitheatre-like space focusing on carefully tended allotment gardens in the fertile valley below. The buildings date from the 15th century onwards and are noted for their unusual chimneys, which are strangely similar to minarets. A series of steep, cobbled paths wind their way between the houses, and to the east side of town stand the 15th-century parish church of Sv Kuzme i Sv Damjana (St Cossimo and St Damian) and a pretty open-sided loggia. Above town, perched on a triangular hill known as Glavica, is Kaštel, a fortress erected by the French in 1810 and now used as a meteorological station. It's worth the climb up for its breathtaking views.

Ubli

The island's main ferry port, Ubli is a curious cluster of modern buildings. Founded by Mussolini as a fishing village in 1936, when the island was under Italy, it was initially populated with fishermen from Istria. However, after just one year they packed up and left, so Il Duce sent a community of Italians from the island of Ponza, instead. There's nothing much to see, but from here a pleasant 3-km coastal road leads to **Uvala Pasadur** (Pasadur Bay), where you'll find Lastovo's only hotel.

Beaches

Through summer, locals transport visitors by boat to the **Lastovčici** (an archipelago of over 40 islets lying northeast of Lastovo) usually stopping at the tiny uninhabited island of **Saplun** where there's a secluded cove with a blissful sand beach.

Essentials

➲ **Ferry** The main ferry port is in Ubli. **Jadrolinija,** jadrolinija.hr, runs a daily ferry and fast catamaran from Lastovo to Split (Central Dalmatia), stopping at Vela Luka (island of Korčula) and Hvar Town (island of Hvar) en route.

◉ **ATM** There is a bank (but no ATM) opposite the tourist office in Lastovo Town.

❶ **Tourist information** Lastovo Town tourist office is opposite the bus stop on the hill above Lastovo Town, T020-801018, lastovo-tz.net.

Lastovo Town.

Sleeping

Old Town
Pučić Palace €€€€
Ulica od Puca 1, T020-326000, thepucicpalace.com.
Map: Dubrovnik, p230.
Overlooking the open-air market, this luxurious boutique hotel is the most romantic (and expensive) place to stay in Dubrovnik's old town. Occupying a restored 18th-century baroque palace, its 19 rooms are furnished with antiques and have extras such as Italian mosaic-tiled bathrooms stocked with Bulgari toiletries. If you're going to splash out for just one night, this could be the place to do it.

Stari Grad Hotel €€€€
Od Sigurate 4, T020-322244, hotelstarigrad.com.
Map: Dubrovnik, p230.
One of only two hotels within the city walls, this old stone building is close to Pile Gate, just off Placa. Inside there are eight guest rooms furnished with reproduction antiques, and a roof terrace where breakfast is served throughout summer.

Amoret Apartments €€
Dinka Ranjine ulica, Old Town, T020-324005, dubrovnik-amoret.com.
Map: Dubrovnik, p230.
Occupying three 17th-century stone buildings in the old town, Amoret has 10 doubles rooms, each with wooden parquet flooring and antique furniture, free Wi-Fi, and a kitchenette so you can cook. The owner, Branka Dabrović, is extremely kind and helpful, and full of local advice.

Karmen Apartments €€
Bandureva 1, T020-323433, karmendu.com.
Map: Dubrovnik, p230.
For a quaint hideaway in the old town, try this delightful little guesthouse run by the Vlan Bloemen family, who also own the Hard Jazz Café Trubador. The four light and airy apartments have wooden floors, colourful painted wooden furniture and handmade bedspreads, and offer views onto the old harbour. The entrance is down a narrow side street between the Rector's Palace and the Aquarium.

Outside the Old Town
Hotel Bellevue €€€€
Pera Cingrije 7, T020-330000, hotel-bellevue.hr.
Map: Dubrovnik, p230.
Built into a cliff face overlooking the sea, halfway between the old town and Lapad Peninsula, this chic hotel reopened in autumn 2006 following total renovation. The 81 rooms are furnished in smart minimalist style with wooden floors, and the 12 suites also have jacuzzis. Facilities include a small beach and a luxurious spa and wellness centre.

Hotel Lapad €€€
Lapadska obala 37, T020-455555, hotel-lapad.hr.
Map: Dubrovnik, p230.
On Lapad Peninsula, overlooking Gruž harbour, this four-star hotel was refurbished in 2008. It has 157 rooms and six suites, with modern minimalist furniture and fabrics in earthy shades of brown, beige and cream, plus slick tiled bathrooms with glass doors so the bedroom is visible. There's an outdoor pool in the garden.

Hotel More €€€
Kardinala Stepinca 33, Lapad Peninsula; T020-494200; hotel-more.hr.
Map: Dubrovnik, p230.
More (pronounced *moor-ay*, which means 'sea') is a smart five-star hotel overlooking Lapad Bay, affording magnificent sunset views. It has 34 spacious rooms and three suites, all with rather sumptuous neo-baroque mahogany wooden furniture and heavy curtains tied by cords with tassels. There's a restaurant with a waterfront terrace, a bathing area, and a wellness centre with sauna, jacuzzi, massage and a gym.

Berkeley Hotel €€
Andrije Hebranga 116A, T020-494160, berkeleyhotel.hr.
Map: Dubrovnik, p230.
Overlooking Gruž harbour, the Berkeley is run by a Croatian family who lived for many years

in Sydney, Australia. There are 16 spacious suites and studios (with kitchenettes), plus eight double rooms, all with wooden floors, slick minimalist furnishing, flat-screen satellite TV and internet. They do an excellent cooked-to-order breakfast, and their 'Stay and Cruise' offer combines several nights at the hotel with a few days exploring the Elafiti islands by motorboat.

Hotel Aquarius €€
Mata Vodopića 8, on Lapad Peninsula, T020-456112, hotel-aquarius.net.
Map: Dubrovnik, p230.
This small, modern hotel is especially good value. It has 20 spacious rooms and four suites, as well as a ground-floor restaurant with outdoor tables in a leafy garden. You pay a little more for a room with a balcony but it's worth it.

Cavtat

Hotel Supetar €€€
Dr Ante Starčevića, T020-479833, hoteli-croatia.hr.
In an old stone building set back a little from the seafront, this basic but welcoming hotel has 28 rooms (sea view and garden view), and a restaurant and waterside summer terrace.

Hotel Villa Pattiera €€€
Trumbićev put 9, T020-478800, villa-pattiera.hr.
On the seafront promenade in the centre of Cavtat, this old stone villa has been refurbished to form a delightful, family-run boutique hotel. There are 12 rooms, all with wooden floors and either a sea or garden view. Breakfast is served in the popular Restaurant Dalmacija on the ground floor.

Elafiti islands

Lopud
Villa Vilina €€€
Obala Iva Kuljevana 5, Lopud, T020-759333, villa-vilina.hr.
Occupying a restored stone villa set in a garden with a terrace overlooking the sea, this hotel has 14 rooms and three suites, a restaurant and a small outdoor pool. It is located just in front of the ferry landing station.

La Villa €€
Iva Kuljevana 33, Lopud, T091-322 0126, lavilla.com.hr.
In a 19th-century villa overlooking Lopud Bay, this small, reasonably priced hotel is run by a young, friendly Croatian couple. The six guest rooms have IKEA-style minimalist modern furniture and coloured Indian fabrics, mosaic-tile bathrooms, and they either look out onto the open sea or the back garden's giant magnolia tree, orange trees and lavender bushes.

Šipan
Hotel Božica €€€
Sudjuradj 13, Šipan, T020-325400, hotel-bozica.hr.
In Sudjuradj, 5 km from the port of Šipanska Luka, this hotel has 22 rooms and four suites, all with wooden floors, simple modern furnishing, internet, minibar and satellite TV, and most with a balcony. There's a restaurant with a terrace, an outdoor pool and a pier where yachts can moor.

Hotel Šipan €€€
Šipanska Luka, Šipan, T020-754900, hotel-sipan.hr.
This three-storey white building is on the edge of town, overlooking the palm-lined seafront promenade. There are 85 slick, modern rooms furnished in minimalist style, a bar and a waterside restaurant with big white parasols. One-day fishing trips and massage can be arranged upon request.

Pelješac Peninsula

Ston
Hotel Ostrea €€€
Mali Ston, T020-754556, ostrea.hr.
This former mill has been restored to form a small luxury hotel, with nine rooms and one suite, all with parquet flooring and antique furniture. Through summer, breakfast is served on a pleasant open-air terrace.

Listings

Orebić
Grand Hotel Orebić €€€
Kralja Petra Krešimira IV 107,
Orebić, T020-798000,
grandhotelorebic.com.
Formerly known as the
Rathaneum, this hotel reopened
in May 2007 following a
complete renovation.
Overlooking the sea, with a small
beach out front, it is a 10-minute
walk along the coastal path from
town. The 173 rooms are smartly
furnished, and most have
balconies and a sea view.
Facilities include a gym, and
bicycles, canoes and surf boards
for rent.

Hotel Indijan €€€
Škvar 2, Orebić, T020-714555,
hotelindijan.hr.
This classy, family-run hotel,
which opened in 2007, overlooks
the beach in the centre of
Orebić. Combining traditional
and modern architecture, it has
17 rooms and two suites, with
pale wood furniture and wooden
floors. Facilities include a
restaurant with a palm-lined
terrace, a lounge bar, an indoor
pool and a sauna.

Adriatic €€
Mokalo 6, 4 km east of Orebić,
T020-714328,
adriatic-mikulic.com.
The Adriatic can be reached on
foot via the pleasant coastal
path. It has 10 apartments, each
with a kitchenette, air
conditioning and satellite TV.

There's a rustic restaurant with a
lovely waterside terrace, a beach
bar perched up above the rocky
shoreline, and an outdoor pool.

Island of Korčula

Korčula Town
Lešić Dimitri Palace €€€€
Don Pavla Pose 1-6, T020-715560,
lesic-dimitri.com.
In the old town, this cluster of
medieval stone buildings has
been lovingly resorted to create a
luxurious 'apartotel' with chic
modern furnishing and quirky
details such as open-plan
bedrooms with free-standing
bathtubs. There are six
'residences' (sleeping two-seven),
all with sleek kitchenettes.

Hotel Marco Polo €€€
Korčula bb, T020-726 100,
korcula-hotels.com.
The waterside Marco Polo
reopened in 2007 following
renovation. There are 94 smartly
furnished rooms (most with sea
views), a new outdoor pool and a
luxurious wellness centre.

Hotel Korčula €€€
Obala bb, T020-711078,
korcula-hotels.com.
Erected in 1871 and originally
used as a café, this building was
converted into the island's first
hotel in 1912. Today retaining its
old-fashioned charm, despite
being in dire need of renovation,
it offers 20 simple rooms and
four apartments, a restaurant

and a lovely seafront terrace,
ideal for watching the sunset.

Lumbarda
Hotel Lumbarda €€
Lumbarda bb, T020-712700,
lumbardahotel.com.
This modern hotel overlooks the
sea and has 44 simple but
comfortable rooms, each with an
en suite bathroom and a balcony,
most with sea views. There's a
small outdoor pool and a
scuba-diving club.

Apartmani Val €
Uvala Račišće bb, T020-712430,
korcula-val.com.
A 20-minute walk from
Lumbarda, in a garden
overlooking the peaceful Račišće
Bay, Val has three apartments,
each with a sea-view terrace. The
host, Toni, used to work as a chef
in Split, and prepares delicious
fresh seafood suppers on
request. He also has bikes and a
small boat to hire, and will collect
you by car if you are arriving
through Korčula Town.

Island of Mljet

Hotel Odisej €€€
Pomena, T020-362111,
hotelodisej.hr.
Lying within the national park, a
pleasant 15-minute walk from
Malo Jezero, this cluster of
modern white buildings,
overlooking Pomena Bay, is
Mljet's only hotel. The best of the
155 rooms each have a sea-view

balcony, air conditioning, TV and minibar. There are also two two-room apartments with jacuzzi and kitchenette. Facilities include bicycles, surfboards and kayaks to rent, plus a small wellness centre.

Stermasi €
Saplunara 2, Maranovici, T020-746179, stermasi.hr.
Overlooking the bay, just a short walk from the lovely sand beach of Saplunara, Stermasi has seven simple but comfortable apartments, each with a kitchenette. The owner also runs a rustic *konoba* serving barbecued fish and meat, and has bikes and small boats to rent.

Villa Mirosa €
Saplunara 26, T020-746133, villa-mirosa.com.
Close to Saplunara sand beach, Villa Mirosa has six basic but comfortable rooms, all with air conditioning and en suite bathrooms. There's a ground-floor restaurant with a lovely, shady terrace. The seafood on offer is caught by the hosts (guests are welcome to join in on fishing trips), and the olive oil, wine and *rakija* are all home-made.

Hotel Solitudo €€€
Ulava Pasadur bb, 3 km north of Ubli, T020-802100, hotel-solitudo.com.
After several years under renovation, this hotel now has 73 rooms all with air conditioning, satellite TV and en suite bathroom. Backed by pinewoods, it overlooks the sea and tiny island of Prežba, which is linked to Lastovo by a bridge. Facilities include a restaurant, rustic *konoba*, wellness centre (sauna, jacuzzi and gym) and scuba-diving centre.

Vila Antica €€
Sv Kuzma i Damjana 3, Lastovo Town, T098-447311.
This lovely old stone cottage has two double bedrooms, a fully equipped yellow kitchen, a slick modern bathroom and a cosy living room with a beamed ceiling. It was renovated in 2006, and makes a romantic escape both in summer and out of season.

Apartments Madirazza €
Pasadur bb, T021-734085, apartmani-lastovo.com.
In a modern white building overlooking the sea, this house has three self-catering apartments, each with a kitchen, sea-view terrace, air conditioning and satellite TV. It's 3 km from the port at Ubli.

Old Town
Proto €€€
Široka 1, in a side street off Stradun, T020-323234.
Daily for lunch and dinner.
Map: Dubrovnik, p230.
In the old town, close to the walk-in tourist information centre, Proto offer tables on a lovely vine-covered, upper-level, open-air terrace. The restaurant dates back to 1886 and has an excellent reputation for traditional Dalmatian seafood dishes such as oysters from nearby Ston, and barbecued meats, notably succulent steaks.

Lokanda Peškarija €€€-€€
Na Ponti bb, overlooking the old harbour just outside the city walls, T020-324750.
Daily for lunch and dinner.
Map: Dubrovnik, p230.
Offering excellent value for money and always busy, this informal seafood eatery stands next to the covered fish market. Indoors there's a split-level, candlelit dining space with exposed stonework and wooden beams, but the best tables are outside with sea views.

Marco Polo €€€-€€
Lučarica 6, T020-323719.
Daily for lunch and dinner.
Map: Dubrovnik, p230.
Located in a side street behind the Church of St Blaise, the dining room here is tiny, but

through summer tables spill out onto a pretty courtyard, making it an old-time favourite of visiting actors and musicians. Seafood predominates, with *crni rižot* (black risotto in cuttlefish ink) a popular choice.

Kamenica €€
Gundulićeva Poljana 8, no phone.
Open all year, but closes at 2000 through winter.
Map: Dubrovnik, p230.
Overlooking the open-air market within the town walls, Kamenica is a down-to-earth eatery much loved by locals for its fresh oysters and simple seafood dishes. The platters of *girice* (small fried fish) and *pržene lignje* (fried squid) make a delicious lunchtime snack.

Taj Mahal €€
Gučetića 2, T020-323221.
Daily for lunch and dinner.
Map: Dubrovnik, p230.
Despite its name, this eatery specializes in Bosnian dishes, not Indian. Come here for barbecued meats such as *čevapi* (rissoles made from minced beef) and *ražnjići* (tiny pieces of pork cooked on a skewer), plus Bosnian favourites *krompiruša* (filo-pastry pies filled with potato) and *zeljanica* (filo-pastry pies filled with spinach and cheese).

Buffet Škola €
Antuninska ulica bb, T020-321096.
Daily for lunch and dinner.
Map: Dubrovnik, p230.
In a narrow side street between Placa and Prijeko, this family-run sandwich bar is known far beyond Dubrovnik. Sandwiches come in delicious home-made bread, filled with locally produced *sir iz ulja* (cheese in oil), *pršut* (dried ham) and tomatoes from the villages of Konavle.

Mea Culpa €
Za Rokom 3, T020-323430.
Daily until 2400.
Map: Dubrovnik, p230.
Locally recommended for the best pizza in town, plus lasagne, this tiny eatery lies within the city walls. It has tables outside on the cobbled street in summer.

Outside the Old Town
Orhan €€€
Od Tabakarije 1, T020-414183.
Open all year for lunch and dinner.
Map: Dubrovnik, p230.
Just outside the city walls, with tables right by the water's edge below Lovrijenac fortress, this highly regarded restaurant offers excellent fresh fish, a romantic atmosphere and discreet service.

Orsan €€
Ivana Zajca 2, Lapad Peninsula, T020-435933.
Daily for lunch and dinner.
Map: Dubrovnik, p230.
This informal eatery has a pleasant, leafy terrace overlooking the small marina in Gruž Harbour. Favourite dishes are *salata od hobotnice* (octopus salad), *svježa morska riba* (fresh fish) and *rozata* (a Dubrovnik dessert similar to crème caramel).

Tovjerna Sesame €€
Dante Alighieria bb, in a side street off Dr Ante Starčevića, T020-412910.
Daily for lunch and dinner.
Map: Dubrovnik, p230.
Just outside the city walls, close to Pile Gate, this romantic eatery is a perfect venue for a light supper over a bottle of good wine. The menu features platters of cheeses and cold meats, truffle dishes and an enticing variety of creative salads.

Cavtat

Leut €€€-€€
Trumbićev Put 11, T020-478477.
Feb-Dec daily for lunch and dinner; closed Jan.
Map: Dubrovnik, p230.
In business for over 30 years, this excellent fish restaurant is in the centre of town, with a large summer terrace overlooking the seafront. The house speciality is scampi cream risotto.

Konavoski Komin €€
Velji Do, Konavle, T020-479607.
Daily for lunch and dinner.
Out of town, 6 km northeast of
Cavtat, this old stone building,
with tables on a series of outdoor
terraces through summer, serves
traditional Dalmatian food and
wine. It's possible to reach via a
marked hiking path from Cavtat.

Elafiti islands

Lopud
Restoran Obala €€€-€€
*Obala Iva Kuljevana bb, Lopud,
T020-759170.*
Daily for lunch and dinner.
Local meat and fish specialities
served at tables on the seafront
promenade, with fantastic sunset
views across the bay. They also
stage occasional live traditional
Dalmatian music.

Konoba Peggy €€
Narikla 22, T020-759036.
Daily for lunch and dinner.
Up a narrow side street above
the ferry quay, this informal
eatery has a pretty terrace with
heavy wooden tables and
benches, and fragrant lemon
trees. Expect typical Dalmatian
fare, notably fresh fish, which the
owner cooks over an open fire.

Šipan
Kod Marka €€€-€€
Šipanska Luka, T020 758007.
Daily for lunch and dinner.
Map: Dubrovnik, p230.

Overlooking the harbour, with
several tables beneath white
umbrellas on the waterside
terrace out front, this informal
eatery serves authentic local
seafood dishes such as
korčulanska popara (Korčula fish
stew) and *rižot na lučki način*
(risotto with lobster, aubergine
and courgette). Be sure to try the
home-made *rakija*.

Pelješac Peninsula

Ston
Bota €€€
*Mali Ston bb, T020-754482,
bota-sare.hr.*
Daily for lunch and dinner.
Occupying the 14th-century salt
warehouse, this restaurant is
recommended for locally grown
shellfish. If you have a sweet
tooth, round off with the *stonski
makaruli*, a bizarre local pudding
made from pasta, nuts, sugar
and cinnamon baked in a
pastry crust.

Kapetanova Kuća €€€
Mali Ston, T020-754 264.
Daily for lunch and dinner.
This highly regarded restaurant
draws connoisseurs from all over
Croatia. The house speciality is
fresh oysters, but there's also a
good choice of seafood risotto
and pasta dishes, plus fresh fish.
It's run by the same family that
own the nearby Hotel Ostrea.

Orebić
Konoba Antunović €€
*Kuna, 16 km east of Orebić,
T020-742035.*
Daily for lunch and dinner.
In the village of Kuna, in a valley
set back from the coast, this
authentic agrotourism centre
serves home produce at heavy
wooden tables and benches in
an old stone building with a
beamed ceiling. Expect platters
of anchovies, olives, *pršut* and
sheep's cheese, plus local stews
and freshly baked bread. Be sure
to try the house wines, the white
rukatac and red *plavac mali*.

Mlinica €€
*Joza Šunja bb, Orebić,
T020-713886.*
Open May-Oct dinner only.
Occupying an old mill, this
popular *konoba* specializes in
meals prepared under a *peka*,
which need to be ordered a
day in advance; more simple
dishes can be eaten without
prior notice.

Island of Korčula

Korčula Town & around
Adio Mare €€€-€€
Svetog Roka, T020-711253.
Open for dinner only.
In a narrow side street in Korčula
old town, close to the Marco Polo
House, this memorable
restaurant has kept the same
down-to-earth menu, including
pašta-fažol (beans and pasta),
brodet (fish stew served with

polenta) and *pašticada* (beef stewed in *prošek* and prunes, served with gnocchi), since it opened in 1974. There's an open-plan kitchen, so you can watch the cooks at work. It's outrageously popular so reservations are recommended.

Konoba Marinero €€€-€€
Ulica Marka Andrijića 13, T020-711170.
Daily for lunch and dinner.
With wooden tables and benches set out on the stone steps in a narrow side street in Korčula old town, Marinero is run by two brothers who are both fishermen. Informal and discreet, it serves the best fresh fish and seafood in the area.

Konoba Mate €€€-€€
Pupnat, T020-717109, konobamate.hr.
Daily for lunch and dinner.
In the village of Pupnat, a 15-minute drive from Korčula Town, this highly regarded agrotourism centre serves delicious home-made ravioli filled with goat's cheese, lamb casserole and seasonal specialities such as wild asparagus omlette. Be sure to round it all off with a glass of homemade *travarica* (*rakija* flavoured with herbs).

Grubinjac €€
Žrnovo bb, T020-711410.
Daily for lunch and dinner.
In an old stone farm building, set amid olive groves, on a hill on the road between Korčula and Žrnovo, this rustic family-run eatery offers tasty local dishes and home-made wine, as well as fantastic views down to the sea.

Pizzeria Tedeschi €€
Šetalište Petra Kanavelića, T020-711586.
Daily for lunch and dinner.
In Korčula old town, with tables lining the seafront promenade, affording views across channel to Orebić, family-run Tedeschi serves the best pizza in town.

Ranč Maha €€
Stiva, Žrnovo, T098-494389.
Open all year for lunch and dinner (weekends only during winter).
This small agrotourism centre occupies a stone building set amid fields near the rural village of Žrnovo, and serves authentic home-made food and wine.

Lumbarda
Konoba Zure €€€-€€
Lumbarda 239, T020-712008.
Daily for lunch and dinner.
Everything on offer at this family-run restaurant is home-made; there's no fixed menu (the choice changes from day to day) but you can look forward to delights such as octopus stew

and lobster with spaghetti, and a plentiful supply of the locally produced *grk*. Guests sit at wooden tables in a walled garden, and are offered a complimentary glass of *travarica* upon arrival.

Island of Mljet

Melita €€€
Otočić Sv Marije, T020-744145.
Open mid-Apr to late Sep for lunch and dinner.
Located on the islet of St Mary, in the middle of Veliko Jezero, this rather formal restaurant serves up a fine selection of barbecued meat and fish dishes. A restaurant boat shuttles guests back and forth from Pristanište.

Franca €€€-€€
Saplunara, T020-746177, saplunara.com.
Daily for lunch and dinner.
At Franca, guests sit together at a long table overlooking the bay, and feast on fresh seafood caught by the owner, who is a fisherman. There are four mooring spaces out front, making it particularly popular with yachting types.

Marijina Konoba €€€-€€
Požura, T020-746113.
Daily for lunch and dinner.
Overlooking the lovely Požura Bay, this family-run gourmet eatery is one of the best places to indulge in fresh seafood such as lobster, as well as locally caught

wild boar. The olive oil is their own, and the bread is freshly baked each day.

Konoba Triton €€
Sršenovići 43, Babino Polje, T020-745131.
Daily for lunch and dinner.
In a cosy old stone building, furnished in rustic style, Triton serves Dalmatian meat and fish specialities, with occasional live music. There's also a pleasant terrace out front with views across the island.

Island of Lastovo

Konoba Augusta Insula €€€-€€
Zaklopatica, T020-801167, augustainsula.com.
Daily for lunch and dinner.
With three terraces above the Zaklopatica Bay, this *konoba* serves up excellent lobster and spaghetti, as well as fresh fish and delicious locally gathered *motar* (rock samphire). They also organize fishing trips, and have several mooring places out front, complete with water and electricity supplies for yachters.

Konoba Triton €€€-€€
Zaklopatica, T020-801161.
Daily for lunch and dinner.
Considered by many to be the best restaurant on the island, Triton is popular with yachters, who moor up directly in front of the summer terrace that has views of Zaklopatica Bay. The owner catches fresh fish daily, and has apartments to rent upstairs.

Konoba Bačvara €€
Požival bb, Lastovo Town, T020-801075.
Open Jun-Oct for lunch and dinner.
Hidden away in an old stone building with a rustic interior in the lower part of Lastovo Town, this traditional *konoba* serves up fresh seafood, locally produced vegetables and wine.

Konoba Portorus €€
Skrivena Luka, T020-801261.
Daily for lunch and dinner.
With tables set out on a terrace looking out over the 'hidden bay', this simple eatery attracts people with smaller boats (the water is shallow here), who can moor up outside and hop ashore for a meal.

Entertainment

Dubrovnik

Bars & clubs
Buža
Od Margarite, T091-589 4936.
Accessed through a small doorway in the city walls, looking out to sea, you'll find this informal bar by following the 'Cold Drinks' sign. Tables are arranged on a series of terraces set into the rocks. The drinks in question are served in plastic cups, but the mellow music and night-time candles make it many people's favourite Dubrovnik bar.

Eastwest
Frana Supila bb, T020-412220, ew-dubrovnik.com.
In a 1970s modernist building, overlooking the old harbour, during the day this chic club runs a café and a private pebble beach equipped with sunloungers and umbrellas, but come early evening, the cocktail bar and restaurant opend and a party mood sets in. There's a rooftop VIP open-air lounge open until 0500, where you might spot some well-known faces from the world of sport and cinema.

Factory
Vukovarska 3, T099-2311399, factory-club.hr.
This big new club, with space for 1500 guests, opened in autumn 2008. It occupies a former paint factory, opposite the Mercante shopping centre, west of the old

town. International DJs such as David Morales and Darren Emerson have played here.

Hard Jazz Café Trubadour
Bunićeva Poljana 2, T020-323476.
In the old town, this cosy bar is crammed with old furniture, candles, jazz memorabilia and signed photos of well-known people who have been here. It stages occasional live jazz concerts on a small stage outside through summer. It's owned by the Van Bloemen family, who founded London's renowned Troubadour Café in Earl's Court in 1954, and moved to Dubrovnik in 1972.

Latino Club Fuego
Brsalje bb (just outside Pile Gate), T020-312870.
Daily until 0600 in summer.
Working through summer, this long-standing club is packed every night. Besides Latino, it also plays disco and techno, and stages occasional live concerts. Woody Harrelson and Tara Reid have been spotted here.

Festivals & events
Sveti Vlaho
3 Feb.
Each year, Dubrovnik celebrates its patron with the Feast of St Blaise. A ceremonial holy service is held in front of the cathedral at 1000, followed by a religious procession around town at 1130; the remains of St Blaise, in the form of relics, take pride of place.

During the time of the republic, those prisoners who did not present a threat to public safety were released on this day to participate in the festivities.

Libertas Film Festival
libertasfilmfestival.com.
Late Jun-early Jul.
Held annually in the old town. Past guests include Woody Harrelson, Nick Nolte and Kevin Spacey.

Dubrovnik Summer Festival
dubrovnik-festival.hr.
Mid-Jul to mid-Aug.
Each year, this highly acclaimed international festival hosts drama, ballet, concerts and opera at open-air venues within the city walls. Shakespeare's Hamlet staged on Lovrijenac Fortress is one of the most popular performances.

Pelješac Peninsula

Bars & clubs
Trstenica
Orebić beach.
Beach bar and disco on Orebić's main beach, day and night.

Festivals & events
Ston Summer Festival
Ston.
Late Jul-late Aug.
This summer festival stages open-air evening music and theatre in the centre of Veli Ston, given partial coverage by Croatian television.

Island of Korčula

Bars & clubs
Cocktail Bar Massimo
Šetalište Petra Kanavelića bb, Korčula Town, T020-715073.
In the old town fortifications, inside the Tiepolo Tower on the tip of the peninsula, this bar is famed for its splendid sunset views over the sea.

Tramonto Cocktail Bar
Šetalište Petra Kanavelića bb, Korčula Town, T020-715401.
This family-run cocktail bar serves great drinks on a waterside terrace.

Festivals & events
Moreška
May-Oct.
This traditional sword dance is performed at 2100 each Monday and Thursday, next to the Land Gate, at the entrance into the old town. Tickets, which should be booked in advance, are available from travel agencies and hotel receptions around town.

Shopping

Books
Algoritam
Placa 8, T020-322044.
The best bookshop for
foreign-language publications
including novels, travel guides
and maps.

Food & drink
Dubrovačka Kuća
*Svetog Dominika bb, near Ploče
Gate, T020-322092.*
Tastefully laid out shop stocking
the best Croatian wines, *rakija*,
olive oil and truffle products.
There's a gallery upstairs.

Souvenirs
Boutique Croata
*Pred Dvorom 2, T020-323526,
croata.hr.*
Sells original Croatian ties in
presentation boxes, with a
history of the tie.

Galerija Buža
Miha Pracat 6, T020-323144.
Close to the Icon Museum and
Orthodox Church, this small
store sells funky handmade
modern jewellery.

Island of Korčula

Souvenirs
Aromatica
*Ulica Depola 96, Korčula Town,
T020-711900, aromatica.hr.*
Delicious-smelling soaps,
shampoos and massage oils
made from local aromatic herbs.

Activities & tours

Dubrovnik

Adventure sports
Adriatic Kayak Tours
*Zrinsko-frankopanska 6,
T020-312770,
adriatickayaktours.com.*
Arranges half-day and full-day
kayaking tours, as well as a
one-day pedal-and-paddle tour
involving kayaking from Lopud
to Šipan then riding a mountain
bike the length of the island.

Diving
Diving Centre Blue Planet
*Masarykov put 20,
T091-899 0973,
blueplanet-diving.com.*

Cavtat

Diving
**Epidaurum Diving and
Watersports Centre**
*Šetalište Žal bb, T020-471386,
epidaurum-diving-cavtat.hr.*

Pelješac Peninsula

Diving
Adriatic
*Mokalo 6, Orebić, T020-714328,
adriatic-mikulic.com.*

Island of Korčula

Boating
Cro Rent
*Obala Hrvatskih Mornara bb,
Korčula Town, T020-711908,
cro-rent.com.*
Rents speedboats as well as cars,
mopeds and motorbikes.

Diving
MM Sub
*Lumbarda bb, Lumbarda,
T020-712288, mm-sub.hr.*

Island of Mljet

Adventure sports
Hotel Odisej
You can rent mountain bikes,
kayaks and canoes, by the hour
or by the day (see Sleeping,
page 258).

Island of Lastovo

Diving
Paradise Diving Centre
*Pasadur bb, Ubli, T020-805179,
diving-paradise.net.*

Contents

268 Getting there
272 Getting around
276 Directory
278 Language

Practicalities

Getting there

 Air

From UK & Ireland

British Airways flies to Dubrovnik from London Gatwick; Croatian Airlines flies to Dubrovnik, Pula, Split, Zadar and Zagreb from Aberdeen, Belfast, Birmingham, Edinburgh, Glasgow, London, Manchester and Newcastle; **EasyJet** flies to Dubrovnik from Liverpool, London Gatwick or London Stansted, and to Split from Bristol, London Gatwick or London Stansted; **Flybe** flies to Dubrovnik from Belfast, Birmingham, Dublin, Edinburgh, Exeter, Newcastle and Southampton, and to Split from Belfast, Birmingham, Glasgow and Southampton; **Jet2.com** flies to Dubrovnik from Belfast, Edinburgh, Leeds and Manchester, and to Split from Manchester and Newcastle; **Ryanair** flies to Pula from London Stansted, and to Zadar from Dublin, Edinburgh and London Stansted; and **Wizz Air** flies to Zagreb from London Luton.

From rest of Europe

There are direct flights to Croatia from most European capitals. Carriers include **Aeroflot**, **Air France**, **Austrian Airlines**, **ČSA**, **Germanwings**, **Lufthansa**, **Malev**, **SAS**, **TAP Portugal** and **Turkish Airlines**.

From North America

There are no direct flights from the US to Croatia.

Airport information

Zagreb Airport (T01-456 2222, zagreb-airport.hr) has two banks, a post office, a duty-free shop, newsagents, a bar and restaurant, plus a number of rent-a-car companies, including **Avis** (T01-467 3603, avis.com.hr) and **HM Rentacar** (T01-370 4535, hm-rentacar.hr). Zagreb airport is 15 km south of the city centre. An airport bus, run by **Pleso** (T01-633 1999, plesoprijevoz.hr) makes regular runs between the airport and Zagreb Bus Station, a ticket costs 30Kn.

    Split Airport (T021-203555, split-airport.hr) has a bank, a post office, a duty-free shop, newsagents, and bar and restaurant, plus car-hire companies including **Dollar Thrifty** (T021-399000, carrentalsubrosa.com) and **Uni Rent** (T021-797 327, uni-rent.net). Split airport is 25 km west of the city centre. An airport bus, run by **Pleso** (T021-203119, plesoprijevoz.hr) runs at regular intervals between the airport and Split's Riva (seafront promenade), a ticket costs 30Kn.

    Dubrovnik Airport (T020-773100, airport-dubrovnik.hr) has a bank, a duty-free shop, a bar, plus car-hire companies including **Avis** (T020-773811, avis.com) and **Budget** (T020-773290, budget.hr). Dubrovnik airport is 21 km southeast of the city centre. An airport bus, run by **Atlas** (T020-442222, atlas-croatia.com) makes regular runs between the airport and Dubrovnik Bus Station, passing the outer walls of the old town en route, a ticket costs 35Kn.

Airline websites

British Airways ba.com
Croatian Airlines croatiaairlines.com
EasyJet easyjet.com
Flybe flybe.com
Jet2.com jet2.com
Ryanair ryanair.com
Wizz Air wizzair.com

ZRAČNA
ZRAČNA LUKA
LUKA ZAGREB
LUKA ZAGREB
ZAGREB ZRAČNA
ZAGREB ZRAČNA
ZRAČNA LUKA
ZRAČNA LUKA ZAGREB
LUKA ZAGREB ZRAČNA
ZAGREB
ZRAČNA LUKA

Rail

Regular daily international trains run direct to Zagreb from Venice, Ljubljana, Vienna, Budapest, Munich, Belgrade and Sarajevo.

The cheapest and fastest route from the UK is London–Paris–Venice–Zagreb, taking **Eurostar** (eurostar.com) through the Channel Tunnel. The entire journey takes about 39 hours and requires an overnight train. Prices vary greatly depending on how far in advance you book. For further details or information about alternative routes, contact **Rail Europe** (raileurope.co.uk), or check out the **Man in Seat Sixty-One** (seat61.com), an excellent website dedicated to travelling without flying.

If you are an EU passport holder and plan to travel across Europe to Croatia, consider buying a 'Global' **Inter Rail** (interrailnet.com) pass, offering unlimited second-class train travel in 30 countries. If you are 26 or under, a 15-day Global Inter Rail pass costs €279; if you are over 26, it costs €399.

Going green

To lessen the environmental impact of your journey, consider travelling across Europe by train. If you are in Italy, Croatia is just a short ferry or catamaran ride away. See opposite for more information.

Road

There are good road links to Croatia from the neighbouring countries of Slovenia, Hungary, Bosnia and Herzegovina, and Serbia and Montenegro. Visitors arriving from Italy or Austria will pass through Slovenia.

Eurolines (eurolines.com) runs a network of long-distance buses all over Europe, though there is no longer a direct bus from the UK to Croatia.

Sea

Croatia is well connected to Italy by overnight ferries the year through, and by additional fast daytime catamarans in summer.

Jadrolinija runs regular year-round overnight services Ancona–Split, Ancona–Zadar and Dubrovnik–Bari. **Blue Line** also cover the Ancona-Split route. **Azzurra Line** operate an overnight service Bari-Dubrovnik several times weekly, summer only.

Regarding prices, if you travel Ancona–Split with Jadrolinija in peak season (August), expect to pay €48 for a one-way deck ticket (or €55 if you travel at the weekend), or €108.50 for a one-way ticket with a bed in a double cabin with a shower and WC (€124.50 at the weekend). A one-way ticket for a car is an extra €63.50 (or €73 at weekends).

In addition, **SNAV** operates fast, summer-only, daytime catamarans, with daily services for Ancona–Split and Pescara–Stari Grad (on the island of Hvar). Expect to pay €60 Ancona–Split one-way (€108 return) for a foot passenger, plus €55 one-way (€99 return) for a car.

In high-season, it is possible to arrive in Istria by boat from Italy. Venezia Lines operates catamarans from Venice to Poreč and Rovinj, and Venice to Pula and Mali Lošinj. **Emilia Romagna Lines** runs catamarans from Ravenna to Rovinj, Rimini to Lošinj, and Pesaro to Lošinj and Zadar.

Ferry & catamaran company websites

Azzurra Line azzurraline.com
Blue Line blueline-ferries.com
Emilia Romagna Lines emiliaromagnalines.com
Jadrolinija jadrolinija.hr
SNAV snav.it
Venezia Lines venezialines.com

Getting around

Rail

All major Croatian cities, except Dubrovnik, are connected by rail. Train travel into more remote regions has been limited by topography, the rocky Dinaric Alps making it extremely difficult to build railways. Trains are operated by **Hrvatske Zeljeznice** (Croatian Railways, hznet.hr).

The most useful long-distance routes are Zagreb–Osijek (4 hrs) covered by six trains daily, Zagreb–Rijeka (4 hrs) four trains daily, and Zagreb–Split (5 hrs 30 mins by day, 8 hrs by night) three trains daily, one is an overnight service with sleeping cars.

For a one-way ticket expect to pay: Zagreb–Osijek 115Kn; Zagreb–Rijeka 97Kn and Zagreb–Split 17Kn. A return ticket is sometimes, but not always, cheaper than two one-way tickets.

The **InterRail Global pass** (interrailnet.com) provides train travel throughout Croatia and the other 29 participating European countries.

Zagreb There are daily train services to Varaždin (2 hrs 30 mins), Čakovec (3 hrs) and Osijek (4 hrs) in inland Croatia. Also to Rijeka (4 hrs) and Split (5 hrs 30 mins) on the coast.

Istria From Pula there are three trains daily to Rijeka (2 hrs) and Zagreb (6 hrs).

Kvarner From Rijeka several trains run daily to Zagreb (4 hrs).

North Dalmatia From Zadar, there are four trains daily to Knin (2 hrs 15 mins), from where it is possible to take connecting trains to Zagreb and Split, though this may involve a long wait.

Central Dalmatia From Split there are daily trains to Zagreb (5 hrs 30 mins).

South Dalmatia Dubrovnik is not connected to the rest of the country by rail.

Road

Bicycle
Croatia is a great destination for mountain biking but be aware that locals drive fast and occasionally a little recklessly on major mainland roads and are not used to cyclists. The islands, however, are perfect for exploring by bicycle.

Bus/coach
Buses tend to be slightly faster and marginally more expensive than trains, and they are generally less comfortable. However, while train services are limited, by using the bus you can get from any major city to the most remote village, albeit with a few changes en route. There are numerous private companies, each operating on their own terms, so there's no such thing as an unlimited travel pass. Prices and quality of buses vary greatly from company to company, and a return ticket is sometimes, but not always, cheaper than two one-way tickets.

For a one-way ticket expect to pay: Zagreb–Osijek (4 hrs, 10 buses daily) 170Kn, Zagreb–Rijeka (3 hrs, 22 buses daily) 151Kn, Zagreb–Split (5-7 hrs, depending on the route taken, 26 buses daily) 180Kn.

For national information contact **Zagreb Bus Station**, T060-313333, akz.hr.

Zagreb Frequent buses run to Kumrovec (1 hr 30 mins), Varaždin (2 hrs), Čakovec (2 hrs 20 mins), Osijek (4 hrs), Vukovar (4 hrs 30 mins) and Plitvice Lakes National Park (2 hrs 30 mins) from the main bus station in Zagreb; also to Rijeka (3 hrs), Pula (5 hrs), Split (5-7 hrs) and Dubrovnik (8-10 hrs).

Istria From Pula, frequent buses run to Rijeka (1 hr 45 mins); Zagreb (4 hrs); Zadar (7 hrs); Split (10 hrs) and Dubrovnik (15 hrs). From Rovinj, regular buses to Pula (45 mins) and Poreč (45 mins). From Poreč there are regular buses to Pula (1 hr 15 mins)

South Dalmatia From Dubrovnik, frequent buses run to Cavtat (40 mins), Sto (1 hr 40 mins) and Orebić (3 hrs), also to Split (4 hrs), Zadar (7 hrs 30 mins), Rijeka (12 hrs) and Zagreb (8-10 hrs).

Car

Having a car obviously makes you more independent, so you can plan your itinerary more freely. However, it also creates various problems that you would not encounter if using public transport. Medieval walled cities such as Split and Dubrovnik are traffic free so you'll have to park outside the walls – even then, finding a place can be difficult (and expensive) as the more central parking spots are reserved for residents with permits. Having a car can also make ferry transfers to the islands extremely problematic: during high season be prepared to sit in queues for hours on end to get a place on the boat (there is no reservation system for vehicles: you buy a ticket and then it's first come, first aboard).

In summer 2005 two new motorways opened, connecting Zagreb and Rijeka, and Zagreb and Split. These are modern and fast, and you have to pay a toll to use them. The coastal road from Rijeka to Dubrovnik offers truly stunning views over the sea, but is twisty and tiring, and gets notoriously slippery after rain. On the islands, roads tend to be narrow and windy and are often less well maintained.

Petrol stations are generally open daily 0700-1800, and often until 2200 in summer. The larger cities and major international roads have 24-hour petrol stations.

Hrvatski Autoklub (Croatian Automobile Club) T987, hak.hr, offers a 24-hour breakdown service.

Car hire Car hire is available at all the main airports. For one week in summer, expect to pay in the region of €247.50 for a small car such as an Opel Corsa 1.2, or €435.50 for an Opel Astra 1.7. Payments can be made by credit card, and your credit card number will be taken in lieu of a deposit. Most companies require drivers to be 21 or over.

and Rovinj (45 mins).

Kvarner Frequent buses run to Zagreb (3 hrs), Pula (2 hrs 30 mins), Zadar (4 hrs), Split (8 hrs) and Dubrovnik (12 hrs).

North Dalmatia Frequent buses run to Zagreb (3 hrs 30 mins), Rijeka (4 hrs 30 mins), Pula (7 hrs), Split (3 hrs 30 mins) and Dubrovnik (7 hrs 30 mins).

Central Dalmatia From Split, frequent buses run to Šibenik (1 hr 30 mins), Makarska (1 hr 30 mins), Rijeka (8 hrs), Pula (10 hrs 30 mins), Dubrovnik (4 hrs) and Zagreb (5-7 hrs).

Car hire websites

Budget budget.hr
Europcar europcar.hr
Hertz hertz.hr

The Croatian Adriatic has 66 inhabited islands, many of which can be reached by ferry. There are regular connections between the mainland ports of Rijeka, Zadar, Split and Dubrovnik to nearby islands.

Prices are reasonable as the state-owned ferry company **Jadrolinija** has been subsidized by the government in an attempt to slow down depopulation of islands. As well as connecting the islands, Jadrolinija operates a twice-weekly overnight coastal service (with cabins available) running from Rijeka to Dubrovnik, stopping at Split, Stari Grad (island of Hvar) and Korčula Town en route.

Sample high season prices are: Rijeka–Split by ferry, one way, passenger 164Kn, car 448Kn; Split–Vis by ferry, one way, passenger 45Kn, car 296Kn; Dubrovnik–Sobra (Mljet) by ferry, one way, passenger 19Kn, car 128.50Kn.

In addition to Jadrolinija, a number of smaller local companies run ferries and catamarans on certain routes. In the Kvarner egion, **Linijska Nacionalna Plovidba** operates ferries from Valbiska (Krk) to Lopar (Rab), while **Rapska Plovidba** runs ferries Jablanac (mainland) to Mišnjak (Rab), and between Rab Town (Rab) and Lun (Pag). In South Dalmatia, **Mediteranska Plovidba**, runs a ferry from Orebić (mainland) to Korčula Town (Korčula) and **G&V Line** connect Dubrovnik (mainland) to Sobra (Mljet) by fast catamaran, stopping at the Elafiti islands en route.

Ferry & catamaran websites

G&V Line gv-line.hr
Jadrolinija jadrolinija.hr
LiniJska Nacionalna Plovidba lnp.hr
Mediteranska Plovidba medplov.hr
Rapska Plovidba rapska-plovidba.hr

Directory

Customs & immigration

EU citizens do not need a visa but do require a passport to enter Croatia for stays for up to 90 days.

Disabled travellers

With a dramatic increase in the number of physically disabled people as a result of the war of the 1990s, Croatia became more aware of the problems faced by those with mobility difficulties. Public buildings, as well as the better hotels, are gradually adding wheelchair access and other facilities.

The **Savez Organizacija Invalida Hrvatske** (Association of Organisations of Disabled People in Croatia, Savska Cesta 3, 10000 Zagreb, T01-482 9394) publish guides for disabled travellers to Zagreb, Split, Pula, Rijeka and Varaždin, available in both Croatian and English.

Emergency

In the case of an emergency requiring police attention, dial 92. For an ambulance, dial 94.

Etiquette

Very few restaurants or nightclubs demand a shirt and tie, but Croatians, and especially Dalmatians, are quite style conscious – so don't turn up at a smart restaurant in shorts and a grubby T-shirt. You should have your legs and shoulders covered when visiting churches. Croatia has many nudist beaches, which are marked 'FKK' (from the German, Freie Kunst und Kulture). In secluded bays it's also acceptable to bare all, but on crowded family beaches you should wear swimming trunks or bikini bottoms.

Croatians like to discuss politics and religion, but following the war there are plenty of thorny issues. Many Croats have heart-rending stories to tell, but remember that many families have mixed marriages somewhere down the line, so do not be too blatant about displaying personal views about who was right and who was wrong.

Families

The family is highly regarded in Croatia and children are welcome in general.

Health

Most EU countries have a reciprocal healthcare agreement with Croatia, meaning that you pay a basic minimum for a consultation and hospital treatment is free if you can show your European Health Insurance Card (EHIC).

For minor complaints visit a *ljekarna* (pharmacy), recognized by its green cross outside; most are open Monday-Friday 0800-1900 and Saturday 0800-1400, and in larger cities at least one will be open 24 hours. In an emergency, go to *hitno pomoč* (casualty). Dial 94 for an ambulance.

Insurance

Travel insurance is highly recommended and should cover theft or loss of possessions, medical and dental treatment, cancellation of flights, delays in travel arrangements, accidents, missed departures, personal liability and legal expenses. Keep any relevant medical bills and police reports to substantiate your claim. Note that many policies exclude 'dangerous activities' or charge a higher premium for them. This may include sailing, scuba-diving, rafting and even hiking. Some companies will not cover people over 65 years old, or may charge high premiums.

Money

The official currency is the kuna (Kn), which is divided into 100 lipa. The kuna is still not fully convertible so you can't buy or sell it outside Croatia, though you can exchange small amounts at border points in neighbouring countries. Before leaving Croatia, you can exchange unused kuna for foreign currency in a bank, but officially you need a receipt showing where you got the kuna from in the first place.

The euro is the most readily accepted foreign currency. Most towns and villages, even on the islands, have a *banka* (bank), generally open Monday to Friday 0700-1900 and Saturday 0700-1300, and most have an ATM too. Major credit cards (American Express, Diners Club, MasterCard and Visa) are widely accepted.

Police

The Croatian *policija* (police) wear dark blue uniforms. In the case of an emergency requiring police attention, dial 92.

Post

Post offices is larger towns work Monday-Friday 0700-2000 and Saturday 0700-1300, while in smaller villages some open mornings only, Monday to Friday 0930-1200. The postal service is run by Hrvatska Pošta and is pretty reliable. Airmail letters and postcards take about five days to reach EU countries and two weeks to get to the US, Canada and Australia.

Safety

Despite the negative image created by the war, Croatia has a lower crime rate than most other European countries. Rare cases of violent crime are usually targeted at specific persons connected to organized crime. Foreigners do not appear to be singled out.

Although military action connected to the war ended in 1995, the problem of landmines, mostly along the former front lines in eastern Slavonia and the Krajina, remains. De-mining is not complete: if you are passing through such areas, exercise caution and do not stray from known safe roads and paths.

Telephone

The prefix for Croatia is +385. International directory enquiries: 902. Local directory enquiries: 988.

Time difference

GMT+1.

Tipping

Tips are not included on bills. At the end of a good meal at a restaurant it is customary to leave 10% extra if you are satisfied with the service. Bar staff do not expect tips.

Tourist information

The Croatian National Tourist Board, croatia.hr, covers the whole coutry. For local offices, see the Essentials boxes for each destination.

Voltage

Croatia functions on 220 volts AC, 50Hz; plugs have two round pins (as in most of continental Europe).

Language

Croatian belongs to the South Slavic branch of the Slavic group of languages – a similar language is spoken by Serbs, Montenegrins and Bosnians. Most people working in tourism, as well as the majority of younger Croatians, speak good English, so you won't have much of a problem communicating unless you get off the beaten track. If you do make the effort to learn a few words and phrases, though, your efforts are likely to be rewarded with a smile of appreciation.

Vowels

a	like 'a' in cat
e	like 'e' in vet
i	like 'i' in sip
o	like 'o' in fox
u	like 'ou' in soup

Consonants

c	like 'ts' in bats
č	like 'ch' in cheese
ć	like 'ch' in future
đ	like 'j' in jeans
dž	like 'dj' in adjust
j	like 'y' in yes
lj	like 'ly' in billion
nj	like 'ny' in canyon
š	like 'sh' in push

Numbers

1	*jedan*	(ye-dan)
2	*dva*	(dva)
3	*tri*	(tree)
4	*četri*	(che-ti-ree)
5	*pet*	(pet)
6	*šest*	(shest)
7	*sedam*	(se-dam)
8	*osam*	(o-sam)
9	*devet*	(de-vet)
10	*deset*	(de-set)
11	*jedanest*	(ye-'da-na-est)
12	*dvanaest*	('dva-na-est)
20	*dvadeset*	('dva de set)
50	*pedeset*	(pe-'de'set)
100	*sto*	(sto)

Basics

yes	*da* (da)
no	*ne*(ne)
please	*molim* (mo-lim)
thank you	*hvala* (hva-la)
hello	*bog* (bog)
goodbye	*dovidjenja* (do-vee-'jen-ya)
excuse me	*oprostite* (o-'pro-sti-te)
sorry	*pardon* (par-don)
that's OK	*u redu je* (oo re-doo ye)
to	*u* (oo)
from	*iz* (iz)
I (don't) speak Croatian	*ja (ne) govorim Hrvatski* (Yah ne 'go-vo-rim 'hr-vat-ski)
do you speak English?	*govorite li vi engleski?* (go-vo-ri-te li 'en-gle-ski?)
good morning	*dobro jutro* (do-bro yoo-tro)
good afternoon	*dobar dan* (do-bar dan)
good evening	*dobro večer* (do-bra ve-cher)
good night	*laku noć* (la-koo noch)
my name is…	*moje ime je…* (mo-ye ime ye…)

Questions

how	*kako* (ka-ko)
when	*kada* (ka-da)
where	*gdje* (g-dyay)
why	*zašto* (za-shto)
what	*što* (shto)

Time

morning	*jutro* (yoo-tro)
afternoon	*popodne* (po-'po-dne)
evening	*večer* (ve-cher)
night	*noć* (noch)
yesterday	*jučer* (yoo-cher)
today	*danas* (da-nas)
tomorrow	*sutra* (soo-tra)
what time is it?	*koliko je sati?* ('ko-li-ko ye sa-ti?)
it is...	*točno...* (toch-no...)
0900	*devet sati* (de-vet sa-ti)
midday	*podne* (po-dne)
midnight	*ponoć* (po-noch)

Signs & notices

Airport	*Aerodrom*
Entrance/Exit	*Ulaz/Izlaz*
No smoking	*Zabranjeno pušenje*
Toilets	*WC*
Ladies/Gentlemen	*Ženski/Muški*

Days

Monday	*Ponedjeljak* (Po-'ne-diel-yak)
Tuesday	*Utorak* ('Oo-to-rak)
Wednesday	*Srijeda* (Sree-ye-da)
Thursday	*Četvrtak* (Che-'tvr-tak)
Friday	*Petak* (Pe-tak)
Saturday	*Subota* ('Soo-bo-ta)
Sunday	*Nedjelja* ('Ne-dyel-ya)

OPASNOST OD PADA PREDMETA S VISINE

Index

A

About the region 22-75
accommodation 54-59
    Central Dalmatia 210-214
    Istria 128-130
    Kvarner 152-154
    North Dalmatia 172-173
    South Dalmatia 256-259
    Zagreb & inland Croatia
        102-104
activities & tours 68-75
    Central Dalmatia 222-223
    Istria 135
    Kvarner 157
    North Dalmatia 177
    South Dalmatia 265
    Zagreb & inland Croatia
        109
air travel 268
airport information 268
alcohol 62-63
Aleja Glagoljaša 127
architecture 38-41
Arheološki Kompleks Salone
    191
art 36-38

B

beaches 69
    Lopar 151
    Makarska Rivijera 198
    Saplunara 253
    Zlatni Rat 16, 201
birdwatching 69, 147, 169
Blue Cave, The 16, 209
boat travel 271, 275
Brač (see Island of Brač)
Brijuni National Park 117
    accommodation 128
bus travel 270, 272-273

C

Čakovec 94
    accommodation 103
    Čakovec Dvor 95
    eating & drinking 107
camping 58
car trave 273, 274
castles
    Čakovec Dvor 95
    Stari Grad 94
    Trakoščan 93
    Trsat 142
    Veliki Tabor 92
Cavtat 238-239
    accommodation 257
    activities & tours 265
    Baltazar Bogišić Collection 238
    eating & drinking 260
    Račić Mausoleum 239
    Vlaho Bukovac Gallery 238
Central Dalmatia 178-223
    at a glance 13
    getting around 272
Cetina, river 197, 222
City Walls, Dubrovnik 229
climate 18-21
climbing 70, 169, 177, 197, 223
Cres (see Island of Cres)
cuisine 60-65
    menu reader 64
currency 277
customs 276
cycling 69, 272 (see also
    mountain biking)

D

Dinaric Mountains 47
Diocletian's Palace, Split 183
disabled travellers 276
discounts 11
diving 70, 157, 177, 222-223, 265
drink 62-63

Dubrovnik 228-236
  accommodation 256-257
  activities & tours 265
  Akvarij 235
  ATM 229
  beaches 236
  Crkva Svetog Vlaha 233
  Dominikanski Samostan 232
  eating & drinking 259-260
  entertainment 263-264
  Franjevačka Samostan 231
  Gradske Zidine 229
  Gundulićeva Poljana 234
  hospital 229
  Islet of Lokrum 236
  Jezuitska Crkva i Samostan
    235
  Katedrala 234
  Knežev Dvor 233-234
  map 230
  Muzej Pravoslavne Crkve 235
  Palača Sponza 232
  pharmacy 229
  Pomorski Muzej 235
  post office 229
  shopping 265
  Stadun (Placa) 231
  tourist information 229
  transport 229
  Velika Onofrio Fontana 231
  Vrata od Pila 231
  Vrata od Ploča 233
  War Photo Limited 236

E

eating & drinking 60-65
  Central Dalmatia 214-219
  Istria 130-133
  Kvarner 155-157
  North Dalmatia 173-175
  South Dalmatia 259-263
  Zagreb & inland Croatia
    104-107
economy 44-45

Elafiti islands 240-241
  accommodation 257
  eating & drinking 261
electricity 277
emergencies 276
entertainment
  Central Dalmatia 219-222
  Istria 133-134
  Kvarner 157
  North Dalmatia 176
  South Dalmatia 263-264
  Zagreb & inland Croatia
    108
environment 46-47
etiquette 276
Euphrasius Basilica, Poreč 14, 123

F

families 276
ferries 271, 275
festivals 48-53
food 60-65
  menu reader 64

G

Glagolitic Alley 127
Glagolitic script 127
Grožnjan 125
  accommodation 130
  ATM 125
  eating & drinking 133
  shopping 134
  tourist information 125

H

health 276
hiking 70, 143, 169, 199
history 24-35
hotels 55
Hvar (see Island of Hvar)

I

immigration 276
insurance 276
introducing the region 6-21
Island of Brač 200-201
  accommodation 212
  activities & tours 223
  ATM 201
  Bol 16, 201
  eating & drinking 217
  entertainment 221
  pharmacy 201
  post office 201
  Pustinja Blaca 201
  tourist information 201
  transport 201
  Vidova Gora 201
  Zlatni Rat 16, 201
Island of Cres 146-147
  accommodation 153-154
  activities & tours 157
  ATM 147
  Cres Town 147
  eating & drinking 156
  Eco-center Caput Insulae 147
  tourist information 147
  Tramuntane 147
  transport 147
Island of Hvar 202-207
  accommodation 212-213
  activities & tours 223
  Arsenal i Kazalište 205
  ATM 203
  beaches 206
  eating & drinking 217-218
  entertainment 221
  Fortica 206
  Franjevački Samostan 205
  Humac 207
  I Ivar Town 16, 203
  Jelsa 207
  Katedrala Sv Stjepan 205
  map 204
  pharmacy 203

Index

post office 203
Stari Grad 206
tourist information 203
transport 203
Trg Sv Stepan 203
Tvrdjalj 206
Island of Korčula 246-251
  accommodation 258
  activities & tours 265
  ATM 247
  beaches 251
  eating & drinking 261-262
  entertainment 264
  Galerija Ikona 251
  Gradski Muzej 249
  Katedrala Sv Marka 247
  Kopnena Vrata 247
  Korčula Town 17, 247
  Kuca Marca Pola 251
  Opatska Riznica 249
  pharmacy 247
  shopping 265
  tourist information 247
  transport 247
Island of Krk 144-145
  accommodation 153
  activities & tours 157
  ATM 145
  Baöka 145
  eating & drinking 155-156
Island of Lastovo 254-255
  accommodation 259
  activities & tours 265
  ATM 255
  beaches 255
  eating & drinking 263
  Lastovo Town 255
  tourist information 255
  transport 255
  Ubli 255
Island of Lošinj 148-149
  accommodation 154
  activities & tours 157
  ATM   149
  eating & drinking 156

Mali Lošinj 149
  tourist information 149
  transport 149
  Veli Lošinj 149
Island of Mljet 252-253
  accommodation 258-259
  activities & tours 265
  ATM 253
  eating & drinking 262-263
  Mljet National Park 253
  Saplunara 253
  tourist information 253
  transport 253
Island of Pag 166-167
  accommodation 172-173
  activities & tours 177
  ATM 167
  eating & drinking 174-175
  entertainment 176
  Pag Town 167
  Novalja 167
  tourist information 167
  transport 167
Island of Rab 150-151
  accommodation 154
  activities & tours 157
  ATM 151
  Bazilika Sv Ivana Evandeliste 151
  beaches 151
  Crkva Sv Junstina 151
  Crkva Svete Marije Velike 151
  eating & drinking 157
  Lopar Peninsula 151
  Rab Town 15, 151
  tourist information 151
  transport 151
  Trg Municipium Arbe 151
  Veli Zvonik 151
Island of Vis 208-209
  accommodation 213
  activities & tours 223
  ATM 209
  beaches 209
  eating & drinking 219

  entertainment 221-222
  Komiža 209
  Modra Spilja 209
  pharmacy 209
  post office 209
  tourist information 209
  transport 209
  Vis Town 209
Islet of Košljun 145
  accommodation 153
  eating & drinking 156
  Katedrala Uznesenja 145
  Punat 145
  tourist information 145
  transport 145
  Vrbnik 145
Istria 110-135
  at a glance 11
  getting around 272

Karneval 49
kayaking 17, 72, 177, 197, 222-223, 265
kitesurfing 177
Koločep, Elafiti islands 240
  (see also Elafiti islands)
Koöljun (see Islet of Koöljun)
Kopački Rit Nature Park 98
  accommodation 103
  eating & drinking 107
Korčula (see Island of Korčula)
Kornati National Park 15, 170
  accommodation 173
  eating & drinking 175
Kumrovec, Staro Selo 91
Krk (see Island of Krk)
Krka National Park 16, 195
Kvarner 136-157
  at a glance 11
  getting around 272

L

landscape 46-47
language 278-280
Lastovo (see Island of Lastovo)
Lonjsko Polje Nature Park 97
 accommodation 103
 eating & drinking 107
Lopud, Elafiti islands 240
 (see also Elafiti islands)
Lošinj (see Island of Lošinj)
Lovran 143
 accommodation 152-153
 eating & driking 155
Lovrec Vineyard 95
Lumbarda 251

M

Makarska 197
 accommodation 211-212
 activities & tours 223
 ATM 197
 beaches 198
 eating & drinking 217
 entertainment 220-221
 Mount Biokovo 199
 tourist information 197
 transport 197
Marco Polo 249, 251
marschino 165
Medvednica Nature Park 88
menu reader 64
Mljet (see Island of Mljet)
Mljet National Park 17, 253
money 11, 44-45, 277
Moreška, The 248, 264
Motovun 125
 accommodation 130
 activities & tours 135
 ATM 135
 eating & drinking 132
 entertainment 134
 Film Festival 15, 125, 134
 tourist information 125

Mount Biokovo 199
mountain biking 69, 223, 253, 265

national parks 47
naturism 59, 71, 198
North Dalmatia 158-177
 at a glance 12-13
 getting around 272
nudist beaches 198

Omiš 197
 accommodation 211
 activities & tours 222
 ATM 197
 eating & drinking 216
 tourist information 197
Opatija 143
 accommodation 152
 eating & drinking 155
 entertainment 157
Opatija-Lovran Lungomare 143
opening hours 11
Orebić 243
 (see also Pelješac Peninsula)
Osijek 97
 accommodation 103
 eating & drinking 107
 Tvrdja 97

P

Pag (see Island of Pag)
painting 36-38
Paklenica National Park
 168-169
 accommodation 173
Pannonian Basin 46
Pelješac Peninsula 242-245
 accommodation 257-258
 activities & tours 265
 ATM 243

beaches 244
eating & drinking 261
entertainment 264
Franjevački Samostan 244
Orebić 243
Ston 243
tourist information 243
transport 243
vineyards 245
Plitvice Lakes National Park
 14, 100-101
 accommodation 104
 eating & drinking 107
police 277
politics 42-43
Poreč 122
 accommodation 129
 activities & tours 135
 ATM 122
 beaches 123
 Decumanus 122
 eating & drinking 132
 entertainment 133
 Eufrazijeva Basilica 123
 hospital 122
 pharmacy 122
 post office 122
 tourist information 122
 transport 122
 Trg Marafor 123
post 277
Practicalities 266-281
Pula 114-116
 accommodation 128
 activities & tours 135
 Arena 115
 ATM 115
 Augustov Hram 116
 eating & drinking 130
 entertainment 133
 Gradska Tržnica 116
 hospital 115
 Kaštel 116
 pharmacy 115
 post office 115

Index

Rimski Forum 115
shopping 134
Slavoluk Sergijevaca 116
toursist information 115
transport 115

R

Rab *(see Island of Rab)*
rafting 71-72, 169, 177, 197, 222
rail travel 270, 272
rakija 63
Rijeka 141
  accommodation 152
  activities & tours 157
  ATM 141
  eating & drinking 155
  entertainment 157
  Gospa Trsat 142
  hospital 141
  Korzo 141
  Most hrvatskih branitelja 141
  pharmacy 141
  Pilgrimage path 142
  Pomorski i Povijesni Muzej 141
  post office 141
  tourist information 141
  transport 141
  Trsat 142
Risnjak National Park 143
  accommodation 153
rock climbing 70, 169, 177,
  197, 223
Rovinj 119
  accommodation 128
  activities & tours 135
  Akvarij 121
  ATM 119
  beaches 122
  eating & drinking 131
  entertainment 133
  hospital 119
  Kuča Batana 121
  Limski Kanal 122
  pharmacy 119
  post office 119

Sv Eufemija 121
shopping 134
tourist information 119
transport 119

S

safety 277
sailing 72, 222
Salona 190
Salona Archaeological Site 191
scuba-diving *(see diving)*
sculpture 36-38
Sea Organ, Zadar 15
sea travel 271, 275
Šetalište Franza Josefa 15, 143
shopping 66-67
  Central Dalmatia 222
  Istria 134
  North Dalmatia 176-177
  South Dalmatia 265
  Zagreb & inland
    Croatia 108-109
Šibenik 194
  accommodation 211
  activities & tours 222
  ATM 193
  eating & drinking 216
  entertainment 220
  hospital 193
  Katedrala Sv Jakoka 195
  tourist information 193
  transport 193
Šipan, Elafiti islands 240
sleeping 54-59
  Central Dalmatia 210-214
  Istria 128-130
  Kvarner 152-154
  North Dalmatia 172-173
  South Dalmatia 256-259
  Zagreb & inland
    Croatia 102-104
South Dalmatia 224-265
  at a glance 13
  getting around 272

Split 182-190
  accommodation 210
  activities & tours 222
  ATM 183
  beaches 190
  Dioklecijanova Palača 15, 183
  eating & drinking 214-215
  entertainment 219-220
  Galerija Meštrović 190
  Galerija Umjetina 189
  Galerija Vidovič 187
  hospital 183
  Katedrala Sveti Duje 187
  map 184
  Marjan 189
  Muzej Hrvatskih Arheoloških
  Narodni Trg 188
  Pazar 187
  Peristil 185
  Podrum 185
  Pomorski Musej 189
  post office 183
  Ribarnica 188
  Riva 185
  shopping 222
  Spomenika 190
  Sustipan 190
  tourist information 183
  transport 183
  Varoš 188
  Zlatna Vrata 187
sports 74-75
Stari Grad, castle 94
Stari Grad, Island of Hvar 206
Ston 243
  (see also Pelješac Peninsula)

T

telephone 277
time 277
tipping 277
Tito, Josip Broz 91, 93
tourist information 11, 277
train travel 270, 272
Trakoščan 93

transport 268-275
Trogir 193
  accommodation 211
  ATM 193
  eating & drinking 216
  hospital 193
  Katedrala Sveti Lovrijenac 193
  tourist information 193
Trsteno Arboretum 237
truffles 14, 126, 132

V

Varaždin 94
  accommodation 103
  eating & drinking 107
  Stari Grad 94
Varadin 94
Veliki Tabor 92
Vis *(see Island of Vis)*
Vukovar 99
  accommodation 103
  eating & drinking 107
vultures, Eurasian griffon 147

W

walking 70, 143, 169, 199
war of indepedence 32-35, 99, 231
War Photo Limited, Dubrovnik
  17, 236
weather 18-21
whitewater rafting 71-72, 169,
  177, 197, 222
wildlife 47, 69, 147
windsurfing 72-73, 177, 222-223
wine 17, 62, 73, 95, 223, 245

Y

youth hostels 59

Z

Zadar 162-165
  accommodation 172
  activities & tours 177
  Arheološki Muzej 164
  ATM 163
  Crkva Sv Donat 163
  eating & drinking 173
  entertainment 176
  Forum 163
  hospital 163
  Katedrala Sv Stošije 164
  Morske Orgulje 164
  Narodni Trg 165
  pharmacy 163
  post office 163
  Riznica 164
  shopping 176
  tourist information 163
  transport 163
Zadarski Pozdrav Suncu 165
Zagreb 80-89
  accommodation 102-103
  activities & tours 109
  Archeološki Muzej 87
  at a glance 10
  ATM 81
  Botanički Vrt 87
  Crkva Svete Katerine 85
  Dolac 81
  Donji Grad 86-87
  eating & drinking 104-106
  entertainment 108
  Etnografski Muzej 87
  Gornji Grad 14, 81-86
  hospital 81
  Hrvatski Muzej Naivne
    Umjetnosti 85
  Kamenita Vrata 84
  Katedrala 83
  Klovičevi Dvori 85
  Kula Lotrščak 85
  Maksimir Park 88
  map 82-83
  Medvednica Nature Park 88

  Meštrović Atelier 84
  Mirigoj Cemetary 88
  Moderna Galerija 87
  Muzej Mimara 86
  Muzej suvremene
    umjetnosti 89
  Muzej za Umjetnost i Obrt 86
  pharmacy 81
  post office 81
  shopping 108-109
  Strossmayerova Galerija
    Starih Majstora 87
  Tkalčićeva 83
  tourist information 81
  transport 81
  Trg Bana Jelačića 81
  Trg Svetog Marka 84
  Umjetnički Paviljon 87
  Uspinjača 86
Zagreb & inland Croatia 77-109
  at a glance 10
  getting around 272
Zlatni Rat 16, 201
Zrmanja, river 169, 177
zvončari 142

Footprint credits

Project Editor: Felicity Laughton
Picture editor: Rob Lunn
Layout and production:
Davina Rungasamy
Maps: Kevin Feeney
Proofreader: Jen Haddington
Series design: Mytton Williams

Managing Director: Andy Riddle
Commercial Director: Patrick Dawson
Publisher: Alan Murphy
Publishing managers: Felicity Laughton,
Jo Williams
Digital Editor: Alice Jell
Marketing: Liz Harper,
Hannah Bonnell
Sales: Jeremy Parr
Advertising: Renu Sibal
Finance & administration:
Elizabeth Taylor

Print

Manfactured in Spain by GraphyCems
Pulp from sustainable forests

Footprint feedback

Every effort has been made to ensure that
the facts in this guidebook are accurate.
However, travellers should still obtain
advice from consulates, airlines etc about
travel and visa requirements before
travelling. The authors and publishers
cannot accept responsibility for any loss,
injury or inconvenience however caused.

Publishing information

FootprintEurope Croatia
1st edition
© Footprint Handbooks Ltd
May 2010

ISBN 978-1-907263-01-9
CIP DATA: A catalogue record for this
book is available from the British Library

® Footprint Handbooks and the Footprint
mark are a registered trademark of
Footprint Handbooks Ltd

Published by Footprint
6 Riverside Court
Lower Bristol Road
Bath BA2 3DZ, UK
T +44 (0)1225 469141
F +44 (0)1225 469461
footprinttravelguides.com

Distributed in North America by
Globe Pequot Press